American Philosophy from Edwards to Dewey

American Philosophy from Edwards to Dewey:

an introduction

Guy W. Stroh
Professor and Chairman,
Department of Philosophy, Rider College

D. VAN NOSTRAND COMPANY, INC.
PRINCETON, NEW JERSEY · TORONTO · LONDON · MELBOURNE

To my mother and father

VAN NOSTRAND REGIONAL OFFICES: *New York, Chicago, San Francisco*

D. VAN NOSTRAND COMPANY, LTD., *London*

D. VAN NOSTRAND COMPANY (Canada), LTD., *Toronto*

D. VAN NOSTRAND AUSTRALIA PTY. LTD., *Melbourne*

Library of Congress Catalog Card No. 68–21148

Preface

The primary purpose of this book is to provide an introduction to the major developments in American philosophy from their Puritan origins to their point of definite maturity in the present century. In the short period from the beginning of the eighteenth century to the middle of the twentieth century—from the time of Jonathan Edwards to that of John Dewey—American philosophy was launched and became firmly established in the mainstream of Western philosophical thinking. This book attempts to show how this development has unfolded.

The study of American philosophy may serve as an excellent introduction to philosophy in general for the American college student or for anyone with a background in American culture and life. Such a reader may appreciate and comprehend the important developments in his own country's philosophy better than that of any other. Moreover, the developments within American philosophy are sufficiently rich, clear, and interesting to offer the beginning student a vivid and solid conception of what philosophy is really all about. American philosophy as such is not narrowly provincial, not simply nationalistic. It offers, rather, a multiplicity of interesting views of man, the universe, science, religion, and all the principal themes of philosophy that give the student much to think about. A distinctive virtue of American philosophical thinking is that it is not of mere academic interest but is also directly connected with human experience.

This book can be used in several types of college courses in conjunction with selected readings from the individual philosophers themselves: a general introduction to philosophy; the history of American philosophy; problems in American philosophy; the history of American civilization; and American intellectual history.

The book focuses attention on the most important and representative of America's philosophers. It does not pretend to describe all the facets of American philosophy, but rather, attempts to introduce the student to its most vital and important tendencies. All the philosophers considered here received their education in American colleges, and all have contributed in some important way to American education and to the development of the highest reaches of the American mind. One major philosopher, George Santayana, who was neither born nor died in America, is included because he was educated in the United States, came to his philosophical maturity under the strong influence of other American philosophers, and has influenced the course of American philosophy. The English philosopher Alfred North Whitehead has not been included. Whitehead composed many of his most important works while he lived in the United States, but he was not educated in America and had already developed his basic philosophic ideas before he came to the United States at the age of sixty-three. Whitehead is more properly thought of as an English philosopher even though he has had considerable influence in America in recent times.

This selection of individual philosophers and their ideas demonstrates that American philosophers do not argue one basic or nationalistic philosophical position. Rather, the selections underscore and clarify the diversity and plurality of the most significant ideas in American philosophy, the ideas that have been most influential and still stimulate serious thought. In order to understand these important philosophical conceptions it is necessary to see them in their historical and intellectual contexts. The situations and issues that give rise to philosophical thinking must be perceived if one is to appreciate the views and reasoned arguments that any philosopher may offer. To understand any philosophical concept it is necessary to see it in its logical development, that is, systematically—in terms of the issues and problems out of which it arises, the thinking and reasoned arguments that make it up, and the criticism and further thought to which it may lead.

The plan of this book is to develop the history of American philosophy in two main parts. Part I, the early period, extends from Puritanism to Transcendentalism—roughly from 1700 to 1860—and includes chapters on Jonathan Edwards as representative of Puritanism; Thomas Jefferson as representative of the American Enlightenment; and Ralph Waldo Emerson as representative of New England Transcendentalism. Part II, the modern period, extending from the Civil War to the mid-twentieth century, includes Charles Sanders Peirce and William James as representative of Pragmatism, and Josiah Royce as representative of Idealism in America; and George Santayana and John Dewey as representative of philosophical Naturalism in America.

Each philosopher is considered as an individual thinker and as representative of an important type. He is explained in terms of those ideas peculiar to his method of philosophizing, and in relation to other philosophers and more general movements that have importance for the whole history of American philosophy and the Western philosophical tradition.

Thomas Jefferson, for example, is interpreted as a typical thinker of the American Enlightenment whose ideas of democracy and freedom merit attention apart from the American Enlightenment. William James is representative of American Pragmatism; he is also a thinker whose ideas, such as those on the freedom of the will and the meaning of truth, merit attention in a wider and deeper sense than the movement of pragmatism itself. Each chapter of the book locates a major American philosopher in the widest possible context in order to show the total scope of his thought. An attempt is also made to break down each philosopher's thought into the significant details of his views and arguments. For example, John Dewey is viewed in terms of the broad concepts of naturalism and instrumentalism which permeate his entire philosophy as well as in terms of such subjects as art and education, ethics and valuation, which represent important subject-matters falling under his basic naturalism and instrumentalism. At the end of each chapter a concluding section discusses the significance and influence of the individual philosopher for the purpose of encouraging the student to evaluate or assess critically the achievements of major American philosophers.

No historical or interpretive study of philosophy is a substitute for the actual works of the philosophers it may attempt to explain. Fundamentally, any written history or interpretation of philosophy presupposes these works, and hence, a serious student will want to read and think through these original sources for himself. Accordingly, incorporated in the plan of this book is a list of suggested readings at the end of each chapter. The student is directed to these readings as primary sources for understanding the fundamentals of each philosopher's thought.

By interpreting the main lines of American philosophical thought from Edwards to Dewey, then, the purpose of this book is to show how American philosophy has come to maturity by the mid-twentieth century. However, no attempt is made to encompass all the recent developments of twentieth-century American philosophy. Therefore, at the end of this book a guide to further readings is provided to show something of the great wealth and variety of careful work by American philosophers in recent years. It is seriously hoped that the study of American philosophy from Edwards to Dewey will provide a meaningful background in terms of which the student may carry his studies further and appreciate the work that is still going on in American philosophy.

Guy W. Stroh

Contents

PART I

American Philosophy
Before the Civil War

The country was new, but the race was tried, chastened, and full of solemn memories. It was an old wine in new bottles; and America did not have to wait for its present universities, with their departments of academic philosophy, in order to possess a living philosophy,—to have a distinct vision of the universe and definite convictions about human destiny.

George Santayana : THE GENTEEL
TRADITION IN
AMERICAN
PHILOSOPHY

Introduction

Early American Philosophy

One of America's most articulate philosophers, George Santayana, once observed that "America is a young country with an old mentality." [1] While this remark no doubt holds true today, it applies with especial force to America before the Civil War. The New England Puritans, the Founding Fathers, and the New England transcendentalists all found new applications for ideas that had already been worked out in Europe. Thus Americans applied old philosophies, borrowed world-outlooks, before any original systems were brought forth in the new land. The individuals who early settled on these shores, who won their independence from England, pushed back the wilderness of the frontier, civilized the country, and prospered with it, were not lacking in practical wisdom. On the contrary, among them were men capable of finding new and better applications for very old ideas. In point of fact, the successes as well as the failures of early American life are inconceivable apart from the ideas, philosophies, and plans of action that defined its hopes and goals.

America's old mentality comprised the religious, moral, political, and social ideas that gave form to the young life in the new world. The practical affairs of life, of surviving and progressing, took precedence over thought and new speculation. At the same time these practical affairs required a meaning or purpose that could be defined only in ideological terms. Practical success in clearing the wilderness, achieving

3

freedom, and creating the worth of the individual person required strong commitments to beliefs. The earliest American philosophers reflect this urgency to find and act on firm beliefs. The Puritans, the men of the Enlightenment, and the New England romanticists, however much they may differ in *what* they believed, all believed in believing, all endorsed an unwavering commitment to what each took to be the greatest good. For the Puritans the Word of God was the source of truth; for the men of the Enlightenment reason was man's guide in life; and for the New England transcendentalists intuition—immediate insight—was the origin of man's true beliefs.

The philosophers of America's past endorsed many of the same virtues and values, but often for different reasons. Thrift, enterprise, justice, honesty, and prudence were virtues in the eyes of all. The differences were ones of emphasis and of relationship to a larger body of other beliefs or creeds. The Puritans valued thrift and the other virtues for their godliness, their power to discipline the soul in conformity to the Creator's will. The Founding Fathers valued thrift and the other virtues for their utility in this life rather than as promoting any supernatural goal. The transcendentalists valued thrift and the other virtues for still different reasons: they believed that virtue entails integrity, that virtue brings a man to find his own whole and better self.

The American Puritans brought with them a complete outlook on life, based on the Christian religion interpreted by John Calvin (1509–1564), that had only to be applied rigidly and piously. They were seeking their own religious freedom; yet they were intolerant of other religious views. This contradiction was coupled with strong differences of opinion about church government which gradually led to the decline of strict Puritanism or Calvinism by the first half of the eighteenth century.

Precisely at this time of strongest internal conflict and decline, Jonathan Edwards gave American Calvinism its most tightly argued philosophical defence. Edwards was armed with a remarkable knowledge of English philosophy as well as a keen and original mind. These powers he turned on the Arminians,[2] the deists, and all groups who would seek to weaken the concepts of God's sovereignty and man's utter depravity and predestination. The Arminians argued for freedom of the will and the deists claimed that reason, not revelation, was the ground of true religion. Edwards not only staunchly argued against any freedom of will or religion based on natural reason, he in fact far outdistanced his opponents in the acuteness of his reasoning and became the first great philosopher on American shores. His writings are the first American works that can be described as profoundly philosophical. His essays, especially those on the mind, freedom of the will, religious affections, and true virtue, establish him as the real starting point of early American philosophy.

But Edwards was defending a decaying tradition. By 1750 the seeds of the Enlightenment and the struggle for independence were beginning to sprout. Although Benjamin Franklin was a contemporary of Edwards, his views and those of Thomas Jefferson and other leaders of the new country had left the strictures of Calvinism far behind. The Founding Fathers, more in tune with the progress of the times, were interested in enlightenment, liberty, and the pursuit of human happiness. They required practical wisdom rather than speculative theology and viewed the counsels of common sense and experimentation as far superior to miracle and revelation. This practical wisdom they found in the already developed ideas of the "free thinkers" of the European Enlightenment. Such men as Francis Bacon (1561–1626), Isaac Newton (1642–1727), and John Locke (1632–1704) were primary sources of knowledge and inspiration for the leaders of the American Enlightenment. To Thomas Jefferson and other men of the Enlightenment, philosophy—indeed, all learning—proved itself by what utility or progress it brought for the betterment of mankind. This kind of philosophy was, therefore, centered in society and political life rather than God-centered. At this time America needed a practical, social, and political philosophy, and Thomas Jefferson supplied this need better than any other man. Jefferson was and is the philosopher *par excellence* of American democracy. He was both a skillful architect and a tireless builder of the new American Republic. His philosophy had what Edwards' lacked—a vital relevance to his own time as well as an enormous influence on succeeding generations. Yet as a philosophy of life it was left unfinished and rough rather than refined. Based on common sense and practical affairs, it defined the dignity and goal of the individual in external and social terms rather than in internal or autonomous ones. By the end of Jefferson's life the need had arisen for a more imaginative and individualistic philosophy of life. America was now a nation, prosperous and still growing—but the quality of its life was in need of interpretation and counsel.

The New England transcendentalists marked the third major phase of early American philosophy. The Enlightenment had fostered social and political advance, but what was still needed was an affirmation of the moral and spiritual value of the individual. The Enlightenment had freed men from oppression, superstition and ignorance, but now the question emerged whether the conformity imposed by society would prevent the individual from being truly himself. Just as obedience to the will of God defined the purpose of Puritanism, and allegiance to a rule of reason and human freedom defined the purpose of the Enlightenment, so self-reliance or the assertion of man's unfettered allegiance to himself defines the meaning of transcendentalism. By the early 1830's the transcendentalists had brought a poetic, highly romantic focus to the problem of the meaning and purpose of man's life. Men like Emerson and Thoreau found new opportunities to make use of age-old ideas. Romanticism in America, like the Enlightenment and Puritanism, followed European antecedents. The reverence for nature, the primacy of feeling, the autonomy and sacredness of the individual person, were upheld by the New England transcendentalists as they had previously been upheld by Samuel Taylor Coleridge (1772–1834) in England and Jean Jacques Rousseau (1712–1778) in France. In contrast to the frank *materialism* and *social* orientation of the Enlightenment, transcendentalism was *idealistic* and oriented toward *individualism*.

Emerson, in his personal influence and the eloquence of his lectures and essays, offered the best formulation of the American romantic philosophy. He extolled the feeling of beauty rather than mere utility or external authority as the measure of truth and the source of values. He upheld the value of justice, not because it was socially useful or commanded by an external God, but because it created an immediately felt harmony between man and nature. To be at peace with oneself and with all other things was the only real way to be alive. Emerson advocated a philosophy of insight rather than analysis or disputation. Each man was to be his own philosopher, to create his own vision of the world, and to make his own peace with all existence.

With the Civil War and its aftermath, transcendentalism declined. It was frankly utopian and out of touch with the life and intellectual climate that developed in the latter half of the nineteenth century. In 1859, on the publication of Darwin's *Origin of Species*, the idea of evolution became a new source of philosophic thought. It is convenient to look upon the idea of evolution as marking the beginning of the modern period in American philosophy. This idea brought about so much critical thought and controversy and gave such prestige to natural science that philosophy was impelled to meet the challenge with new methods and ideas. The major philosophical movements in America subsequent to the Civil War—philosophies more analytical, scholarly,

and original than any that had appeared in America before—represent a]
break with early American philosophy.

Early American philosophy, then, passed through three major phases:
religious, political, and literary. Puritanism represents the religious phase|
during which philosophy was in the hands of the clergyman. Accordingly, the earliest form of philosophical activity in America is theological,
involving an attempt to give a systematic justification for the view that
man lives in a God-centered universe. The Enlightenment represents the
political phase, during which philosophy was in the hands of the statesman. Accordingly, the second form of philosophical activity in America
is primarily social, involving an attempt to give a rational justification for
democracy. Finally, transcendentalism represents the literary phase of
early American philosophy, during which philosophy was in the hands
of the poet. Accordingly, the third form of philosophical activity in
America is romantic, involving an imaginative attempt to set man free
from all restrictions and to view him as purely self-reliant and creative.
Edwards, Jefferson, and Emerson are the ablest spokesmen for these
three major currents in early American thought. They represent high
points of early American intellectual life—Edwards the Theologian-
Philosopher, Jefferson the Statesman-Philosopher, and Emerson the
Poet-Philosopher.

NOTES

1. George Santayana, "The Genteel Tradition in American Philosophy,"
in *Winds of Doctrine and Platonism and the Spiritual Life* (New York:
Harper Torchbooks, 1957), p. 187.
2. The Arminians began as a Dutch religious sect who took their name
from Jacobus Arminius (1560–1609). Their influence spread to England, and
by 1734 they were gaining many converts in America. Edwards, in fact,
viewed them as a serious threat to Calvinism, since the Arminians believed in
the freedom or self-determining power of man's will. This implied that man
could freely choose to sin or not to sin which in turn implied a denial of
man's predestination or absolute dependence on God.

SUGGESTED READINGS

G. N. Grob and R. W. Beck, eds., "The Puritan Mind" (Part I); "The Mind
of the Enlightenment" (Part II); "Transcendentalist Interlude" (Part III,
Ch. XV); in *American Ideas: Source Readings in the Intellectual History
of the United States*, Vol. I (New York: Free Press of Glencoe, 1963).
Paul Kurtz, ed., "The Colonial Period" (Part I); "Reason and Revolution"
(Part II); "Transcendentalism" (Part IV); in *American Thought Before
1900: A Sourcebook from Puritanism to Darwinism* (New York: Macmillan, 1966).

W. G. Muelder and L. Sears, eds., "Early Philosophical Theology and Idealism" (Part I); "The Period of the American Enlightenment" (Part II); "Transcendentalism" (Part III); in *The Development of American Philosophy: A Book of Readings*, 2nd ed. (Boston: Houghton Mifflin, 1960).

1 *Jonathan Edwards*

Puritanism and Determination

Jonathan Edwards (1703–1758) was the first real philosophical talent to appear in early America. Born October 5, 1703, at East Windsor, Connecticut, he was descended from two generations of Protestant ministers. He received his education at what is now Yale University, where he studied theology and prepared for his lifelong career as a minister of the gospel in the strictest Calvinist sense. His active career as a clergyman and preacher of hell-fire sermons was complemented by carefully reasoned meditations on basic philosophical and theological themes. His written works represent a lifetime of devotion to the cause of unraveling for himself and communicating to others a detailed justification of (1) the majesty of the divine being, (2) the total depravity and predestination of man, and (3) the glorious work of the redemption of man through divine grace.

The themes of Puritanism and determination permeate Edwards' system of thought: Puritanism for the purity or holiness of the objective to be reached, and determination for the strictness of the methods whereby this objective could be secured and defended. Thus Edwards is the best exponent that America has ever produced of uncompromising Calvinist Puritanism. Calvinist Christianity requires an unflinching adherence to definite, firmly decided principles, from the absolute majesty and rule of the divine being to the utter depravity and determination of the will of man. Edwards was admirably suited in mind and temperament to the

9

carrying out of these strict principles, both in theory and in practice.

His theism forms the center of his world-view. Theist Christianity is based on the idea of God as creator and absolute ruler of the world. But it also requires that a sharp separation be made between God and His creation. The divine being is characterized by omnipotence, omniscience, and perfect benevolence, while the world, including man, is set off against this as temporal, limited, and totally dependent on God. In fact, with the fall of Adam, men were left in such a state of sin and depravity that they are powerless to perform any truly good actions or salvage their damaged souls. Only by supernatural assistance—by miracle—can man be saved. Man's will is so depraved that only a determination of it by a divine source can turn it away from selfishness and worldliness. According to Edwards' theism, it is absolutely essential that the start of anything good in man must proceed from the free grace of the divine being. Since all men have sinned against a God of perfect justice and love, all deserve eternal damnation. The divine being is under no obligation to save any man, but miraculously elects a few for saintliness as a free gift of his divine mercy. To Edwards, this meant that all men, without qualification, should be reminded, to their terror, of the misery of their lives and the peril of their souls. If they could only be brought to realize the hopelessness of their meager self-reliance, men might then pray for divine help and deliverance.

Edwards formulated his theism in the most rigid terms and made it an all-inclusive doctrine. He was convinced that it was right and realistic and sought to communicate his definiteness to others. To accomplish this, it was essential for him to defend strict Calvinist theism against the attacks of deists, Arminians,[1] and anyone else who might weaken the notions of man's predestination and the absolute sovereignty of the divine being. The encroachments of rationalism and the belief in the freedom of the will had to be put down if pure theism was to be maintained. Therefore, keenly aware of these dangerous tendencies, Edwards kept up a running attack against them in his major philosophical and theological writings. His resolve to set out a pure Calvinist position was matched only by the rigidity of the doctrine itself. His arguments became carefully measured disputations in which he defined basic terms and premises and then, with ruthless logic, proceeded to establish the inevitable conclusions of his doctrine, demolishing all other alternatives. His method suited his purpose perfectly, since the inevitable conclusions of logical reasoning simply illustrated to him the wonderful, ultimate determination of all things by the divine will.

For Edwards it is clear that man is not even given sufficient power to account for his own depravity. With great argumentative skill, he shows that men are certainly not the ultimate causes of their own existence or even of their coming into the world to do evil. A determination from a higher source is needed to explain man's creation. Edwards argues further that the existence of an absolute being or power is involved in the very question as to why there is *anything* in existence rather than *nothing*. Either there is absolute nothing or absolute being. But the former is a contradiction in terms, a logical impossibility; the thought that there *is* absolute nothing contradicts itself. Therefore, there must be an absolute something, an all-comprehending being, since the mind falls into absurdity or contradictions in trying to form an idea of its denial.

All things are ultimately determined by an eternal, infinite, and perfect source or cause: this is Edwards' leading principle. He even uses it to explain the final cause of evil and man's depraved condition. Man could not be depraved unless the infinite power of God permitted it. The divine being is not the direct cause of man's evil ways, but rather the indirect cause of them, since God, after the disobedience of Adam, simply took away the element in the soul or will of man necessary to achieve true virtue and prevent corrupt choices. Men are left with their natural wills, which are determined by self-love rather than divine or pure love. Men on their own are determined to make choices which reflect their limited and fallen nature. Even the divine being works according to the determination of the will. The divine will is determined by the most perfect and holy motives. God necessarily chooses what is perfectly good and virtuous. Man, on the other hand, by necessity chooses or wills what is imperfectly good or not really good at all, this being the result of the determination of his will by limited and selfish desires. Determination of the will is thus argued consistently and completely, for the divine being as well as for man.

Edwards formulated his basic theological ideas very early in life and throughout his career remained unwavering in his resolution to set out his principles decisively and piously. As a young student at Yale, he discovered the ideas of the English philosopher John Locke and the great scientist Isaac Newton. He decided to make use of their ideas in defending his own. Locke provided him with the inspiration that all knowledge must come from experience, and Newton provided a basis for Edwards to argue the universal causation of all things.

In the last year of his life, Edwards, because of his fine reputation as a thinker and clergyman, was called to be president of the College of

New Jersey, now Princeton University. He did not live long enough to take on the new responsibilities, but died of a smallpox infection on March 22, 1758, having assumed office only two months before.

EMPIRICISM AND IDEALISM   Jonathan Edwards was not yet thirteen years old when he entered Yale College. There, in his second year, he began to read and study John Locke's *An Essay Concerning Human Understanding*. As Edwards tells us, he received more pleasure from reading this essay than the greediest miser finds in gathering up handfuls of gold. That Edwards was prepared to appreciate and assimilate Locke's empirical philosophy with its emphasis on careful observation and analysis is indicated by his having composed earlier, at the age of twelve, an essay entitled *Of Insects*. This remarkable little essay shows him to have been a keen observer of fact with a talent for analyzing things. Edwards' discovery of Locke enabled him to bring his own latent ideas on fundamental philosophic topics into the open at an incredibly early age. Immediately upon reading Locke, Edwards composed his own *Notes on the Mind*, which showed not only that he had assimilated Locke's ideas, but that he had actually gone a long step beyond them, pushing Locke's position to what he thought was its logical conclusion. The maturity and originality of thought manifested in *Notes on the Mind* rank it as the *first* significant piece of American philosophy, and one of the most interesting items in the history of original philosophical thinking.

Locke had begun with the intention of finding the origin, certainty, and extent of human knowledge. He assumed, as did common sense, that both material bodies and minds existed. But he was not satisfied with the grounds philosophers gave for these common beliefs. The philosophy of Descartes, for example, had supported the ordinary beliefs in material things and mental substance by a strong rationalism and a doctrine of innate ideas, neither of which Locke could accept. Locke therefore argued for an empirically built philosophy according to which all ideas had their origin in experience. For Locke, the mind was analogous to a *tabula rasa* with only the two powers of (1) receiving ideas of the senses and (2) combining these ideas in various ways by reflection. The root of Locke's empiricism was that all the ideas of the human mind can ultimately be traced back to experience or sensation. All simple ideas had to be derived from experience: How could a person form an idea of, for example, the color yellow without recourse to sensation or experience? And if simple ideas can come only from experience, then complex or compound ideas can be analyzed as the result of the mind's reflecting upon, combining, and separating the original simple ideas or sensations. Innate ideas are impossible. The mind has no power to frame any ideas in which the simple ideas obtained by direct experience have no part.

Locke also distinguished between qualities of things and *ideas* of these qualities in the mind. Primary qualities—solidity, extension, figure, motion, rest, and number—are simply powers in objects capable of producing ideas in us which are resemblances of these qualities. For example, someone may have the idea that an apple is a solid object. Since solidity is a primary quality of bodies, this would mean that the solidity is really in the apple or solid body itself and that someone's idea of the apple's solidity actually resembles the solidity present in the apple. Secondary qualities, on the other hand—color, sound, smell, taste, etc.—are powers in things capable of producing ideas in us which are not resemblances of these qualities. The apple may taste sweet, according to Locke, yet sweetness is not a primary quality of the apple itself, it is merely an idea or experience in us. The apple may look red, but redness is not a property of the apple itself. Rather, it is an idea or experience only in our minds. Thus ideas of secondary qualities do not resemble any qualities in things themselves, but are purely mental. What might be termed tertiary qualities—the powers of objects to produce sensations of warmth or cold, pleasure or pain—certainly are not elements in things themselves. A needle may cause me to feel pain, but the pain is not in the needle; rather, it is in me or in my experience.

Locke's empirical theory thus brought all ideas to the test of observation and experience and at the same time provided the ground for a strong common-sense dualism—belief in material as well as mental realities. Edwards liked the empirical test of careful observation and the tracing of all ideas back to experience. But unlike Locke, he had no particular allegiance to common sense or to the material world. In fact, early in life he had developed a mystical affection for a supernatural sense and for the superior order of the spiritual world. He therefore began to drive Locke's empiricism to what he believed must be its inevitable result—idealism. Edwards would show that empiricism implies idealism. If *all* ideas come from experience, then even ideas of material bodies with their solidity, extension, and motion must come from experience or exist only in our mind. If the color is not really in the apple, but only in our mind or experience of the apple, then the solidity, shape and the whole so-called material body itself can be found nowhere but in experience or in the mind.

Edwards argues in *Notes on the Mind* that as the pain is not in the needle, nor color in the thing colored, so also all the other properties of a thing cannot be outside the mind or experience, but rather must be within the mind or experience. The solidity of material bodies, for example, is known to us by the resistance they offer to our sense of touch. But what is the feeling of resistance except an idea or mental existence? What can resistance or solidity be apart from any idea or sensation of it? Edwards concludes that it is impossible to know what resistance or solidity is apart from any ideas of it. Other so-called primary qualities are analyzed in terms of the idea of resistance itself. Extension or shape is the termination of resistance; motion is the termination of resistance from place to place. In so arguing, Edwards sought to reduce all material existence to mental existence. All things to be or to be known must come from experience or ideas; but ideas exist only mentally or in the mind; therefore all things including material bodies exist and are known only mentally, only in terms of ideas. Even divine things or the divine being itself must be known in terms of experience or a supernatural sense imparted to man by God. Edwards' empiricism carries over into religion: the basis of all religious knowledge must be a real experience or sense of the divine being.

> There is a difference between having an opinion that God is holy and gracious, and having a sense of the loveliness and beauty of that holiness and grace. . . . There is a wide difference between mere speculative rational judging anything to be excellent and having a sense of its beauty and sweetness. The former rests only in the head, speculation is only concerned in it; but the heart is concerned in the latter. When the heart is sensible of the beauty and amiableness of a thing it necessarily feels pleasure in the apprehension.[2]

Note that Edwards did not imply that all things exist only in the narrow compass of one's brain; the brain too, he maintained, exists only as an idea in some mind. To be is to be perceived or experienced by some mind, and to account for the permanence and orderliness of the world's existence Edwards drew the conclusion that all things exist as ideas in the infinite mind of the divine being. Edwards' idealism therefore implies the existence of an all-comprehending mind from which all things take their existence. His idealism thus suits his Calvinist theism insofar as the world, in order to exist, requires some mind to realize its existence. The world could not exist outside of a mind, and the mind of the divine being is omniscient, the knower of all things.

Edwards also argued for a Chain of Being that would correlate being or existence with mental or spiritual perfection. He held, for example, that an archangel has more being or existence than a worm because the worm does not exist for itself but only as an idea in some mind. The more mental existence or ideas a thing has, the more being or perfection that thing has. God has absolutely perfect existence since the divine being has an infinite mental existence or a perfectly consistent and comprehensive series of ideas in His mind.

The originality and maturity of Edwards' idealism, composed before he was twenty years of age, are all the more striking when we recall that virtually the same idealistic conclusions were developed by the famous English bishop and philosopher, George Berkeley, at about the same time. Berkeley argued essentially the same consequences of Locke's original empiricism and thereby became an important link in the chain of the development of modern empirical philosophy. That Edwards, independent of Berkeley and at so early an age, arrived at so nearly the same idealistic conclusions from Locke's original empiricism is all the more remarkable. Edwards' *Notes on the Mind* went unnoticed, however, and has been uncovered only in historical retrospect. Although Edwards never received the philosophical recognition that the power of his thought merited, he did lay a foundation for both empirical and idealistic philosophies which were to appear again and again in the course of development followed by other American philosophers.

THE FREEDOM OF THE WILL   In 1754 Jonathan Edwards published *A Careful and Strict Enquiry into the Modern Prevailing Notions of That Freedom of Will Which Is Supposed to Be Essential to Moral Agency, Virtue and Vice, Reward and Punishment, Praise and Blame.* In important respects, this work is Edwards' greatest achievement. On the one hand, it established him as America's most articulate theologian; on the other, it shows him as perhaps the foremost philosophical determinist since Spinoza. Formally considered, this work is a defence of Calvinism by way of a refutation of the Arminian notion of the freedom or self-determining power of the will.

In Edwards' mind the problem of man's will—its freedom or its determination—was of both contemporary and lasting importance. During his time strict Calvinist theism was threatened by the Arminian belief that men could freely choose to sin or not to sin. Theologically, i.e., in terms of basic religious principles, Arminians denied man's utter depravity, his utter helplessness apart from God. If the practice of strict Calvinism was to be preserved, it had to be purged of any such current heretical notion of freedom as would imply a denial of man's absolute dependence on the divine being. Philosophically, the whole notion of man's moral responsibility required careful explanation so that the notion of man's responsibility for sin could be squared with the condition of man's will. And this explanation had to apply to all men since the fall of Adam.

A theory was required, therefore, that would contain, in its negative aspect, a refutation of man's autonomous will, and in its positive aspect, a justification of man's moral responsibility. The dilemma can be put as follows: Unless freedom of the will is refuted, predestination cannot be maintained; and unless man's responsibility for sin is affirmed, he cannot be condemned to eternal damnation. The entire theory as well as the practice of Calvinism thus hinged on the notion of the will. And Edwards set for himself the task of explaining in minute detail how the will can be both predestined and responsible for what it does.

He begins with a definition. Will means choice; to will is to choose. Will is the power of a person's mind to choose or refuse, to accept or reject anything. Any voluntary preference is a choice; hence to will is to choose voluntarily. But as there are no preferences apart from inclinations or desires, Edwards argues that a man never wills or chooses anything contrary to his desires. Even though choice or will is conscious or voluntary, it is nevertheless a function of preference or desire. The will is therefore determined by something—by desire, or motives. What determines the will? The strongest motive before the mind. The will or one's choices always follow what the person conceives to be the greatest apparent preference or good. A man's will always follows the last dictate of his understanding, what he considers to be to his best advantage. This is not always that which is momentarily the most agreeable, nor that which is in the long run the best possible advantage; it is, rather, that which is estimated or understood to be advantageous at the time of understanding.

Will, then, according to Edwards, is conscious or voluntary choice that is determined by the strongest desire. If choice involves a selection among alternative objects, the selection fixes upon whichever object has the stronger desire or motive behind it. This connection between the strongest motive on the one hand and choice or will on the other is a cause-effect relationship. Edwards holds that it is impossible for anything to happen without a cause: if choices occur, if men will or choose anything, there must be a cause for the choice. Choices are determined by their causes; the will is determined if all events have causes.

But is the causal relation between motives and choices necessary or is it only contingent? Edwards takes the strict position that the causal relation between motive and choice is a necessary relation. That is, real necessity means *certainty* for Edwards. If between A and B there is a real causal connection, then it is certain that B will follow A. Any perfect knowledge of causal relations (such as that of the divine being) must according to Edwards, be founded upon "the certainty that is in things themselves." If the divine being knows that certain effects will necessarily follow certain causes, he knows this only because the causal relation in reality is inevitable. Because B will or must follow A, a perfect mind can have a foreknowledge of this fixed relation.

With this strong conception of causal necessity in mind, Edwards next draws a distinction between natural and moral necessity. A morally necessary effect is simply that which follows a moral cause; that is, a motive to which praise or blame can be applied. Natural necessity involves no moral choice. An earthquake, for example, may kill thousands of people not because it made a choice to do so, but simply through the inevitability of natural causes and effects. In contrast, a man, out of hate, may kill another man because he chooses to do so—because his choice is determined by the strongest motive (in this case, hate).

Edwards also speaks of moral inability and contrasts this with natural inability. The difference is based on the distinction between being unable to will or choose and being unable to perform something. A child, for example, may be unable to choose to kill his father because of a strong inclination of love toward his father. This is moral inability, not natural inability, since the child presumably is physically capable of killing. On the other hand, a person may be unable to kill someone because of natural inability—if he does not have sufficient strength to perform the action—even though he may have the desire to do it. Edwards says:

> A strong habit of virtue and a great degree of holiness may cause a moral inability to love wickedness in general . . . or to choose a wicked life. . . . And on the other hand, a great degree of habitual wickedness may lay a man under an inability to love and choose holiness.[3]

A very malicious man, for example, may be unable to act benevolently toward an enemy, not because of any physical inability, but out of moral inability of the will or motivation.

After arguing that the will or choice is under causal necessity, Edwards considers the questions of freedom or liberty of will and action. He admits that men are able to do what they choose or will but denies that they have free choices. A moral agent, to be responsible for his actions, to be blamed or praised, must have the power to do what he wills or chooses. No one, Edwards admits, can be blamed or praised for involuntary acts—actions that he is forced to do against his will. Edwards therefore uses the words "liberty" and "freedom" to apply to actions which are the results of voluntary choices. But, he adds, "to talk of liberty or the contrary as belonging to the very will itself is not to speak good sense.[4] . . . the will itself is not an agent that has a will; the power of choosing itself has not a power of choosing." [5] That which has the power of choosing is the man and not the will of the man. A bird, he argues, may be said to have the power of flight or the freedom to fly— but the power of flight itself does not have the freedom to fly. The agent is the only thing that can be responsible or free, not some ability or power within the agent.

The Arminians whom Edwards vigorously opposes claimed that the will is self-determining or free—that men are free to choose this or that. Edwards denies this on the grounds that it conflicts with the principle that every effect has a cause and that cause and effect must be logically distinct. Nothing that comes to pass or exists in time can be the cause of itself. The will cannot be determined by itself since nothing that happens is its own cause. To say that the will is free or that men have free choices implies that choices make choices. This leads to an infinite regression, according to Edwards. If will determines the will, then a person chooses to choose, and if a person chooses to choose then a person chooses to choose to choose and so on to infinity. On the other hand, if there is said to be a first choice, a choice that is itself not chosen, then the will is not determined by itself, since we have a choice that is not determined by any further choice or will.

From this Edwards concludes that it does not make good sense to say that the will is self-determined or free. He adds that it is in agreement with good sense to hold that actions, not volitions, may be free. All that is required by common sense or even morality is that a person be free to do what he chooses, not that he be free to choose. As a later philosopher phrased it, men are free to do what they choose but not free to choose what they choose.

Edwards brings his doctrine of determinism to completion by pointing out that the will of the divine being is not free either. He argues that God is morally perfect—that the divine being necessarily wills or chooses only holy or benevolent actions. God's moral excellence is necessary, yet praiseworthy, according to Edwards. He then asks this pointed question: If God is under the moral necessity to choose only what is holy, if the divine being is incapable of any unholy or evil action, then how is it that *even the Arminians* praise the divine being? The answer is clear to Edwards. Praise applies to the nature of motives, not to their freedom. Holy motives are praised because they are good—and if they are necessary then they are perfectly or inevitably good. Bad motives are blamed because they are bad, and when they are necessary they are all the more deserving of blame. A creature whose motives are necessarily wicked is absolutely detestable or sinful. The more tightly connected the bad cause and the bad effect, the greater the evil. The more tightly connected the good cause and the good effect, the greater the good.

In this manner Edwards drew the inevitable conclusions of his logic, refuting the freedom of the will not just for man but also for the divine being. With this he accomplished two important results: he defended the Calvinist notion of predestination which was under attack from the Arminians, and he laid an important cornerstone for his moral philosophy. The problem for moral philosophy as Edwards saw it was to define the nature of true virtue. But if the will were not determined, if the will were in fact free, then there could be no genuine virtue, since then virtue would be uncaused or a matter of caprice. For a Puritan like Edwards it was inconceivable that moral virtue could be left to chance or caprice. For a Puritan there would have to be a strict cause for virtue and a strict cause for vice. The proof that the will is not free, but determined by strict necessity, serves, for Edwards, the important purpose of laying the solid foundations of a sturdy ethics—an ethics which includes the strictest obligations, and in which the will must be precisely determined.

TRUE VIRTUE AND RELIGIOUS EXPERIENCE   Edwards' consummate skill as the ablest philosopher of Puritanism is nowhere better demonstrated than in his carefully reasoned attempts to explain the nature of true virtue and true religion. In 1755 he composed *The Nature of True Virtue*, having written *A Treatise Concerning Religious Affections* in 1746. Both of these works manifest Edwards' steadfast intention of establishing the truth of strict Calvinism on solid foundations and of defending its genuine value from misconceptions and criticisms. Edwards strongly believed that the nature of true virtue and true religion had to be clearly set out and distinguished from their counterfeits—false virtue and false religion. To acquire a clear, logical understanding of virtue and religion was itself a form of Puritan virtue and piety.

What Edwards tried to show, therefore, in these two essays (the one in moral philosophy, the other in the philosophy of religion) was that moral virtue can be genuine or true only if it is based on strict piety or the love of God. This mutual implication of morals and religion, or virtue and piety, is essential to his entire argument in both treatises. The religious tone of his moral philosophy and the moral tone of his conception of real religion simply indicate the basic unity of his thought and the unity of the doctrine he was expounding.

Both religion and morality must be based on affection or love, but not on any mere human or partial affection. Religion and morality both require perfect or universal love—a combination of Platonic and Christian love. It is in this insistence on perfect love or pure benevolence for both morality and religion that we see evidence of Edwards' efforts to unite Platonism and Christianity. Platonic love signifies an ideal affection that is purified of any selfish or worldly interests. It must be completely universal and impartial. Christian love, on the other hand, must be completely sincere and spiritual. In short, both Platonic love and Christian love require the complete conversion of the soul from any earthly or temporal affections to purely ideal and everlasting benevolence.

Edwards begins his analysis of true virtue by focusing attention step by step upon its exact defining characteristics. This means explaining what virtue is not, as well as what it is. First, it is subsumed under excellence or beauty as opposed to non-excellence or deformity. But not all excellence or beauty can be called virtue, only that which pertains to creatures with understanding and will. Moral virtue cannot exist without the mind and its power of choosing or deciding. The beauty of flowers or the singing of birds, for example, cannot be called moral excellence or beauty. But not all operations of the mind or decisions of men can be characterized as moral in quality either. Only those decisions of the mind that are based on the heart, that is, affections and choices that deserve praise or blame, can be called moral.

Moral qualities, whether good or bad, depend upon emotion and choice. Only those actions which result from choices of the heart—the affections—are morally praiseworthy or blameworthy according to Edwards. Honest or good actions, therefore, are morally founded on love, whereas dishonest or bad actions are founded on base motives. In either case, affection determines the will and is therefore the foundation of virtue.

What is the foundation, then, of true virtue? It must be some affection, some benevolence or love. But love of what? Love in relation to what? Men by nature operate on the principle of self-love, choosing courses that they consider to be in their own interest. But self-love on the human scale is too narrow to serve as the principle of true virtue. Since man's will is limited and depraved, it cannot serve as the defining criterion of real virtue. Altruistic affection for others, whether family, neighbors, or even humanity at large, is also not sufficient, since it is interested and not disinterested affection. On his own, man is simply not capable of real, impartial, and complete love. Man's own affections, no matter how great, are not infinite, are not completely universal. Edwards draws the conclusions that true virtue is love toward the divine being or being in general, and that human virtue must fall short of this goal. True virtue is here distinguished from both apparent virtue and vice. Selfish dishonesty, for example, is morally bad, since it is obviously not based on good will or even limited benevolence. Natural honesty, based on humanly good will, while not malevolent or wicked, is nevertheless not completely good. The natural virtues that men are capable of by their own powers, according to Edwards, are all forms of limited benevolence. They are good only in a limited way, and are not infinitely good or based on an infinitely good will.

The only proper object of true virtue is being in general, the divine being. Acts of justice based on the altruistic motive of doing good to men have only a limited basis. But acts of justice based on the motive of universal love or benevolence to God have a perfectly complete basis. Completely impartial love is therefore a requirement of true virtue. True virtue is a function of the motives behind choices and depends on the kind of emotion that moves the will. Virtuous actions are caused by virtuous choices, and virtuous choices themselves must be determined by entirely good motives. But only the divine being has necessarily good motives. Therefore, if man is capable of true virtue at all, it is not because of his limited affections, but solely because the divine being imparts from his perfectly good will these gracious affections to man. We have here the inevitable dependence of morals on religion which Edwards staunchly defends. Man's moral responsibility is complete, but his moral ability is incomplete. Man ought to act according to principles of perfect justice and benevolence; this is his moral responsibility. But he is unable to accomplish this on his own; this is his moral weakness. Man has the freedom to do what he chooses, but is unable by himself to choose what is absolutely good.

True religion, therefore, becomes the foundation of true morality. Human morality, morality not founded on truly spiritual causes can only be an inferior type of morality by comparison with a completely God-centered morality founded on purely spiritual causes. Human morality is tainted by the weaknesses of the flesh, while spiritual morality overcomes worldly desires and is completely free from corruptions of the flesh. The real nature of virtue is thus, for Edwards, bound up with the real nature of religion.

Religion, like morality, is based on emotion. In fact, emotion gives the incentives for all actions, whether moral or religious. But how is one to determine what affections are truly religious? By what signs is one to ascertain whether a practice or sentiment has a truly spiritual character? This problem was a vital one for Edwards, both in a practical and in a theoretical sense. Religious revivals were frequent during his lifetime; the Great Awakening began in Edwards' own village, Northampton, Massachusetts, in 1734 and subsequently spread over the eastern coast from Maine to Georgia. For about fifteen years New England was the center of religious stirrings and conversions. Edwards defended these revivals because he believed he saw in them the miraculous workings of the divine will. These emotional religious awakenings were consistent with his general view that religion is fundamentally a matter of the heart, of the affections. It was Edwards' fundamental conviction that religion depends upon feeling, that no conversion could really take place except through an emotional upheaval. The true basis of religion was spiritual love, and unless men's hearts were driven by divine love, they could have no real religion in their souls.

Yet Edwards was also keenly aware of the problems raised by emotional religious conversions because he saw that emotions may be both excessive and superficial. An outward appearance may be mistaken for a real spiritual transformation. He saw the practical as well as the philosophical need for distinguishing the reality of religion from the appearance, and in his *Treatise Concerning Religious Affections* he set himself the painstaking task of unraveling, one by one, the distinguishing features of true religion.

Consistent with his basic Calvinist position is Edwards' notion that the practice of true religion depends upon divine election. The elect, those who are truly religious, are so by virtue of divine intervention in their lives. Election, or conversion to the practice of true religion, can take place only by virtue of a supernatural cause producing the supernatural effect of transforming man's natural sinfulness into a truly spiritual life. Divine grace, in the form of a supernatural light, must be added unto man if his footsteps are to be infallibly guided in holy ways. Ordinary experience and man's natural powers of understanding are insufficient to bring him onto the path of true religion. A supernatural sense is required to see the spiritual light of true religion, and this sense can supervene only as a miraculous gift from the divine being. Against the deists Edwards argues that reason cannot take the place of divine revelation. He points out that reason is no substitute for sense experience. Reason cannot prove that honey is sweet or that ice is cold. "The truth of the numberless particular propositions cannot be known by reason, considered independently of the testimony of our senses, and without an implicit faith in that testimony." [6] Likewise in matters of religion, reason alone is insufficient to give man a sure sense of what to do and what to believe. Particular revelations are required if men are to possess certain and definite knowledge where reason would either be silent or fall into insoluble paradoxes.

Edwards observes that a union of inclination and practice, of affection and action, is necessary for true religion. "A man's having much affection does not prove that he has any true religion: but if he has no affection, it proves that he has no true religion." [7] But also, "Herein chiefly appears the power of true godliness, viz., in its being effectual in practice." [8] In other words, true religion is not distinguished by outward display but rather by a certain inward *control* of mind and body that the truly religious person possesses. Edwards goes into great detail enumerating twelve signs by which the presence of true religion may be identified. These signs show a spiritually controlled or holy life through such divinely received powers as understanding the divine will, the determination to set divine things above all others, ability to practice true humility, ability to beget and provoke all the Christian virtues, and finally, ability to persist in making Christian practice the chief business of one's life.

True religion, then, is only true as it becomes the center of life itself. This is in agreement with Edwards' basic theoretic position that men are entirely dependent upon the will of the divine being. True religion implies submission to benevolent love in general, with the attendant consequence of a change in man's nature and way of life. Moral energy and an eagerness to perform true virtue in all its forms are the consequences of religious experience. True religion implies a causal necessity between man's affections or feelings and man's will and actions. It involves the inevitable following of holy practices as the results of holy affections or experiences. True religion for Edwards signifies the determination to submit to and live by the predetermined plan of the divine being. There can be no caprice, no indecision, no wavering in true religion once it is understood to be perfectly determined in the divine schema of all things.

THE SIGNIFICANCE AND INFLUENCE OF EDWARDS   Jonathan Edwards stands head and shoulders above all other American thinkers of his time. Neither Samuel Johnson (1696–1772), who developed a similar form of philosophical idealism and who founded Kings College (now Columbia University), nor Cadwallader Colden (1688–1776), who developed philosophic theories of matter and mind and who also tried to explain Newtonian science, measures up in acuteness and originality to Jonathan Edwards. Although Edwards' importance for the course of early American history and the whole history of religion in America has long been clearly recognized, his philosophic importance has not. True, he stands as the most articulate spokesman for early American Puritanism. The nineteenth-century historian George Bancroft thus acknowledged Edwards' historical position: "He that would know the workings of the New England mind in the middle of the last century, and the throbbings of its heart must give his days and nights to the study of Jonathan Edwards."[9] And Edwards received recognition during his own lifetime as the most skillful exponent of Calvinism in America. Through his sermons and writings he came to stand for the pure mind and character of American Puritanism.

Meanwhile Edwards' reputation as Puritan sage has almost entirely eclipsed his importance as a philosopher. His original philosophic talent is not generally recognized, and even when recognized, appears only in historical retrospect. Historically, Edwards is associated with all the narrowness and moral fanaticism of the movement he defended, and his philosophic influence is almost nil. Santayana,[10] writing about the American philosophic tradition, associated Edwards with "the religion of the agonized conscience." This identification has remained, and we cannot point to any prominent American philosopher who received philosophical inspiration from the works of Edwards. In fact, it is only recently that Edwards' stature as a creative philosopher has come to be seriously considered.

His early fame depended upon his being identified as a preacher of hell fire. His famous sermon "Sinners in the Hands of an Angry God" seemed to seal his reputation as a fanatical rather than a dispassionate thinker. His philosophical essays on freedom of the will, true virtue, the mind, and the religious affections made little impact on philosophical thought in America as it later developed. Although both Emerson and Royce were in their time to fashion forms of philosophical idealism similar to Edwards', they were not inspired or influenced by him, but rather by English and German thinkers.

Philosophically, therefore, Edwards was neither followed nor refuted; he was neglected. His intellectual impact, consequently, was felt only in the course of the development of religious and theological ideas. One explanation for this neglect can perhaps be found in the fact that American intellectual history in general is more noticeable for its borrowings from European and other sources than for its concern with its own history and traditions. American thinkers, generally, were schooled in European thought and maintained a rather neglectful attitude toward their own history. The prestige of older European thought in part accounts for this. William James is really the first significant American philosopher to derive any of his ideas from another American philosopher.

Another explanation for Edwards' neglect is perhaps found in the fact that he was defending, during his lifetime, a decaying world outlook. Puritanism, by the first half of the eighteenth century, was dying out. By 1750 the forces of the American Enlightenment were sufficiently strong to encourage abandonment of the Puritan world view. The Puritans themselves had encouraged learning and had contributed to the education of men. In this sense they prepared the way for the demands of political and religious freedom which were characteristic of the last half of eighteenth-century American life. Puritanism counted learning and industry as virtues, but it did not stand for democracy or religious tolerance or freedom. It therefore paved the way for an outlook of cosmopolitan, secular enlightenment which oddly enough was the very antithesis of its provincial, religious theocracy. Consequently, during his own lifetime Edwards actually defended a view of life and the world that did not fit the spirit of the times.

Yet a philosopher's significance cannot be entirely measured by his historical influence. In fact, it is to be regretted that Edwards' carefully argued philosophical treatises were eclipsed in the course of identifying him with merely the religion of an agonized conscience. Although virtually unnoticed, his philosophical essays represent the very high note upon which American philosophy actually began. His significance, if measured in logical and conceptual terms, has to be weighed as considerable.

He succeeded in articulating a carefully consistent philosophical system. In his epistemology he began with an empirical framework and derived a metaphysical idealism and coherence theory of truth. Starting with the view that all ideas must be derived from experience, he drew the conclusion that all ideas of so-called "externally existing material things" must depend upon the experience of the mind. The material world is therefore known to us only through our ideas, and can only be known to exist mentally. Truth itself can reside nowhere but in the mind, according to Edwards. A true idea is one that corresponds to reality; and if all reality is mental, then all truth is mental. Truth is the perception of the relations between ideas. Falsehood is the supposition of the "relations between ideas that are inconsistent with those ideas themselves; not their disagreement with things without." [11]

In making his theory of knowledge or truth consistent with his theory of reality Edwards achieved a remarkable philosophical synthesis in his own thought. His view that all ideas must come from experience—his empiricism—is also applied in his moral philosophy and in his theory of true religion. Morals and religion must also be based on experience, even though the bases offered by human ideas or specifically human experiences are insufficient. He therefore postulates the notion of divine grace, which is imparted to man from the divine being, to account for true virtue and true religion. The occurrence of miracles thereby comes within the purview of experience and is empirical, since miraculous occurrences are all experiences of the divine being which may be imparted to man.

Perhaps Edwards' greatest achievement is his synthesis of his philosophic and religious views. Not only did he tie his philosophical ideas together, but he integrated them within the framework of his Calvinism. Every one of his philosophical conclusions was of service to him in establishing his religious outlook. His arguments for idealism—that all existence is within the mind—established for him the superior reality of spiritual or immaterial being. His coherence theory of truth led to the identification between absolute truth and the divine mind, since the standard of truth must, he argued, be the perfectly complete and consistent infinite series of ideas in the mind of God. Even the analysis of true virtue leads to the conclusion of a perfectly good or holy will as the standard or measure of all moral values. The only object of true virtue is disinterested benevolence, or love of being in general.

What is perhaps Edwards' most important philosophic effort, at least the effect sustaining the greatest amount of careful argumentation and drawing of subtle distinctions, is his analysis of the freedom of the will. The distinction he draws between being free to choose and being free to do as one chooses enables him on the one hand to remain a strict determinist and yet on the other hand account for moral responsibility. Moral responsibility, he argues, does not depend on the will's being free to choose. All that is necessary for the moral responsibility of any agent is power—ability or freedom to do what is chosen. Moral consequences must have moral causes, according to Edwards. Moral choices must be determined by good or bad motives or desires.

Edwards' philosophical importance has to be mainly located in his synthesis of all the parts of his philosophy within the framework of Calvinist religion. He is the first systematic theologian-philosopher that America produced. It is all the more remarkable that such a system of tightly argued philosophy was constructed as early as 1758. One has to wait more than a hundred years to find a rival for Edwards in the development of systematic thought in America. Not until after the Civil War does one find any systems of philosophy in America that are as meticulously argued.

NOTES

1. For the Arminians, see note 2 on p. 7.
2. Jonathan Edwards, in C. H. Faust and T. Johnson, eds., *Jonathan Edwards: Representative Selections*, p. 107, from "A Divine and Supernatural Light."
3. *Ibid.*, p. 279, from "The Freedom of the Will."
4. *Ibid.*, p. 280.
5. *Ibid.*
6. Jonathan Edwards, in Vergilius Ferm, ed., *Puritan Sage: Collected Writings of Jonathan Edwards*, p. 94, from "The Insufficiency of Reason as a Substitute for Revelation."
7. Edwards, in Faust and Johnson, eds., *op. cit.*, pp. 223–224, from "Religious Affections."
8. *Ibid.*, p. 251.
9. *Ibid.*, pp. xiv–xv, from "Introduction."
10. See Part II, Chapter 4, p. 209 of this volume.
11. Edwards, in Ferm, ed., *op. cit.*, p. 17, from "The Mind."

QUESTIONS FOR DISCUSSION

1. To what extent does the Puritanism of Jonathan Edwards offer a complete and coherent philosophy of life?
2. How does Edwards argue from empiricism to idealism? Is his view cogent that all existence is mental?
3. If man has no freedom of the will, how can he be held morally responsible for his actions, according to Edwards?
4. Does Edwards present a good case for his view that true virtue and true religion go hand in hand?
5. What would you say is the most important legacy of Edwards' philosophy?

SUGGESTED READINGS

Notes on the Mind. Edwards' early formulation of his empiricism and idealism. [In Faust and Johnson, eds., *Jonathan Edwards: Representative Selections*, pp. 27–37.]

A Divine and Supernatural Light. Edwards extends empiricism to include a supernatural sense. [In Faust and Johnson, pp. 102–111.]

The Insufficiency of Reason as a Substitute for Revelation. Edwards' arguments against deism or mere natural religion based on reason alone. [In Ferm, ed., *Puritan Sage: Collected Writings of Jonathan Edwards*, pp. 93–109.]

Freedom of the Will. Edwards' definition of the will (Part I, Section I); determination of the will (Part I, Section II); distinction between natural and moral necessity (Part I, Section IV); difference between being free to choose and being free to do as one chooses (Part I, Section V); whether any events can exist without causes (Part II, Section III); moral virtue, necessity, and praise (Part III, Section I). [In Ferm.]

The Nature of True Virtue. Definition of true virtue (Ch. I); analysis of self-love (Ch. IV). [In Ferm.]

A Treatise Concerning Religious Affections. Edwards defines true religion (Part I); distinguishes signs of truly gracious and holy affections (Part III). [In Ferm.]

PRIMARY SOURCES

Jonathan Edwards, *The Nature of True Virtue*, Foreword by W. K. Frankena (Ann Arbor: University of Michigan Press, 1960).

C. H. Faust and T. Johnson, eds., *Jonathan Edwards: Representative Selections* (New York: American Book, 1935).

Virgilius Ferm, ed., *Puritan Sage: Collected Writings of Jonathan Edwards* (New York: Library Publishers, 1953).

Perry Miller, gen. ed., *The Works of Jonathan Edwards*, Vol. I, *Freedom of the Will*, ed. by Paul Ramsey; Vol. II, *Religious Affections*, ed. by John E. Smith (New Haven, Conn.: Yale University Press, 1957, 1959).

SECONDARY SOURCES

Alfred O. Aldridge, *Jonathan Edwards* (New York: Washington Square Press, 1964).

Perry Miller, *Jonathan Edwards* (New York: Meridian, 1959).

2 *Thomas Jefferson*

Enlightenment and Freedom

The figure of Thomas Jefferson (1743–1826) is unique in the history of
American life and thought. His accomplishments were so varied, his
interests so rich, and his life so much a part of his times that any simple
characterization of him is bound to be too restrictive. He might best be
compared to the Roman emperor and philosopher Marcus Aurelius as
one of the few individuals in history who have achieved intellectual as
well as political eminence. Even this comparison is too limited to do
justice to the breadth and vitality of Jefferson's accomplishments and
concerns.

Born in Virginia in 1743, Jefferson was heir to the aristocratic life
of a gentleman farmer and landowner. He received a fine classical education at the College of William and Mary, and was later admitted to
the practice of law. His earliest interests were directed to all those
worldly pursuits that bring some genuine usefulness or good for the
progress of man. His attachment to the land, to learning, and to civic
duty remained with him throughout his long life. Jefferson was especially
fortunate in that he possessed the advantages and endowments necessary
to help him become a forceful leader in the eventful times during
America's struggle for freedom and self-government. He was, during
this formative period, a Universal Man among Universal Men. No one
had mind and hand more involved in shaping the life of the new Ameri-

29

can Republic than did Jefferson. And no one conceived the life of the new, struggling Republic in broader humanistic terms than he.

Jefferson expressed in his thoughts and carried through in his activities all the principal concerns of the American Enlightenment. His wide range of reading and personal contacts gave him access to political, scientific, and philosophic ideas of all ages from ancient Greeks to Enlightenment thinkers in eighteenth-century France, England, and America. He succeeded Benjamin Franklin as president of the American Philosophical Society, which was concerned with promoting and publishing all forms of useful knowledge that would contribute to the betterment of mankind. Along with Franklin, he represented the United States as minister to France and joined in the intellectual activities of French cultural life. As a free thinker and humanist, Jefferson brought as much to France by way of Enlightenment as he took away. Both he and Franklin were perfectly at home in French intellectual circles; in fact, Jefferson kept up a steady life-long correspondence with many of the leading philosophers and scientists of Europe. The spread of knowledge and the discovery of useful information were of vital concern to all men who counted themselves as free thinkers and who believed in the fundamental freedom of man.

The American Enlightenment, in the last half of the eighteenth century, represents an interesting reaction to and contrast with Puritanism. The growth of learning, the development of commerce, and the growth of urban life and population in general hastened the end of the provincial and religiously authoritarian way of Puritanism. Interest in the world and in social life took the place of interest in otherworldliness and sin. The spread of learning as well as the growth of science and useful knowledge brought to its end the Puritan age of miracle and the depravity of man. The interests and needs of the times required a belief in the innate goodness and perfectibility of man.

Very near the heart of the Enlightenment was a concern for religious freedom. In Europe and in America there appeared during this period many prominent figures who strove for the exercise of independent thinking and the elimination of intolerance and oppression in matters of religion. Jefferson, during his long lifetime, was an outspoken crusader for religious freedom. He asserted, "I can never join Calvin in addressing *his* God . . . , his religion was daemonism. If ever man worshipped a false God, he did."[1] Jefferson's strong opposition to Calvinist theism was based on his concerns for human freedom, happiness, and the growth of practical knowledge. Calvinism considered man depraved, was intolerant of other religious views, and placed miracle and revelation ahead of reason and experiment. Jefferson, as an advocate of *deism*, considered man good and perfectible, stood for religious tolerance, and favored the growth of natural knowledge as showing the benevolent design of the divine being in all the laws and parts of nature.

Deism, to which many prominent men of the age subscribed, asserts, in opposition to Calvinist theism, that religion is based on human reason and observation rather than on revelation or miracle. This *natural religion*, as it is also called, held that the natural powers of man are sufficient to reveal the purposeful arrangement of things as due to the superintending power of a divine being. For deism the existence of a divine being is required as a creator of the universe, and the universe is conceived as orderly and rational, changing in accordance with natural laws. Once created with orderly laws, nature accounts for all occurrences. Divine intervention (through miracles) is not necessary to account for the course of events, and in fact would represent a flaw in nature's orderly mechanism. Jefferson, in defending deistic views, was giving expression to his fundamental concern for the well-being and progress of man. Deism was the form of religion that was open to the growth of new knowledge; its orientation was, above all, humanistic. Calvinist theism was God-centered; deism was man-centered. Calvinism was for the elect; deism was open to all men.

The American Enlightenment was also devoted to political freedom. Just as religious freedom implied a sense of man's importance and essential goodness, so political freedom involved an awareness of man's right to self-government. Here again, Jefferson was a leader in the cause of political liberty and self-determination. He showed himself to be both a man of action and a man of thoughtful concern for the broad problems of political life. As a man of the Enlightenment, Jefferson saw that political organizations too often represented a tyranny of the few over the many. His confidence in the people to decide their own manner of government was based on his optimistic view of the possibilities latent within human nature: men could perfect themselves as knowledge was allowed to grow and education to flourish. He viewed political freedom, therefore, as both a natural right and a continuing experiment. A man's freedom cannot be infringed upon without denying the essential worth, perfectibility, or goodness of mankind. The birthright of freedom can easily be usurped and is therefore in need of ever-vigilant defence. According to Jefferson, enlightenment and freedom had to be taken together; unless men were educated and enlightened, their freedom would either bring on mob rule or be easily dissipated. And unless men were free to inquire, form their opinions, and test their hypotheses, they could never be enlightened.

In Jefferson's view, highly typical of the Enlightenment, men in society could devise orderly ways of pursuing their mutual well-being through reason and experiment. Social law could come under the guidance of reason and could benefit from the advancement of knowledge. These beliefs coincide with a strong faith in the essential rational makeup of the whole universe. This *rationalism* in Jefferson is fundamental; it ties together his strong concern for both political and religious freedom. The author of the *Declaration of Independence* was also the author of the *Bill Establishing Religious Freedom in Virginia.* In Jefferson's eyes, political and religious freedom were demands of reason. Deism was for him a religion of reason; democracy was simply the politics of reason. Yet, his rationalism was always tied to a strong realistic respect for facts and common sense. If he assumed that the natural universe and the social world were controlled by reason at all, this could only mean that observed facts or effects of rational order were open to careful inspection. Claims of reason had to be tested by experience or observation. In fact, to Jefferson the value of men's reason signified just this—that it can pass the tests of experience and observation.

Thomas Jefferson's style of writing is a further indication of the perfect manner in which he represents the American Enlightenment. Compared with Jonathan Edwards, Jefferson's language is uninvolved and essentially simple. He shows little faith in elaborate arguments. Unlike Edwards, he found himself in agreement with common sense on many important philosophical topics, and his ideas, therefore, did not require metaphysical refinement on such topics as man's basic moral sense, the existence of the material world, or the freedom of the will. Jefferson took a common-sense attitude when he asserted that men have a basic sense of moral uprightness and are free to follow honest or dishonest intentions. To argue that men are incapable of true, moral virtue or unable to make free moral choices would be, for Jefferson, simply to oppose all good sense. The view that all existence is really mental or that matter really is not substantial would appear pure whimsy to a man of Jefferson's strong common-sense belief in the real existence of material bodies.

The unsophisticated character of many of Jefferson's basic ideas may give the impression that he was not philosophical at all or that he left his basic notions unargued and philosophically unexamined. This misunderstanding is encouraged by the fact that Jefferson never wrote a systematic treatise expounding his basic philosophical views. Nevertheless, the philosophical character of his thought is quite apparent if two points are kept in mind: he advocated a common-sense position in philosophy, and he embodied the Enlightenment's broad, untechnical, unspecialized view of philosophy. Jefferson believed that knowledge grew by the communication and usefulness of ideas, and ideas, to have any real human meaning, have to be intelligibly communicated and have to possess some human use. Since knowledge requires the efforts of many minds and since it must be tested by the standard of human progress, it must be formulated in terms related to the natural powers of man's understanding.

The Enlightenment view held that knowledge is common knowledge. Knowledge cannot be esoteric and at the same time serve any humanitarian purpose. Philosophy, rather than being a specialized branch of academic learning or speculation, is the sum of all the branches of useful knowledge. The Enlightenment philosopher must be a universal man. He cannot separate political ideas from ideas of science; he cannot compartmentalize his learning or experience, nor become an expert in just one subdivision. All knowledge worthy of the name must contribute to man's progress. Improved methods in agriculture, in regulating trade, or in reasoning or predicting the weather are philosophical in their fundamental character insofar as they prove useful. It is apparent that Jefferson's thought ties together under a rule of reason or common sense if one examines his basic views on science and education.

Basic in Enlightenment thought was the view that the growth of science and education implied human progress. The happiness of man was to be the result of overcoming ignorance and finding useful applications of knowledge. Experimentation and invention were looked upon as positive goods. In this humanistic conception of science, the importance of observation and collection of useful information was emphasized. Science itself was conceived as an inductive growth from carefully collected facts. The conclusions of science were its applications, since there would be no utility in merely collecting facts if they did not establish a worthwhile result. This utilitarian view of science, which Jefferson shared with Franklin and others, implied that the terms *science, knowledge,* and *philosophy* were interchangeable. Science was organized knowledge, information from which useful results could be obtained. And philosophy simply stood for the integrated or systematic pursuit of knowledge for the well-being and progress of man.

For this reason, Jefferson was a staunch advocate of liberal education for all men. His interest in a broad-based, useful education can be seen in his activities in founding the University of Virginia. He took part in planning its scientific curriculum, drew up the architectural plans for its buildings, supervised its construction, and served as its first president. He saw to it that agricultural studies, Greek and Roman classics, Newtonian science, and English and French humanistic thought were included in its curriculum. The purpose of its system of education was to produce enlightened, free men who could function as responsible citizens and contribute leadership and inventiveness to the progress of mankind. Enlightenment required the learning and preservation of worthwhile attainments of men in the past. Freedom required courage and experimentation with an eye turned to the future. These themes of enlightenment and freedom are central to Jefferson's view of man and his whole conception of philosophy. His vigorous interest in maintaining them, both in theory and in practice, make him the most perfect embodiment of Enlightenment philosophy that America produced.

MATERIALISM AND COMMON-SENSE REALISM   Since Jefferson never composed any detailed, systematic treatise on basic philosophical topics, his views on the nature of knowledge and the makeup of the universe have to be gathered largely from his correspondence. Throughout his long life he kept up an active interest in the problems of cognition and the nature of reality and was eager to examine the results of other thinkers on these matters.

Like Edwards, Jefferson accepted an empirical basis for knowledge: all knowledge must be based on experience or observed fact. But his conception of the empirical basis for all knowledge differed in important respects from that of Edwards. For Jefferson, experience and observation signified a disclosure of real facts about real things existing in an outside world. There sounds throughout his empiricism the strong note of common-sense realism, which holds that observation and experience are not of mere *ideas,* but of *things* outside the mind. The word "fact" signified to Jefferson just the opposite of "fancy" or mere mental existence. Experience and observation could serve as a basis for knowledge in his view simply because they, unlike fancy, revealed real facts about real things. "A single sense may indeed be sometimes deceived, but rarely; and never all our senses together, with their faculty of reasoning. They evidence realities, and there are enough of these for all the purposes of life without plunging into the fathomless abyss of dreams and phantasms." [2]

Common-sense realism was therefore strongly opposed to skepticism as well as to immaterialism or idealism. Complete skepticism regarding human knowledge, the idea that man cannot truly know any real existences at all, seemed idle speculation to Jefferson. Such skeptical theories had neither the common assent of mankind nor a justification in daily living or practical affairs. As a reader of ancient classics, Jefferson was acquainted with skeptical doubts regarding knowledge, which he called "pyrrhonisms" after Pyrrho, the founder of the Skeptic School of philosophy in ancient Greece. Jefferson asserted in opposition to skepticism, " 'I feel, therefore, I exist.' I feel bodies which are not myself: there are other existences then. I call them *matter*." [3]

He sided with what he thought to be simply the common-sense view that man can directly experience real existences, whether mental or material. Immaterialism or idealism, the view that one never has any experience of material bodies as such, but only an experience of ideas or mental existences, he dismissed as inconsistent with good sense. Edwards and other immaterialists had argued that matter is dependent upon ideas or thought, that matter is not substantial at all. Jefferson reversed this and held that ideas and thoughts are dependent on matter. "I can conceive *thought* to be an action of a particular organization of matter. . . . To talk of *immaterial* existences, is to talk of nothings." [4] Matter is real and can be known to be real by direct experience. In this respect, he believed that by numerous experiments the advancing science of his day supported the dependence of thought on matter.

Citing the work of several French scientists on the functions of the nervous system and on the structure of animal organisms, Jefferson asserted that "the cerebrum is the thinking organ; and that life and health may continue, and the animal be entirely without thought, if deprived of that organ. I wish to see what the spiritualists will say to this." [5] This appeal to experimental results is typical of Jefferson's empirical approach to knowledge. He looked to experimental findings as both supporting and extending the common stock of human knowledge and had no respect for reasonings unsupported by objective facts of some kind.

The sources of Jefferson's materialism and realism lie in the ancient Greek materialists, the Epicureans, and in certain modern English, Scottish, and French authors. Jefferson took from such thinkers as Epicurus,

Bacon, Locke, Newton, Condorcet, and Stewart what he considered to be sound empirical teachings in natural philosophy. He identified all of these men with a strong respect for fact and a common-sense approach to human knowledge. He admired the Epicurean philosophy for its frank materialism and its conception of knowledge obtained through sense perception. He found in ancient materialism support for his basic conviction that all existence is sustained by material agencies moving through space. He approved the humanistic outlook of the Epicureans, their concern for man's happiness, and also their utilitarian view of knowledge. They believed that man can find lasting happiness and the good life only by understanding the material conditions and forces that support his existence.

Jefferson admired the seventeenth-century English philosopher Francis Bacon for his views on human knowledge. Bacon's emphasis on the discovery of new and useful truths, by framing inductive hypotheses based on the collection of factual samples, was congenial to Jefferson's strong sense of experimental knowledge and realism. He admired the work of John Locke and Isaac Newton for similar reasons. Locke had devised an empirical account of knowledge and remained consistent with common sense in his view that man can have knowledge of both material and mental existences. Jefferson took Locke's *Essay Concerning Human Understanding* to be a leading example of the drawing of sound philosophical conclusions by an appeal to observation and carefully ascertained fact. On the other hand, Jefferson was an admirer of Newtonian science because he saw in it a bold and successful attempt to prove that the natural world conforms to laws. The mathematical laws of motion and universal gravitation convinced him that the mind of man is able to discover real and important natural laws inherent in nature's intricate mechanism. The appeal to observed, experimental evidence in Newton's hypotheses impressed Jefferson's mind and supported his conviction that knowledge is progressive and real.

Condorcet and other French materialists impressed him by their detailed collection of facts and by their explanations of man and culture as dependent upon material conditions. Since material conditions could be improved through the advance of scientific knowledge, Jefferson believed that human life would be enhanced by such knowledge. He conceived man's culture and happiness as rooted in material factors and believed they could be advanced by the improvement of medical science, agricultural science, meteorology, and all natural sciences. The French materialists, with their humanistic concern for better understanding of these factors, were thus admired by Jefferson, as he was in turn admired by them. Jefferson was eager to communicate his scientific findings to these thinkers and kept up a stream of correspondence with them in the pursuit of the useful spread of information.

Jefferson had personal contact with and greatly admired his younger contemporary, the Scottish philosopher and proponent of common-sense realism, Dugald Stewart (1753–1828). Stewart carried forward the tradition of Scottish realism initiated by Thomas Reid and had a strong influence in bringing common-sense realism to America. The tenets of this realism were congenial to the practical interests of Americans, and in fact a good many Scottish common-sense philosophers were to be found in America and American colleges during the nineteenth century. In New Jersey, Princeton had a long line of presidents from Witherspoon and Smith in the late eighteenth and early nineteenth century to James McCosh in the latter half of the nineteenth century, who maintained a strong adherence to the same kind of common-sense realism which Jefferson adopted as a basic part of his empiricism. He was convinced that man can know directly (1) the existence of mental existences, (2) the existence of material things, and (3) the existence of basic moral truths. These three tenets were basic to his realism. What he found to his liking in this philosophy was its support of his basic humanism. Jefferson believed human values were based on man's innate goodness or sense of morality. He therefore could accept a common-sense philosophy which placed moral truths on the same sure sound footing as material facts.

INNATE MORAL SENSE AND NATURAL RIGHTS   Jefferson was above all a humanist and so must be understood fundamentally as a moral philosopher. He sought to locate a moral basis for his views of science, religion, and government and tried to find humanitarian goals for all the plans and projects of his own life. In his sense of the term, good moral goals or values were simply those which guide the efforts in life that are honestly productive of genuine human happiness. It is therefore understandable that Jefferson looked back to the whole humanistic tradition in Western thought, as well as to common sense, for support of his moral philosophy.

Although Jefferson wrote no systematic treatise or essay expounding his moral philosophy, his thoughts fall together in the consideration of several important problems: (1) What is the basis of morality in man; that is, through what faculty or manner of apprehension can man make moral distinctions between right and wrong, good and bad? (2) What is the standard or test of the moral worth of actions; that is, what is the criterion by which moral truths can be proved and actions justified? And (3) what is the makeup of the good life for man and what are the results of applying principles of moral conduct to human life as a whole?

Consistent with his view that the basis of all true knowledge is the direct perception of matters of fact, Jefferson held that moral truths could be directly perceived by an innate moral sense implanted in man. Sometimes he called it a moral instinct, at other times he called it conscience. What he wanted to claim was that morality is neither a matter of reasoning, which can go astray, nor of artificial convention adopted by some and not by others, but is, rather, natural to man. "The moral sense, or conscience, is as much a part of man as his leg or arm. It is given to all human beings in a stronger or weaker degree, as force of members is given them in a greater or less degree." [6] According to Jefferson, men are held morally accountable for the uprightness, not for the rightness, of their decisions. Reasoning and science may often be necessary to determine whether a particular judgment or decision is the true one or the right one; but only a sense of honesty is needed to determine whether one's decision is forthright or morally sound: "He who made us would have been a pitiful bungler, if he had made the rules of our moral conduct a matter of science. For one man of science, there are thousands who are not." [7] Speaking of the moral sense, Jefferson declared, "This sense is submitted, indeed, in some degree, to the guidance of reason; but it is a small stock which is required for this; even a less one than what we call common sense." [8]

In support of his position that the basis of morality is a moral sense natural to mankind, Jefferson considers a number of alternative views and possible criticisms of the whole notion of a moral sense innate in men. Some have asserted that truth is the proper foundation of morality, that we discover moral distinctions between good and bad in the same way that we discover what is true or false in general. This is unacceptable to Jefferson, who claims it reverses the situation. Truth, he contends, is indeed an aspect or part of morality, but not its foundation. No one is morally to blame for making an honest mistake of fact. A dishonest action itself is morally bad not simply because it is in error, but because it is a deliberate or chosen act of deception. Others, including Jonathan Edwards, have made the love of God the foundation of morality. But this, too, according to Jefferson, is but a branch of our moral duties, not the source of them. Jefferson asks, "If we did a good act merely from the love of God and a belief that it is pleasing to Him, whence arises the morality of the Atheist? It is idle to say, as some do, that no such being exists." [9] The fact that a disbeliever in religion could be morally honest in his intentions and actions was sufficient proof to Jefferson that morality could not be based on religion. In fact, he considered the reverse to be the case. Religion itself was to be judged in terms of its moral results and had to be based on moral qualities in order to be genuine.

Jefferson conceived religion as a "matter between our Maker and ourselves." Religion is a private matter between an individual and the divinity. Morality, on the other hand, is essentially social, involving our relations with others. "But I consider our relations with others as constituting the boundaries of morality. With ourselves we stand on the ground of identity, not of relation, which last, requiring two subjects, excludes self-love confined to a single one. To ourselves, in strict language, we can owe no duties, obligation requiring also two parties." [10]

Jefferson's reply to those who would base morality on self-interest is, first, that morality is essentially social, involving duties and relationships with other human beings, and second, that selfishness "is the sole antagonist of virtue, leading us constantly by our propensities to self-gratification in violation of our moral duties to others. . . . Take from man his selfish propensities, and he can have nothing to seduce him from the practice of virtue." [11] The more sophisticated arguments of "egoism" —the view that men act altruistically for the sake of the pleasure they receive from altruistic acts rather than out of a genuine regard for the welfare or happiness of others—Jefferson dismisses as shortsighted and not based on all the real facts. He asks how it is that these acts (for the good of others) give us pleasure, and answers: "Because nature hath implanted in our breasts a love of others, a sense of duty to them, a moral instinct, in short, which prompts us irresistibly to feel and to succor their distresses." [12] Man by his very nature has social dispositions, a moral sensitivity which inclines him to take account of the good of others.

Jefferson also makes a distinction between taste and morals, between what is aesthetically pleasing and what is morally good. The sense of beauty is exercised chiefly on subjects addressed to the fancy or imagination in contradistinction to the moral sense, which is applied to the realm of real facts about real persons.

Jefferson raises what may perhaps be considered the most serious objection to the existence of a moral sense in man, the fact that "the same actions are deemed virtuous in one country and vicious in another." [13]

Cultural relativity or divergent opinions of moral judgments would seem to imply that there can be no true moral sense in man. Jefferson answers this objection by holding that "nature has constituted *utility* to man the standard and test of virtue. Men living in different countries, under different circumstances, different habits and regimens, may have different utilities; the same act, therefore, may be useful, and consequently virtuous in one country which is injurious and vicious in another differently circumstanced." [14] The basis of morality is one thing, the standard or criterion another. The basis of morality is the natural sense in man by which he directly discerns the honesty or forthrightness of his intentions and actions. The standard of morality is the test by which applications of this sense may be judged.

Jefferson holds that all sensible men may naturally be expected to feel and to hold that honesty is morally good, but the same acts of honesty in different circumstances may not have the same utility in relation to human well-being. Moral or forthright actions are themselves good because of their general utility in the production of human happiness. But Jefferson never conceived of human well-being as either definable by rigid formulas or independent of variable circumstances. If utility is the test of virtue—and for Jefferson it must be—then anything that deserves to be called useful to man's well-being must have a practical application in actual fact or the circumstances of life. The circumstances in one place or at one time differ from those of another place or time; but, Jefferson claims, this does not mean that the same standard of morality is not applied in all cases, but rather that it imposes different demands in relation to the goal of human well-being.

Jefferson's utilitarian conception of morality is connected with his adoption of the principal features of the Epicurean ethical philosophy. Not only were the Epicureans materialists and empiricists in their conceptions of reality and knowledge, but they also considered utility the test of virtue. Human happiness was the aim of life for Epicurus, and virtue, including prudence, temperance, fortitude, and justice, was the means by which this goal could be achieved. The absence of pain was considered more important than active pleasure, and the highest pleasures were conceived to be those of the mind. Peace of mind through the avoidance of desire was held to be the supreme good for man. Jefferson included all these points in his moral philosophy, adopting the rather ascetic conception of human happiness held by the ancient Epicureans. He concurred with them in believing that man is a free agent and capable of perfecting himself by discipline. However, this agreement did not prevent him from finding fault with their moral philosophy. He considered their ethics defective on its social side. Their moral philosophy emphasized the individual discipline of a man rather than his social ties and obligations, and therefore was not progressive. Jefferson conceived morality as bound up with social life. He could not separate moral progress from political progress. It is understandable therefore that he was an enthusiastic exponent of the natural rights of man in both a moral and a political sense.

That Jefferson conceived the moral sense in social terms is evidenced by the way in which he formulated the need for justice in a "short syllogism": "Man was created for social intercourse; but social intercourse cannot be maintained without a sense of justice; then man must have been created with a sense of justice." [15] This sense of justice with which men are said to be created is therefore assumed to be both natural to men and socially necessary. Jefferson could not conceive justice and society either as mere conventions—social contracts—or as merely founded upon force or power. When he asserted that there is a right independent of force, that is, natural rights belonging equally to all men, he was at the same time asserting a moral and political principle grounded in the facts of human nature. His famous doctrine of the natural rights of man, which he shared with Thomas Paine and others, is therefore an assertion of the requirements of justice. His classic formulation of this doctrine in the *Declaration of Independence* is intended as a persuasive and simple statement of the moral basis of human nature and, hence, of any human society. "We hold these truths to be self-evident: that all men are created equal; that they are endowed by their creator with [inherent and] unalienable rights; that among these are life, liberty, and the pursuit of happiness." [16]

Natural rights are not merely legal or chartered privileges that can be granted or denied to men. Natural rights are human freedoms or moral necessities possessed by man *qua* man, precisely because man is human. And what is precisely *human* about man is his moral sense, his need for an awareness of justice. Man, therefore, has no natural rights in opposition to his social duties, or, "no man has a natural right to commit aggression on the equal rights of another; . . . every man is under the natural duty of contributing to the necessities of the society." [17] Natural rights are not only human freedoms, but also human responsibilities. Jefferson insisted that the whole notion of natural rights should be tested by reason and experience, that rights should be consistent and derived from observed fact. Natural rights are therefore demanded by reason and are reasonable demands. To be reasonable they must be equal human rights. No man can claim them for himself without at the same time claiming them for all men. Jefferson believed that life, liberty, and the pursuit of happiness, as broad requirements of human life, could be reasonably claimed by every man, insofar as he claimed these rights for all men. However, it is because these rights are so very broad and may conflict with one another that governments are required to secure and protect them. That the problems of coordinating and protecting these rights are immense, Jefferson never doubted. But he fervently believed that they could be instituted and maintained. It was to this unwavering belief that he devoted the greatest share of his activity and thought. The reality of a free republican or democratic government was what Jefferson strove to put into working order; a government based on man's innate moral sense and instituted for the purpose of securing man's natural or human rights.

DEMOCRACY AND THE CHALLENGE OF FREEDOM   Thomas Jefferson's political philosophy is a perfect illustration of the basic liberalism and realism that permeate his thought. Jefferson could never conceive the social life of man as narrow, static, or authoritarian. Rather, he viewed man in the broadest possible light, allowing for the greatest possible degree of human liberty and progress. He could never allow flights of idealistic thought to take the place of realistic appraisal of the complexities of social life. His liberal views answer to his strong conviction that a law of reason governs both the natural rights of man and the motions of the universe. Jefferson was a progressive because he was a realist, believing that man's basic condition *needed* improvement. He was a humanist because he was a liberal, believing that man's basic condition *could* be improved.

The whole purpose of government, according to Jefferson, is to secure and maintain the natural rights of man: life, liberty, and the pursuit of happiness. Both the importance and the limitations of government can be seen to follow from this basic purpose. Governments are important in that they set the basic framework within which human affairs can function; they can make for freedom or for oppression. Without the control of government, life is precarious, liberty unprotected, and happiness reduced to an uncivilized kind. Yet if governments are not limited in their power they may simply seek the advantage of the few through the oppression of the many. Jefferson therefore argued that only a democratic or republican form of government based upon the natural rights of man could fulfill the important role of governing within the proper limitations. That is, only if the people are sovereign and hold the reins of government can society be orderly and just.

To be just, a society or government must uphold the natural rights of man in the widest possible sense. To be orderly, a society must maintain the rights of man in consistency with one another. Jefferson viewed these two principal tasks of government as both essential and difficult. For this reason, he insisted that we can never make a constitution perpetual and that our constitution must have a bill of rights to insure that the government will not overstep its proper bounds. If government is really to belong to the people, it must belong to the "living." One generation cannot bind over another generation if a government is in reality to reflect the will of the governed. Any constitution, therefore, is in continual need of revision. Jefferson tended to conceive a free or republican government as an experimental enterprise. He argued,

> laws and institutions must go hand in hand with the progress of the human mind. As that becomes more developed, more enlightened, as new discoveries are made, new truths disclosed, and manners and opinions change with the change of circumstances, institutions must advance also, and keep pace with the times. . . . let us provide in our Constitution for its revision at stated periods. What these periods should be, nature herself indicates.[18]

In this regard, Jefferson even included the right to revolution as one of man's basic natural rights. Even though he had held law and the rule of reason in high esteem, he did not regard man-made laws as absolute or infallible.

Jefferson also considered the question whether "circumstances do not sometimes occur, which make it a duty in officers of high trust, to assume authorities beyond the law" as "easy of solution in principle, but sometimes difficult in practice." [19] He asserted:

> A strict observance of the written laws is doubtless one of the high duties of a good citizen, but it is not the *highest*. The laws of necessity, of self-preservation, of saving our country when in danger, are of higher obligation.[20]

This reflects Jefferson's strong insistence upon the basic utilitarian attitude toward all laws and values.

Perhaps the strongest note of realism to be found in Jefferson's political writings marks his views on corruption in government:

In every government on earth is some trace of human weakness, some germ of corruption and degeneracy, which cunning will discover, and wickedness insensibly open, cultivate and improve.[21]

However, this frank admission of the reality of corruption increased rather than lessened Jefferson's faith in the sovereignty of the people and in free democratic process of government:

The influence over government must be shared among all the people. If every individual which composes their mass participates of the ultimate authority, the government will be safe; because the corrupting the whole mass will exceed any private resources of wealth; and public ones cannot be provided by the levies on the people.[22]

Jefferson's defence of democratic government is consistent with his Enlightenment view of man and human nature:

One may conclude too hastily, that nature has formed man insusceptible of any other government than that of force, a conclusion not founded in truth nor experience.[23]

Jefferson admitted that democracies had not been sufficiently put to the test. Experiments with democracy, he believed, had not been carried far enough. Greek democracies were small and unable to maintain themselves on a larger scale or with changing times. In England, the will of everyone was permitted an influence, but only to a slight degree. And even in the United States there were suspicions that the masses were unfit for rule and that a strong federal government based on a natural aristocracy was needed. Jefferson considered it a fallacy accredited to Montesquieu and other political writers that only small states are fitted to be republics. According to Jefferson,

We have chanced to live in an age which will probably be distinguished in history, for its experiments in government on a larger scale than has yet taken place. But we shall not live to see the result.[24]

The success of these experiments depends upon the education of all men and on the assumption that education is a public trust:

If a nation expects to be ignorant and free, in a state of civilization, it expects what never was and never will be.[25]

A truly republican government should see as one of its primary responsibilities the diffusion of knowledge more generally through the mass of people. Jefferson looked for

> the diffusion of light and education as the resource most to be relied
> on for ameliorating the condition, promoting the virtue, and advancing the happiness of man.[26] . . . Education is here placed among
> the articles of public care, not that it would be proposed to take its
> ordinary branches out of the hands of private enterprise, which
> manages so much better all the concerns to which it is equal; but a
> public institution can alone supply those sciences which, though
> rarely called for, are yet necessary to complete the circle, all the
> parts of which contribute to the improvement of the country, and
> some of them to its preservation.[27]

Jefferson accepted the challenge of freedom in all of its terms. Broad human freedom requires the fullest participation of the people in the affairs of government. This entails the education of all the people as one of the responsibilities of government. Freedom of the press is required if freedom of thought and speech are to be actualities. But freedom of the press also requires fidelity to the truth and an enlightened reading public to be able to judge what is read. Freedom of religion requires the separation of church and state and the cultivation of peaceful religious attitudes among people to enable them to live in harmony with differing beliefs. Jefferson believed that all of these freedoms could be attained under able leadership and the will of the majority, but that none could be maintained without struggle and experiment. However, the only leadership that could sustain these broad humanistic views would be one based on virtue and talent. The only aristocracy in a truly enlightened democracy would be one based on a moral sense and on all the practical talents necessary to mold plans and decisions experimentally, with a progressive view to the future and the continued advancement of man.

THE SIGNIFICANCE AND INFLUENCE OF JEFFERSON   Thomas Jefferson's lifetime spans the entire period from Jonathan Edwards to Ralph Waldo Emerson, from the end of Puritanism to the beginning of transcendentalism in New England. Though Jefferson lived well beyond the revolutionary times and American Enlightenment of which he was so much an integral part, his historical significance is contained in the fact that the essential features of what may be called the American mind were formed during his lifetime, in large measure through his own perfect embodiment of these features. Consequently, he has come to have an influence and importance that is both staggering in its proportions and impressive in its dramatic grandeur. He is important not only because of his times or because he contributed so much to them, but even more for what he has meant to later times. For generations of Americans, and others as well, he has become a symbol of human freedom, the individual rights of man, and all that is progressive and good in a democratic way of life. Historically, he is a much greater figure than Jonathan Edwards, even though Edwards was just as perfect an embodiment of the times in which he lived. The difference is that Jefferson has been adopted by later ages as a symbol for all of the principal attainments, hopes, and aspirations of a living American democracy. This great influence, in all its diversity, is quite intelligible if we bear in mind the remarkable broadness of Jefferson's views and the dual character of his thought.

Jefferson's liberalism was combined with an equally strong realism. His high regard for individual freedom was combined with a recognition that it could not be obtained without struggle or without maintaining a sense of social justice and responsibility. His high regard for the will of the people and for self-government was combined with a worldly awareness of the corruptions of any government and the continual need to revise and improve legislation, both domestic and foreign. It is therefore understandable that Jefferson's broad-based political position could, over the years, cut across party lines and find favor among Republicans and Democrats, conservatives and liberals, alike. Men as far apart as Lincoln and Calhoun could claim allegiance to important principles in the Jeffersonian tradition. Lincoln could refer to the basic equality of all men and to government of the people, by the people, and for the people as simply following in Jefferson's footsteps. Calhoun could use the principles of self-preservation, natural aristocracy, and the sovereignty of the individual states to defend slavery in the South. This points up the fact that just as the issue of slavery was not resolved in Jefferson's own time, neither was it easily resolvable in later times on the basis of his own principles. He held that human bondage is opposed to the natural rights of man, but he also held to the principles of utility, self-preservation, and self-determination by the people concerned. The latter could be used against the former. The whole Jeffersonian concept that common sense and the inherent reasonableness of man could be counted upon to resolve social problems conflicted in certain ways with his realistic attitude toward the primacy of action and getting things done.

It has been pointed out[28] that Jefferson's own career as statesman and Chief Executive involved a number of good illustrations of the disparity between principles he professed and actions he took. The implication would seem to be that principles for Jefferson were either makeshifts or expedient policies for action, or that they were mere rationalizations and hence too vague to do justice to the concrete situations of action. But these alternatives are not fair to Jefferson and do not do justice to things he really stood for. Jefferson was neither infallible nor superficial in his best and basic thoughts. He tried to maintain an admittedly difficult balance between necessary principles on the one hand and their useful applications on the other. That his principles were not vague platitudes or superficial rationalizations is manifest through the difficulties they give rise to in practice and the problems that they expose rather than brush aside or conceal. Because Jefferson insisted that all principles must be judged by their utility, he could not simply validate his principles *a priori* or in a purely theoretical sense. But because he had confidence in the perfectibility and good sense of men, he believed that through effort, and even great difficulty, men themselves could be counted on to find worthwhile solutions in practical affairs that would be consistent with their innate sense of justice. Jefferson never advocated obedience to rules or principles for their own sake, but only for the sake of improving human welfare or happiness. Equally, he never stood for the breaking of rules, except in unforeseeable circumstances or emergency situations. And he always advocated the location of some greater human good to balance the loss of some lesser one.

Jefferson has a place of recognized importance in American political and intellectual history, but like Edwards, he has a philosophical importance that is hardly acknowledged. Unlike Edwards, Jefferson cannot be accurately characterized as an original philosophical thinker. Also, unlike Edwards, Jefferson cannot at all be termed a systematic and carefully rigorous thinker. Judged in terms of the Western philosophic tradition from Plato through Kant, Jefferson clearly belongs with such amateur *philosophes* as Franklin and Voltaire. But, although his ideas were eclectic and unsystematic, he nevertheless possessed in fine measure several tendencies of thought that indicate his philosophic importance. According to John Dewey, Jefferson "was the first modern to state in human terms the principles of democracy." [29] This means that he was indeed a practical philosopher—a thinker who always sought **to** locate a useful, moral application for his ideas. The fact that he conceived democracy in broadly human and common-sense terms indicates why he is admired by humanists and humanistically oriented philosophers. Since he viewed democracy in human and experimental terms, the "issues Jefferson raised are still of fundamental importance for our life and times." [30]

Although he had no direct effect on the subsequent development of American philosophy in the nineteenth and twentieth centuries, he nevertheless embodied the maxims of independent and comprehensive thought and encouraged naturalistic, pragmatic, and common-sense tendencies found in later American philosophers. Jefferson was a philosopher at least in the sense that he embodied a truly independent sense of judgment and thought on fundamental human problems. He must also be considered a real philosopher because of his strong attachment to comprehensive or broad lines of thought within which to see these human problems. In this respect, Jefferson rises above the other universal men of his times not merely because he was one of America's greatest and most influential presidents, but because of the quality, intensity, and thoroughness with which he so perfectly embodied the spirit of the Enlightenment.

NOTES

1. Thomas Jefferson, in Adrienne Koch and William Peden, eds., *The Life and Selected Writings of Thomas Jefferson*, pp. 705–706, from "Letter to John Adams, Monticello, April 11, 1823."

2. *Ibid.*, p. 701, from "Letter to John Adams, Monticello, August 15, 1820."

3. *Ibid.*, p. 700.

4. *Ibid.*, pp. 700–701.

5. *Ibid.*, p. 717, from "Letter to John Adams, Monticello, January 8, 1825."

6. *Ibid.*, pp. 430–431, from "Letter to Peter Carr, Paris, August 10, 1787."

7. *Ibid.*, p. 430.

8. *Ibid.*, p. 431.

9. *Ibid.*, p. 637, from "Letter to Thomas Law, Esq., Poplar Forest, June 13, 1814."

10. *Ibid.*, pp. 637–638.

11. *Ibid.*, p. 638.

12. *Ibid.*

13. *Ibid.*, p. 639.

14. *Ibid.*, pp. 639–640.

15. Thomas Jefferson, in John Dewey, *The Living Thoughts of Thomas Jefferson*, p. 101.

16. *Ibid.*, p. 41.
17. *Ibid.*, p. 100.
18. Jefferson, in Koch and Peden, eds., *op. cit.*, pp. 674–675, from "Letter to Samuel Kercheval, Monticello, July 12, 1816."
19. Jefferson, in Dewey, *op. cit.*, p. 75.
20. *Ibid.*
21. *Ibid.*, p. 51.
22. *Ibid.*
23. *Ibid.*, p. 55.
24. *Ibid.*, p. 60.
25. *Ibid.*, p. 123.
26. *Ibid.*, p. 125.
27. *Ibid.*, p. 138.
28. See L. W. Levy, *Jefferson and Civil Liberties: The Darker Side* (Cambridge, Mass.: Harvard University Press, 1963).
29. John Dewey, *Freedom and Culture* (New York: Putnam, 1939), p. 155.
30. Sidney Hook, *The Paradoxes of Freedom* (Berkeley: University of California Press, 1964), p. 1.

QUESTIONS FOR DISCUSSION

1. In what important ways do Jefferson's Enlightenment views offer a significant departure from Puritanism?

2. How valid are Jefferson's appeals to common sense and science in support of his realism and materialism?

3. Does it make sense to believe, as Jefferson did, that men have inborn natural rights and moral sense?

4. How reasonable is the Jeffersonian conception of democracy?

5. Are Jefferson's philosophical and intellectual achievements as great as his political and practical ones?

SUGGESTED READINGS

Letter to John Adams, August 15, 1820. Formulation of Jefferson's materialism. [In Koch and Peden, eds., *The Life and Selected Writings of Thomas Jefferson,* pp. 700–701.]

Letter to William Short, October 31, 1819. Jefferson's adoption of the ancient Greek Epicurean philosophy with its strong emphasis on materialism and human happiness. [In Koch and Peden, pp. 693–697.]

Letter to John Adams, April 11, 1823. Jefferson's objections to Calvinism and the formulation of his own deism, including his argument from design for a divine being. [In Koch and Peden, pp. 705–707.]

Letter to Isaac McPherson, August 13, 1813. Jefferson's view of the value of ideas and the spread of knowledge. [In Koch and Peden, pp. 629–630.] See also John Dewey, *The Living Thoughts of Thomas Jefferson,* Section V, for Jefferson's views on intellectual freedom and progress.

John Dewey, *The Living Thoughts of Thomas Jefferson.* Jefferson's views on morals, religion, and education (Sections IV and VI).

John Dewey, *The Living Thoughts of Thomas Jefferson.* Jefferson's political philosophy (Section II).

PRIMARY SOURCES

John Dewey, *The Living Thoughts of Thomas Jefferson* (New York: Fawcett, 1940).
Adrienne Koch and William Peden, eds., *The Life and Selected Writings of Thomas Jefferson* (New York: Modern Library, 1944).

SECONDARY SOURCES

Stuart G. Brown, *Thomas Jefferson* (New York: Washington Square Press, 1963).
Adrienne Koch, *The Philosophy of Thomas Jefferson* (Gloucester, Mass.: Peter Smith, 1957).

3 *Ralph Waldo Emerson*

Transcendentalism and Self-Reliance

Ralph Waldo Emerson (1803–1882) had a greater effect on the minds of generations of Americans than any other thinker. For countless Americans, and others as well, Emerson was the source of fresh inspiration and the prophet of unbounded aspirations and hope for man. He did not possess the systematic mind and argumentative skill of Jonathan Edwards, nor the vigorous inventiveness, enterprise, and statesmanship of Thomas Jefferson. He could neither identify himself with a particular religious movement or sect as did Edwards, nor become part of any particular political movement or social reconstruction as did Jefferson. He had neither the otherworldly interests of Edwards and the Puritans nor the worldly interests of Jefferson and the men of the Enlightenment. Rather, Emerson found all genuine values and ideals within the infinitely rich poetic imagination or genius of man. The task which he set for himself throughout his life was to bring this message to all men—to act as a seer and sympathetic touchstone to the spiritual greatness inherent in every man.

Born in Boston in 1803, Emerson was descended from several generations of Protestant clergymen. He was educated at Harvard and in 1829 accepted a pulpit in the Second Unitarian Church of Boston. However, by 1832 he resigned his position as minister because of a growing awareness that his own convictions were not orthodox and that he could not hold his faith within the strictures of any single creed. Thereafter he traveled, lectured, and wrote and thus became a notable leader in the flowering of literary activity in New England. As editor of *The Dial* and as friend of Thoreau, Hawthorne, Whitman, and Parker, Emerson became the acknowledged leader of New England transcendentalism or romanticism. As poet, critic, and lecturer, he was throughout his long life the untiring prophet of the creative genius and divinity of all mankind.

Transcendentalism marks an important reaction against the period of Enlightenment, and against materialism and orthodoxy as well. The sense of individualism which clearly characterized the progress of the Enlightenment in men like Franklin, Jefferson, and Paine had all but disappeared by the first quarter of the nineteenth century. The Age of Reason, with its broad program of progress, came to a halt as the needs of security and orthodoxy of belief, along with a narrowing concern for economic opportunity and advantages, took its place. The orthodox philosophy of Scottish common sense more and more dominated the academic life of a good number of American colleges. Conservative and uninspiring religious ideas prevailed in the thought and sermons of many clergymen. Deism itself declined as a viable religious creed, for its impersonal and unemotional tone proved uninspiring.

Growing into manhood during these times, Emerson and other sensitive individuals were searching for a world view which would inspire their enthusiasm as well as engage their intellects. This they found in such sources as the European romanticism of Coleridge and Wordsworth, the revival of Greek literature and the classics, Oriental mysticism, and their own meditations on life and fondness for nature and the beauties of the great outdoors. All of these sources conspired to a unity for Emerson and other transcendentalists; each rich perspective taught the lesson that man is essentially a poet, and the world simply an appearance for the individual soul or mind.

Just as we can describe Jonathan Edwards as the best exponent of the philosophy of American Puritanism, and Jefferson as the best embodiment of the philosophy of American Enlightenment, so we can observe in Emerson the clearest formulation of the philosophy of American transcendentalism. For all three figures the term "philosophy" implies an entire *view* of the universe, as well as a *way* of life in the world. Emerson gave what has to be counted as the fullest and most enthusiastic expression of the transcendental outlook.

The term "transcendentalism" is borrowed from the German philosopher Kant, but with an important change of meaning. Emerson asserts that Kant succeeded in

> showing that there was a very important class of ideas or imperative forms, which did not come by experience, but through which experience was acquired; that these were intuitions of the mind itself; and he denominated them Transcendental forms. The extraordinary profoundness and precision of that man's thinking have given vogue to his nomenclature, in Europe and America, to that extent that whatever belongs to the class of intuitive thought is popularly called at the present day *Transcendental*.[1]

For Emerson and other romanticists the term "transcendental" really referred to an infinite array of the mind's own intuitions or direct insights. These intuitions were not only sources of knowledge, but sources of the deepest and most important truths. For Kant, however, there was no such thing as intuitive knowledge. He allowed only two pure intuitions or forms of consciousness, the pure intuition of space and the pure intuition of time. Kant contended that space and time were not themselves ultimate realities, but merely appearances or forms through which experience was ordered or organized by the mind.

In borrowing the term "transcendentalism" from Kant, Emerson breathed a new and essentially romantic meaning into the word. Following the lead of Coleridge and other romanticists, Emerson used "intuition" to signify the poetic faculty of seeing things creatively, seeing things with a freshness and richness such as only the widest exercise of the imagination could contemplate. Therefore, Emerson can say: "The sensual man conforms thoughts to things; the poet conforms things to his thoughts."[2] The poet, because of his creativeness, is by nature a transcendentalist or idealist, since he is truly self-reliant. Rather than conform his ideas to things, he makes things conform to his ideas. The poet makes his vistas or world from his imagination, or from the intuitions of the mind itself. "The Imagination may be defined to be the use which the Reason makes of the material world."[3] Here Emerson implies the identity of imagination, reason, and intuition. Each is simply the expression of the creativeness of the mind or thought. Intuition suggests a direct seeing by the mind, reason suggests a comprehension or knowing by the mind, and imagination suggests a fabrication or creating of things known.

Emerson's transcendentalism is therefore simply "romantic idealism."
As he says: "What is popularly called Transcendentalism among us, is
Idealism; Idealism as it appears in 1842." [4] For Emerson, romantic idealism implies both a fresh and a comprehensive outlook on all things.
Religiously, it implies pantheism; morally, it implies self-reliance or individualism; and, as an outlook on nature and society as well, it signifies
spiritualism or mysticism. In all cases it means a release from limitation
and the dullness of routine and the awakening of ever-new perspectives
on life. Pantheism rejects both theism and deism because both cut off or
alienate man and nature from the divine source. Pantheism finds divine
life in all things—in nature, in man—since all are, in a poetic sense,
infinitely rich and inexhaustible.

Pantheism is a religion of sympathetic feeling which, for Emerson,
does away with the Calvinist or Puritan notion of depravity. Depravity,
meanness—these are transcendentally too low and limited as representations of man, representations which can be transcended by taking a higher
viewpoint. Even deism, with its clockwork of natural laws and its religion of common sense and the goodness of man, is not high enough.
Common sense or ordinary reason is too limited, too mundane, for true
religious aspirations. Since religion involves an idealism of infinite aspirations, it must, according to Emerson, find the divine reality at all points
of the compass, especially within man himself. Religion, to convey any
moral truth, must uphold the divinity or self-sufficiency of the soul itself, since the soul is the source of all perspectives. It is through the
intuitive powers of men's souls that the divine and the moral reality finds
a unity. The more self-reliant or self-existent a soul is, the more divine
it is. The more self-reliant or integrity-bound it is, the more it aspires
to the highest moral goals. True individuality, for Emerson, means fullness of self, a realization of the infinite universal self. The more truly
individual a man is, the more he is a whole man, a harmony of complementary parts. The theme of unity in Emerson's transcendentalism
indicates the mystical turn of his thought. Mysticism not only involves
the assertion that the soul of man and the divine reality are capable of
union or oneness, it also involves the assertions that both are infinite or
essentially without limitation, and that the achievement of oneness is
possible only through intuition or direct knowledge of the truth. Nature
and all things remain lowly appearances until the flash of intuition
presents the eternal as fully revealed in a momentary experience.

In his essays, poems, and lectures, Emerson sought to convey this
"high spiritual truth" to all who would pay heed. His fellow transcen-

dentalists, however, were not all so thoroughgoing, eloquent, or positive in their adoption of the same basic position. For Hawthorne the transcendental movement was an episode not wholeheartedly to be engaged in. For Parker it did not involve an absolute break with Unitarianism; and for Thoreau it involved a more restricted or concentrated form of existence. Emerson said of Thoreau that he seemed to need something to argue against, that there was too much of the negative or too much denial in his fundamental attitude toward life. He claimed that Thoreau descended to argumentation and controversy, and thereby only found real life and peace away from the crowd and alone in the woods at Walden Pond. Emerson maintained that although there are no pure transcendentalists alive, for no man is so perfect, a transcendental perspective is intuitively possible at all times and in all places. He did not advocate any retreat from the world or the society of men. Rather, he declared: "It is easy in the world to live after the world's opinion; it is easy in solitude to live after our own; but the great man is he who in the midst of the crowd keeps with perfect sweetness the independence of solitude." [5]

It is in this sense that Emerson stands as the best exponent of transcendentalism—not merely because he formulated its ideology more coherently than any other romantic, but by the manner in which he succeeded in tying his thoughts together to exhibit, simply and poetically, the inspiring character of the transcendental position. He worshiped great men and celebrated their lives, not in order to disparage the ordinary man, but rather to fire the ordinary man with enthusiasm to discover his own unbounded greatness and worth. Emerson not only emphasized self-reliance (an essential of transcendental doctrine) but he also united it with a complete scheme of values for man that combined religion, morality, nature, and society. In short, he brought transcendentalism "out into the world" in such a way as to reach a wider audience than any other transcendentalist, and by his positive espousal of promise and beauty, seemed to offer more to mankind. This perhaps means that Emerson attempted more, that he considered extravagant hope the very essence of his message.

Intuition and Romantic Idealism   Emerson's essay entitled *The Transcendentalist* was originally delivered as a lecture in Boston in 1842 and was printed in *The Dial* in 1843. This work is perhaps the best single formulation of his philosophic position, as well as the clearest statement of the essence of transcendentalism itself. In the essay, Emerson makes a declaration of intellectual independence in general, and a declaration of independence from empiricism in particular. The dominant notes in American philosophic thought prior to Emerson are its dependence upon borrowed intellectual traditions in general and empiricism in particular. One thing common to the best American Puritan and Enlightenment thought is the reliance upon an empirical basis for knowledge. Even though Edwards drove Locke's empiricism to the position of idealism, and Jefferson interpreted it in the form of materialism, neither Edwards nor Jefferson questioned its foundations. It is therefore significant to note that Emerson's call for self-reliance or integrity of mind represents not merely a stimulus to individual initiative, but also a demand for a freer, more creative view of the human mind itself. Any view of the mind which restricts or limits its horizons is unacceptable to Emerson. In fact, for transcendentalism, any passive or restricted conception of the human mind presents itself as simply a poor, unimaginative representation of the mind's true capabilities. This is the heart of the transcendentalist's position—that everything conceivable or imaginable is simply a point of view or perspective. Transcendentalism, therefore, is frankly idealistic in holding that "mind is the only reality, of which men and all other natures are better or worse reflectors." [6]

Emerson draws a distinction between experience and consciousness, between sense experience and intuition. He claims that consciousness is both more inclusive and more fundamental than sensory experience. Sense experience is external, a looking outside a visible, audible thing; consciousness is internal, a direct self-awareness of the mind itself. There is consequently much more in consciousness than there is in experience. Emerson is a Platonist here, in holding that the mind's conscious awareness of perfect justice, beauty, or the soul itself could never be derived from mere experience. Sense experience is limited, scattered, and transitory and could never of itself give man ideas of the infinite, the eternal, or the absolute. Consciousness, then, is more fundamental than experience, since all experiences involve consciousness but not all consciousness involves experience. The mind, or self, must be aware of itself to be aware of other things. This heightened self-awareness—the mind's recognition of itself in all that it notes—is what Emerson terms intuition.

Experience is only one form of consciousness. To start with the data of the senses or experience is to start from a mere part rather than the larger whole. Hence, empirically built philosophies are defective. To trace all ideas back to experience or to base all knowledge or truth on sense experience is simply not to carry the process back far enough to its real origin. Ideas must be traced not to the senses or experience, but to consciousness or the direct operations of the mind itself. For Emerson, consciousness basically signifies direct awareness. Direct awareness or intuition is involved in all the operations of the mind. Indirect awareness, or the representation of things by the mind, is secondary and passive. Direct awareness or intuition is primary and essentially active.

Transcendentalism therefore asserts that the data of the senses and the whole outside world are only appearances, not ultimate reality. The hard facts of the materialist, for example, are just so many symbolic representations. Facts are not substantial, since they are relative to their interpretations. The angle from which we view the facts determines how they shall be seen. A stick immersed in water may seem bent to the viewing eye and feel straight to the hand. Which is the basic fact? In transcendentalist eyes, neither is basic; both are secondary or subjective facts. The only absolute or ultimate fact is the activity of the mind itself, since this underlies all appearances. Emerson claims we have all that empiricism claims and much more, if we start with consciousness rather than the senses. Transcendentalism includes the data of the senses in its much wider view of reality.

However, according to Emerson we must give up the view that the mind is simply a *tabula rasa,* a blank tablet, a passive receptacle for ideas and knowledge. The mind fabricates or creates its own ideas, even its lowliest ones. As one possible view of what the mind actually is, the *tabula rasa* theory is, in fact, an extremely poor or unimaginative one. Every theory or view of the mind is in reality a confession of its originator. If the mind were really a blank tablet it could neither conceive itself to be one, nor conceive itself at all. The mind's self-awareness is a function of intuition or imagination. The transcendentalist view of the mind allows for the widest possible latitude with regard to its self-existence or self-awareness. It envisions an infinite consciousness through its own imaginative power or intuitions.

Emerson's idealism is essentially romantic: it upholds the infinite aspirations of the mind to break all bounds. Romantic idealism proclaims the divinity of the mind, since it finds an affinity between spirit and all things. By sympathetic feeling or intuition the spirit or imaginative consciousness of man is able to empathize with all existence. Man is essentially a poet; the mind is always poetic, in that it conforms things to itself. In the Emersonian scheme of things, Newton was no less a poet than Shakespeare, since Newton's scientific theories were first of all imaginative interpretations of nature. Newton arranged the forces and motions of nature according to his own ideas. Less creative men do the same thing, but less imaginatively, less ingeniously. Philosophers are no exception to this rule. Every philosophy is a poetic construction, a spiritual contemplation of existence. Materialism, no less than idealism, is a spiritual representation of existence; the difference being that materialism denies its own basis. The materialist forgets or fails to take notice of his own focus of attention, or of the fact that it is *he* who has represented things in a certain way.

The common-sense realist considers that he has touched rock bottom when he admits the existence of carefully observed hard facts. He will not be a romanticist and confuse fact with fancy; but he gives himself away, according to Emerson, by claiming a direct observation of fact. Direct observation is only possible within intuition or the mind itself. The only thing the mind can directly know is itself. It can know other things only indirectly or sympathetically, or by becoming imaginatively those other things. Emerson quotes the French materialist Condillac as admitting this very point: " 'Though we should soar into the heavens, though we should sink into the abyss, we never go out of ourselves; it is always our own thoughts that we perceive.' " [7] Emerson asserts: "What more could an idealist say?"

Emerson's conceptions of the intuitive character of the human mind and the romantically ideal nature of reality are complementary to each other. Both are based upon what he takes to be an exposure of the limitations of empiricism. Transcendentalism asks empiricism for its basis or credentials. How does empiricism know that all ideas or knowledge come from experience or the senses? Transcendentalism drives empiricism back into the mind and finds that all truth or knowledge is intuitive; it is directly given by the operations of the mind itself. Transcendentalism is thus able to admit frankly that the only basis of truth is the self-sufficiency or self-reliance of the mind upon itself or its own flashes of awareness. Gathering evidence is secondary and derivative; immediately seeing that something is true is primary and original.

Only intuition can know that mind is the only reality and that reality is infinitely rich. Emerson considers arguments to be inconclusive. Long chains of reasoning are no substitutes for direct insight. Reasoning itself depends upon intuition, since it depends upon flashes of insight, on inspiration. The skeptic, on the other hand, who denies that the mind can attain absolute truth is only confessing his lack of imagination. The romantic idealist follows his highest impulses, and these, because they are poetically inspired, carry him to the eternal. The skeptic also follows his impulses, but not his highest ones. If the skeptic would take his self-reliance seriously, he would see that his skeptical self is only a small part of his larger universal self.

Thus, Emerson holds forth romantic idealism and intuition as embodiments of the quality of genius in all men. The more self-reliant men are, the more intuitive and romantically ideal they are. The *whole* or complete man is the intuitive or self-aware individual who romantically aspires to be without restrictions—infinite and free.

MAN, MYSTICISM, AND SPIRITUAL LAWS   To understand Emerson's basic outlook on the nature of man it is instructive to look back to the earlier Puritan and Enlightenment viewpoints. For Puritanism, man's position in life was determined by an uncontrollable source external to him. Man's essential condition was alienation from the true goodness possessed only by the divine being. Good works or progress in man, if possible at all for Edwards and Puritanism, had to be the effects produced by a cause outside man. The Enlightenment changed this picture of man's position in life. During the Enlightenment, man's position was conceived as open for possible progress through reason and the acquisition of practical knowledge. Nature was conceived as controllable by man as he came more and more to understand its mechanisms and laws. The Enlightenment conceived man's condition, especially his social condition, as capable of improvement through the use of human talents and reason. However, the Enlightenment conceived man's well-being or happiness as bound up with improvements in the environment, both physical and social. It frankly admitted that man's position in life was determined by causes external to him; this much, at least, it had in common with the Puritan outlook. Both conceived man's position in life as a function of external causes, and both conceived the deity as externally defined. For Puritanism, goodness was outside of men's reach and even undeserved by them. For the Enlightenment, goodness in all its forms was within men's reach and deserved by them, but nevertheless dependent upon and a function of environmental change, especially social improvements.

Emerson considered that he stood in sharp contrast to all external views of man and man's true good. "All men plume themselves on the improvement of society, and no man improves. Society never advances. It recedes as fast on one side as it gains on the other. It undergoes continual changes; it is barbarous, it is civilized, it is christianized, it is rich, it is scientific; but this change is not amelioration." [8] Man scatters his force and can never find his true worth unless he acquires self-knowledge and finds his center of gravity within. Emerson's dictum that "Nothing is at last sacred but the integrity of your own mind" [9] is not only a repudiation of Calvinist depravity, but is also a rejection of any scheme of values that bases its authority on anything outside of man's inner nature. Emerson considers that any view of man which compromises the soul or character by making it dependent upon circumstances, environment, or any limitations is doomed to failure. Transcendentally, any view of man is a reflection of the character of the viewer. The highest view of man is pantheism, since it deifies man's soul. Both theism and deism limit man; they conceive him as essentially dependent on conditions outside his mind or center of being.

In his essays, especially *Character, Self-Reliance,* and *The Over-Soul,* Emerson drives home his central point: the essence of man's being and worth involves a radiation from what is within to what is without, and never the other way round. What a man *is* is primary, what a man *has* is secondary. What a man *is* is fundamental, what a man *does* is derivative. What man *is* cannot be discovered empirically by looking outside, or piecemeal by merely looking at what happens at a certain time or place. Empirical philosophies of man treat the soul or self merely as a symbol, and its sensory experiences as reality. For Emerson it is the soul which is reality; its experience and its possessions are only symbolic of it. Natural laws become spiritual laws when seen as symbolic of the soul's beauty. Natural laws reflect what the mind *reads into* nature, and what the mind reads into nature is its essence, its unified purpose. For romanticism, the soul only finds *itself* in ever richer forms through its contemplation of nature. Emerson asserts "All things are moral. That soul which within us is a sentiment, outside of us is a law." [10]

The basic pantheism involved in Emerson's view of the universe finds all laws or uniformities to be spiritually unified. Man finds principles within himself, in his moral makeup. He also finds that nature has its own principles. These inner and outer principles become unified when nature is taken to be a symbolic rendering of the soul's own life, and when the life of the soul achieves a sympathetic appreciation of the natural universe. For Emerson the experience of beauty in nature signifies the harmony between the soul and nature, man and the universe, inner feelings and outside phenomena. When a flower is observed as beautiful, it is erroneous to assume that the beauty is just in the particular flower, or just in the limited consciousness of the observer. For Emerson the beauty lies in the principle or law of the natural phenomena, as well as in the deeper soul or over-soul of which the observer is only a part. The experience of beauty is an intuitive demonstration that all things are moral and harmonious. At certain moments in our lives we may experience the genuine integrity of both our inner nature and the outer world. Pantheistically or mystically, man's soul and nature are unified and one. Ordinarily, they are both scattered and incomplete.

Emerson's insistence upon the divinity of man and the spiritual character of nature and natural laws derives from his basic mysticism, his Platonism. "Mysticism finds in Plato all its texts." [11] Emerson's high regard for Plato is based on his finding inexhaustible inspiration and aspiration for man in the Platonic philosophy. Plato is regarded as the right teacher for mankind because he maintains that all genuine learning is from within or acquired by self-instruction and that the soul of man has a special affinity for such eternal forms as beauty, justice, and truth. It is instructive to see that Emerson's own mystical pantheism finds in Plato all those qualities which Jefferson's practical sense could never accept or admire. Jefferson regarded Plato's mysticism as unintelligible to the human mind and useless for the practical affairs of life. He saw in Plato a departure from tangible fact and common sense in favor of the pursuit of illusory ideals and dangerous deceptions for the human race. Poetic philosophy and utopian justice were no philosophy and no justice to Jefferson's way of thinking.

However, in Emerson's view an unpoetic philosophy would lack vision and inspiration, and mere tangible justice would be only a partial appearance of a greater reality. To live with and for only the empirical world is to live without hope, to live without eternal beauty, infinite goodness, or absolute truth. Man aspires to fulfill himself, to overcome his limitations, and to live in the presence of his ideals of goodness, truth, and beauty. As a transcendentalist, Emerson freely admitted the extravagant nature of his mysticism and never conceived that it could be proved scientifically or experimentally. His romantic conception of man, mysticism, and spiritual laws did not call for proof. They called, as he often insisted, only for sympathetic appreciation.

MORAL OPTIMISM AND SOCIETY In his lectures and essays Emerson touched on a vast variety of topics from politics to religion, from nature to art, and from wealth to culture, with one thing continually in mind. He found in everything a single moral, presented with an infinite variety of appearances or ramifications. Whether he discussed manners or heroism, farming or literature, he sought to remind men of the potential spiritual greatness within themselves. As a moralist, Emerson was always also a poet. The moral he saw in every aspect of life and the world had to be gathered, expressed, and received by the poetic imagination. The lesson that all things are just and beautiful for a truly self-reliant soul could never be gathered from empirical evidence or any ordinary means. This moral insight could be expressed only in the superlatives of poetry and could be received only by a kindred poetic sympathy. Virtually everything that Emerson wrote, therefore, pointing up this essential moral message, was couched in poetic superlatives. In his essays he attempted to show the superior character of the moral law or higher freedom in every aspect of the universe and even in the face of apparently strong contrary evidence:

> An inevitable dualism bisects nature, so that each thing is a half, and suggests another thing to make it whole. . . . the same dualism underlies the nature and condition of man. Every excess causes a defect; every defect an excess. Every sweet hath its sour; every evil its good. . . . For every thing you have missed, you have gained something else; and for every thing you gain, you lose something.[12]

The moral law, the inevitable retribution of all things, is written in the depths of nature:

> Commit a crime, and the earth is made of glass. Commit a crime, and it seems as if a coat of snow fell on the ground, such as reveals in the woods the track of every partridge and fox and squirrel and mole.[13]

The universal justice of things also implies a moral solution to the problems of evil and suffering in the world:

> The soul will not know either deformity or pain. . . . All loss, all pain, is particular; the universe remains to the heart unhurt. Neither vexations nor calamities abate our trust. No man ever stated his griefs as lightly as he might. Allow for exaggeration in the most patient and sorely ridden hack that ever was driven. For it is only the finite that has wrought and suffered; the infinite lies stretched in smiling repose.[14]

Emerson's moral optimism determined the manner in which he viewed society, politics, and the whole institutional life of man.

Society is something secondary, an appearance or part of a more universal reality. The individual is primary, and the stamp of individual character is the only good that society can possess. In every society, according to Emerson, there is the lurking danger of the mob, of conformity, of placing the lower before the higher. The only society to which men really belong is the infinite, immortal kingdom of human nature in which all men are deified. Particular societies, governments, and institutions are only so many partial symbolic appearances of the invisible spiritual society where all men are different and also one. The only real society for Emerson is the mystical society which accords dignity and divinity to each and to all. It is precisely in this sense that Emerson calls attention to the difference between the moral and political law, even the difference between nature and democracy. The moral law is absolute, but every political law is only relative.

> Nature is not democratic, not limited-monarchical, but despotic, and will not be fooled or abated of any jot of her authority by the pertest of her sons: and as fast as the public mind is opened to more intelligence, the code is seen to be brute and stammering.[15]

His observations on American government indicate that the state is secondary or relative, while the character or soul of men is primary or absolute:

> In this country we are very vain of our political institutions, which are singular in this, that they sprung, within the memory of living men, from the character and condition of the people, which they still express with sufficient fidelity—and we ostentatiously prefer them to any other in history. They are not better, but only fitter for us. We may be wise in asserting the advantage in modern times of the democratic form, but to other states of society, in which religion consecrated the monarchical, that and not this was expedient. Democracy is better for us, because the religious sentiment of the present time accords better with it. Born democrats, we are nowise qualified to judge of monarchy, which, to our fathers living in the monarchical idea, was also relatively right.[16]

In declaring the state to be secondary to the individual, Emerson is not simply voicing the protest that every state is in some way corrupt. He is in fact asserting the primacy of the moral law which admits no higher authority than the divinely inspired character of each individual man:

> To educate the wise man the State exists, and with the appearance of the wise man the State expires. The appearance of character makes the State unnecessary.[17]

But Emerson also held that men are wiser than they know. The wisdom of men is intuitive or self-taught; therefore, their proper education must reside in the stimulus and opportunity to do their own work:

> Hence the less government we have the better—the fewer laws, and the less confided power. The antidote to this abuse of formal government is the influence of private character, the growth of the Individual; the appearance of the principal to supersede the proxy; the appearance of the wise man; of whom the existing government is, it must be owned, but a shabby imitation.[18]

Emerson's doctrines of self-reliance and transcendentalism come together in his insistence on the secondary importance of governments and society. The genuine transcendentalist cannot join any limited or partial cause without scattering his force. Emerson was not a reformer and could not join others in his day in their narrow enthusiasm for religious causes or social reforms. The reformer must begin by finding himself. Reliance on a limited cause expresses itself as the want of self-reliance. In this regard Emerson was an untiring critic of superficial allegiances, pointing out the way in which men look away from themselves to such things as philanthropy, property, and travel. He remained a mystic and moral optimist throughout his life, holding that the more men rely upon their individual souls, the more they will find universal harmony, beauty, and peace.

The recurrent optimism in Emerson's philosophy indicates the moral and poetic focus of his vision. However, his optimism is not based on chance or circumstances or a denial of unpleasant facts. Fate, necessity, and disaster must all be included in the large infinite whole of reality:

> No picture of life can have any veracity that does not admit the odious facts. A man's power is hooped in by a necessity, which, by many experiments, he touches on every side, until he learns its arc.[19]

But he also asserts:

If we must accept Fate, we are not less compelled to affirm liberty, the significance of the individual, the grandeur of duty, the poser of character.[20] . . .

Fate is limitation but

fate has its lord; limitation its limits; is different seen from above and from below; from within and from without.[21]

When seen from below fate is ugly, but when seen from above, with serene perspective, it is beautiful. The poet or tragedian can see and represent in the inevitable unfolding of character a poignant beauty. The destiny of man to be born and to die, to be inevitably human, implies something beyond. Everything implies its opposite; every part belongs to an all encompassing whole. If man looks outward he discerns his limitations, his insignificance. If he turns within, he can begin to see his significance and universal worth.

THE SIGNIFICANCE AND INFLUENCE OF EMERSON   By his simple eloquence Emerson succeeded in reaching a very wide audience. He stands as the finest representative of his age and has indeed outlived his age through his untiring celebration of the spiritual dignity of man. Emerson succeeded in spreading the doctrine of intuition and self-reliance thanks to the fact that countless individuals found their own inner aspirations and half-beliefs resounding in his poetry and prose. He spoke to all men, not from any derivative or external authority, but from what he believed was original, direct insight. He told men what they were eager to hear and convinced them without argument or experiment. He did not prove anything, nor did he venture any likely hypothesis; he simply presented his insights with sincerity and poetic beauty. Unlike Edwards, he did not argue for idealism, nor did he present a refutation of alternative conceptions. Emerson counted on the sympathetic intuitions of his listeners to convince themselves of all the higher truths. He did not find himself defending a dying tradition as did Edwards, but rather he viewed himself as the harbinger of something fresh and new. Intuitively he cut through or bypassed controversy, and managed always to include all the minor parts in his major whole. Virtually all that Edwards claimed for God, Emerson claimed for the spiritual genius in every man. Like Jefferson, he was an optimist about human nature, believing that men had an innate sense of justice which could win out over wrong. But

Emerson was in the long run more extravagant than Jefferson in his claims for man. Jefferson's common sense and penchant for science left no room for metaphysical ideals. But Emerson was at heart a metaphysical poet. Like Jefferson, he had no taste for Calvinism. But unlike Jefferson, he had an insatiable taste for the eternal and the infinite. Emerson found the supernatural in the natural, the metaphysical in the physical. The poetic experience of beauty was all the guarantee that he needed to show that things as they existed were right and true and sublime.

Emerson's impact and influence on American intellectual life is as great as the countless themes he touched on or celebrated. His impact on Thoreau is perhaps the most noteworthy. For Thoreau, Emerson was a touchstone to the divinity and self-existence of the soul. In this respect, Thoreau should not be counted as Emerson's disciple—Emerson wanted no followers—but rather as a fellow witness to the same vision. Emerson encouraged Thoreau to be self-reliant where it matters most, in the innermost conscience of one's being. That Thoreau went further than his guide along the paths of anarchy and individualism indicated to Emerson the militance of the younger man's personality. Emerson was a man of peace and found it easier to reconcile his person with the nature of things. But Emerson himself distinguished between personality and character and considered the former to be a mere appearance and the latter the genuine reality. He saw in Thoreau's character a tower of strength and a fresh reflection of nature's own beauty brightly revealed.

Emerson's importance for the development of American philosophic thought is paradoxical. On the one hand he has been regarded as the purest and greatest philosopher that America has produced, and on the other he has been put down as a mere poet or pure mystic with no systematic philosophy at all.[22] On the one hand he has been regarded by millions of sympathetic followers as the "peoples' philosopher," and on the other he has been regarded as no "philosopher's philosopher" at all. Emerson has been quoted more often than any other American writer, but all too often out of context and for purposes alien to his own intended meaning. His aphorisms have become mottos for the intellectually immature or the pseudo-individualist. How are we then to explain the fact that although Emerson is America's most popular philosopher, his philosophy is neither original nor supported by argumentation or proof?

Emerson is a paradox philosophically in that he heralded and celebrated what he could not actually carry out himself. He was the first to call for Americans to do their own philosophical thinking. In his first published essay, *Nature* (1836), he demanded: "Why should not we also enjoy an original relation to the universe? Why should not we have a poetry and philosophy of insight and not of tradition?"[23] Yet Emerson was not himself original in his philosophy. He borrowed ideas from Plato, Kant, and many others insofar as he found them inspiring. He did not subject these thinkers to probing analysis, since he was interested in appreciation rather than argumentation. He firmly believed that the ideas of great philosophers could be grasped intuitively by the mind—by insight without extended reasoning. But since the ideas of Plato, Kant, and others that Emerson admired were in fact based on analysis, on argumentation, and on much involved reasoning, it is quite clear that Emerson did not really understand these philosophers.

A case in point is Emerson's own statement (see above, p. 53) concerning his adoption of the term "transcendental" from Immanuel Kant. Emerson interpreted this term to refer to intuition or direct insight, but this is not at all what the term indicates in Kant's *Critique of Pure Reason*. Kant's famous work is one of the most intricate in the whole history of philosophy. His notion of the transcendental method is abstract and complex; and this method cannot at all be understood apart from other ideas equally complex. In fact, Kant's transcendental method involves the very opposite of what Emerson took it to mean, since in Kant's system it is principally a critical method of analysis and not a method of direct insight. What Emerson did, therefore, was to take the word and leave the idea behind. Further, he popularized transcendentalism in a way that is quite remarkable. He made use of a high-sounding philosophical term to spread a simple doctrine, one that all men could grasp and appreciate. He used the name "transcendentalism" to teach the view that truth is directly revealed to every man if man will only turn within and become truly self-reliant.

Emerson made easy, then, what Edwards had absolutely denied and what Jefferson claimed took hard work. Emerson preached the self-improvement and self-importance of the common man. He was concerned with the quality of human life, but the essential point is that he believed that the highest quality of life was within the grasp of every man. It has been remarked that this view is distinctively American, and insofar as it is, Emerson is the most eloquent and influential spokesman for the American people. In this sense he is America's most popular philosopher, the most eloquent spokesman for the dignity and greatness of the common man.

Like Puritanism and the Enlightenment, however, transcendentalism eventually declined. By the mid-nineteenth century it had already lost its vitality. The Civil War and the doctrine of evolution ushered in new problems and ideas. Since transcendentalism offered neither a constructive social philosophy nor a positive scientific one, it was virtually bypassed in the rapid growth of science and industrialization in the last half of the nineteenth century and after. It has remained principally as a literary achievement, having produced a good number of works of poetry and prose that have become American classics. Transcendentalism did not survive as a philosophy because it was paradoxically both much more than a philosophy and much less.

Emerson, however, like Jefferson, has become an American institution, a hero who is worshiped from afar. If both men were great as thinkers at all, it is because they were great as men. Even though their influence enhanced respect for the mind and ideas in American life, neither man can be counted as a significantly original or systematic thinker. Both were at heart more interested in man than they were in philosophy. It is not until after the Civil War that one finds in America any strong or pronounced interest in philosophy for its own sake.

NOTES

1. Ralph Waldo Emerson, in Brooks Atkinson, ed., *The Complete Essays and Other Writings of Ralph Waldo Emerson*, p. 93, from "The Transcendentalist."
2. *Ibid.*, p. 29, from "Nature."
3. *Ibid.*
4. *Ibid.*, p. 87, from "The Transcendentalist."
5. *Ibid.*, p. 150, from "Self-Reliance."
6. *Ibid.*, p. 89, from "The Transcendentalist."
7. *Ibid.*, p. 88.
8. *Ibid.*, p. 166, from "Self-Reliance."
9. *Ibid.*, p. 148.
10. *Ibid.*, p. 175, from "Compensation."
11. *Ibid.*, p. 472, from "Plato; or, the Philosopher."
12. *Ibid.*, pp. 172–173, from "Compensation."
13. *Ibid.*, p. 183.
14. *Ibid.*, p. 190, from "Spiritual Laws."
15. *Ibid.*, p. 423, from "Politics."
16. *Ibid.*, pp. 426–427.
17. *Ibid.*, p. 431.
18. *Ibid.*
19. Ralph Waldo Emerson, *The Conduct of Life*, p. 18, from "Fate."
20. *Ibid.*, p. 9.
21. *Ibid.*, p. 19.
22. For interpretations of Emerson by James, Santayana, Dewey, and others, see Milton Konvitz and Stephen Whicher, eds., *Emerson: A Collection of Critical Essays*.
23. Emerson, in Atkinson, ed., *op. cit.*, p. 3, from "Nature."

QUESTIONS FOR DISCUSSION

1. In what ways does Emerson's transcendentalism present a new angle of vision and a departure from the Enlightenment and Puritan viewpoints?

2. If intuition is not based on experience, how can it present us with genuine and important knowledge, according to Emerson?

3. How sound is Emerson's idea that the discovery of self-reliance is the key to unlocking man and the good life?

4. How would Emerson meet the objection that his views on society and the individual are one-sided and unbalanced?

5. To what extent is Emerson's greatness due to the cogency of his ideas? To what extent is it due to the beauty and eloquence of his words?

SUGGESTED READINGS

The Transcendentalist. Emerson's romantic idealism and objections to empiricism and materialism. See also *Nature*, Part VI, for further clarification of why Emerson adopts idealism as a philosophy. [In Atkinson, ed., *The Complete Essays and Other Writings of Ralph Waldo Emerson*, pp. 87–103.]

Self-Reliance. Emerson's strong individualism. Connection between self-reliant existence and genuine or real existence; the reliance on intuitive knowledge. [In Atkinson, pp. 145–169.]

The Poet. The poet as the intuitive knower, the man of the best creative insight. [In Atkinson, pp. 319–341.]

Fate. Optimism and idealism in Emerson are woven in with the admission of fate, limitation, and necessity. [In Emerson, *The Conduct of Life*, pp. 9–35.]

Politics. Emerson's views on the secondary importance of society and governments and the primary importance of man. [In Atkinson, pp. 422–434.]

PRIMARY SOURCES

Brooks Atkinson, ed., *The Complete Essays and Other Writings of Ralph Waldo Emerson* (New York: Modern Library, 1940).
Ralph Waldo Emerson, *The Conduct of Life* (New York: Dolphin Books).

SECONDARY SOURCES

Milton Konvitz and Stephen Whicher, eds., *Emerson: A Collection of Critical Essays* (Englewood Cliffs, N.J.: Prentice-Hall, 1962).
Stephen Whicher, *Freedom and Fate: An Inner Life of Ralph Waldo Emerson* (Philadelphia: University of Pennsylvania Press, 1953).

PART II

American Philosophy Since the Civil War

One of the most familiar traits of our time is the tendency to revise tradition, to reconsider the foundations of old beliefs, and sometimes mercilessly to destroy what once seemed indispensable.

Josiah Royce ⋮ THE PHILOSOPHY OF LOYALTY

Introduction

Modern American Philosophy

After the Civil War an important change began to take place in American philosophical thought, moving at a pace to match that of other great changes. During the last half of the nineteenth century and the first part of the twentieth century the stature of America grew from that of a small nation to a world-leader. This rapid rise not only involved an increase in population, industrialization, and urbanization, but also brought with it an increase in learning and an amazing development in scientific and intellectual endeavors. In tune with this great expansion, American social life became much more complex and specialized. The growing society demanded specialization in industry and the professions, and in areas of learning as well. The evolution of American colleges during this period is marked by a sharp upsurge in the number of courses and degrees that were offered. Before the Civil War it was not possible to specialize in the study of philosophy, or to take advanced degrees in this or other subjects. In fact, before the Civil War, philosophy in America was not really conceived of as a distinct realm of study. In Edwards' time, philosophy was wedded to religion, in Jefferson's time it was identified with worldly wisdom, and in Emerson's time it was identified with self-culture. During this early period American philosophical thought remained well behind its European counterpart.

In its later or modern period, however, American philosophy came to be recognized as a distinct and mature form of study, both in America and throughout the world. Several small but highly significant phenomena throw light on the nature of this transition from early to modern American philosophical thought: (1) *The Journal of Speculative Philosophy*, first published in 1867 at St. Louis, Missouri; (2) the so-called "Metaphysical Club," organized in Cambridge, Massachusetts, during the early 1870's; and (3) the influence of Chauncey Wright (1830–1875), a little known but brilliant thinker of this period.

The Journal of Speculative Philosophy, established by W. T. Harris, was the first American journal specifically devoted to original thinking on distinctively philosophical topics. It provided a forum for the discussion of metaphysical and epistemological questions, such as had never been available in America. Although the journal was organized by men sympathetic with German idealism (Kant and Hegel in particular), spokesmen for many diverse and original philosophic viewpoints were given the opportunity to present their positions in the journal's pages. The greatest American pragmatists—Charles Peirce, William James, and John Dewey—all contributed to the journal, as did America's greatest idealist, Josiah Royce. In particular, it contained some of the earliest essays of Charles Peirce—essays in which he criticized the notions of intuition and self-evident truths, and argued instead that thought is essentially a matter of drawing testable inferences and must be based on the use of signs or symbols which convey definite meanings. The originality and quality of these early essays by Peirce mark them as the real beginning of modern American philosophy.

When Peirce published his early essays in the journal he was an all but unknown figure. His essays, as a consequence, made little impression at the time. Meanwhile, in the early 1870's Peirce met with a small group of individuals known as the Metaphysical Club—William James, Chauncey Wright, John Fiske, Oliver Wendell Holmes, Jr., and others—for the discussion of philosophical topics. A central topic discussed by this remarkable and subsequently famous group was the concept of evolution, perhaps the most significant idea of the nineteenth century.

Chauncey Wright, as the acknowledged leader of the group, exercised a considerable influence on Peirce and James. Although not well-known, Wright possessed high philosophic intelligence and was considerably ahead of his time in his work in the philosophy of science. His ideas set the scene for the development of pragmatism and the analytic character of modern American philosophy. Wright objected to philosophy having any ulterior basis in religion, morality, or metaphysics. He argued that only by a dispassionate and impartial consideration of the facts could philosophy clarify or explain anything at all. Just as science must painstakingly try to verify its theories, so also must any fruitful philosophic idea be open to objective verification. However, philosophic explanations cannot be verified by any simple, uncritical appeal to the facts or by so-called common sense. According to Chauncey Wright we cannot solve philosophical problems merely by appealing to common sense, because genuine philosophical concepts involve *interpretations* of the facts and not simple statements or summaries of them. Further, he objected to any intuitive method of grounding knowledge and claimed that the notion of an intuitive self-consciousness or mental substance was a meaningless combination of words having no testable consequences. Thus, in effect, Wright criticized some of the main tendencies in European and early American thought. He attacked the philosophy of Scottish common-sense realism (which had a strong hold in America during the nineteenth century) as uncritical and superficial, and he attacked New England transcendentalism on the same grounds.

In 1872 Chauncey Wright traveled to England. There he met Charles Darwin, whom he impressed by his interpretation of the idea of evolution. Wright considered the idea of evolution important for a scientific philosophy and maintained that it called for analytical interpretation rather than vague, metaphysical speculation. He attacked Herbert Spencer's interpretation of evolution (which enjoyed a large audience in the United States) as an unscientific use of generalizations which do not explain any facts. Wright opposed vague generalizations and the pronouncement of any ultimate law of evolution pertaining to the whole cosmos. These were premature and unverifiable. Good theories should throw light on specific facts. Bad theories simply pretend to explain phenomena by making vague and untestable assertions. Wright asserts:

> Mr. Spencer's law is founded on examples, of which only the facts of embryology are properly scientific. The others are still debated as to their real characters. Theories of society and of the character and origin of social progress, theories on the origins and changes of organic forms, and theories on the origins and causes of cosmical bodies and their arrangements are all liable to the taint of teleological and cosmological conception—to spring from the order which the mind imposes upon what it imperfectly observes rather than from that which the objects, were they better known, would supply to the mind.[1]

Chauncey Wright's positivistic scientific approach to philosophical problems had considerable impact on Peirce and James. Along with the foundation of *The Journal of Speculative Philosophy* in St. Louis, the informal meetings of the Metaphysical Club in Cambridge after the Civil War mark the awakening of original and full-fledged American philosophical activity. From such small beginnings we may say modern American philosophical thought took root and developed major philosophical movements. Peirce, James, and Dewey carried pragmatism to prominence in contemporary thought. Josiah Royce, influenced by both Peirce and James, constructed what he termed an "absolute pragmatism," thus bringing American idealism to its point of highest prestige. In turn, George Santayana, who developed under the philosophical influence of both Royce and James, reacted to both their positions by constructing a form of critical realism and naturalism which represents a major phase of twentieth-century philosophical thought. The works of Peirce, James, Royce, Santayana, and Dewey represent the coming to maturity of just those tendencies that had their beginnings shortly after the Civil War.

NOTE

1. Edward H. Madden, ed., *The Philosophical Writings of Chauncey Wright: Representative Selections*, pp. 20–21.

SUGGESTED READINGS

G. N. Grob and R. W. Beck, eds., "Evolution and the Rise of Naturalism" (Ch. 1); "Pragmatism: An American Philosophical Adventure" (Ch. 2); in *American Ideas: Source Readings in the Intellectual History of the United States*, Vol. II (New York: Free Press of Glencoe, 1963).

Paul Kurtz, ed., "Evolution and Darwinism" (Part VI), in *American Thought Before 1900: A Sourcebook from Puritanism to Darwinism* (New York: Macmillan, 1966).

Edward H. Madden, *Chauncey Wright* (New York: Washington Square Press, 1964).

———, *Chauncey Wright and the Foundations of Pragmatism* (Seattle: University of Washington Press, 1963).

———, ed., *The Philosophical Writings of Chauncey Wright: Representative Selections* (New York: Liberal Arts Press, 1958).

W. G. Muelder and L. Sears, eds., "Evolution" (Part IV); "William T. Harris and *The Journal of Speculative Philosophy*" (Part V); in *The Development of American Philosophy: A Book of Readings* (Boston: Houghton Mifflin, 1960).

Philip P. Wiener, *Evolution and the Founders of Pragmatism* (Cambridge, Mass.: Harvard University Press, 1949).

4 *Charles Sanders Peirce*

Pragmatism and Logic

Charles Sanders Peirce (1839–1914) is a pivotal figure in the development of American philosophical thought. Not only did he originate the philosophy of pragmatism and thereby influence the subsequent course of American philosophy, but he is also the central figure in turning philosophy in America toward autonomous inquiry. Peirce was an original thinker who pioneered studies in the foundations of logic, the philosophy of science, and metaphysics. Although his work went unnoticed by the larger world during his lifetime, he reached a small audience of outstanding philosophers—in particular William James and Josiah Royce. His impact on James and Royce is the first instance of one major American philosopher molding the philosophical thinking of other major philosophers. Peirce is the first American philosopher to devise an original philosophic method—pragmatism—which has since come to be recognized as one of the major movements of twentieth-century thought.

Peirce conceived of philosophy as a form of inquiry that must be scientific and a pure search after truth. Philosophy cannot have an ulterior purpose or thrive by ingeniously defending preconceived values or goals. If philosophy is to discover or even hope to find out what the truth really is, it cannot allow religious, moral, or aesthetic purposes to determine its course. According to Peirce, philosophy must become scientifically objective and maintain the integrity of the laboratory method which treats all ideas as hypotheses to be tested, rather than as beliefs to be accepted as conclusive. Previous philosophers, according to Peirce, had blocked the way to real inquiry by claiming absolute certainty for their conclusions or infallibility for their methods. Philosophy, if it is to be fruitful, requires both methods and concepts that are open to correction and clarification. First, philosophy must have a method of clarifying the meaning of its basic concepts, or they will remain obscure and confused. Second, philosophy requires a method of testing the validity of its conclusions. Peirce's pioneering work in pragmatism and logic stands out as just such an attempt to furnish philosophy with the suitable methods for carrying on its work. Pragmatism implies a philosophy that always looks to practical, that is, testable consequences. Pragmatism demands an explicitly experimental philosophy.

Since Peirce neither published any full-length books on philosophy during his lifetime nor held any influential academic position for very long, it is all the more remarkable that he should have had the philosophical influence that he did. The recognition given Peirce during his lifetime was due to the efforts of William James. James saw in Peirce a thinker of the first magnitude, and he gave him full credit for originating American pragmatism, which has come to be recognized as the most important and original development in American philosophy.

Charles Peirce was born in Cambridge, Massachusetts, in 1839, the son of Benjamin Peirce, a great American mathematician and Professor of Mathematics at Harvard. Peirce asserts of himself:

> I was born and reared in the neighborhood of Concord—I mean in Cambridge—at the time when Emerson, Hedge, and their friends were disseminating the ideas that they had caught from Schelling, and Schelling from Plotinus, from Boehm, or from God knows what minds stricken with the monstrous mysticism of the East. But the atmosphere of Cambridge held many an antiseptic against Concord transcendentalism; and I am not conscious of having contracted any of that virus.[1]

Charles Peirce was a gifted youth and received from his father a broad and intensive early education in science, mathematics, and philosophy. Before he entered Harvard in 1855, he had already made the acquaintance of many scientific and philosophic ideas that he was later to develop in his pragmatic or "laboratory" philosophy. Peirce's father taught his son the importance of science as discovery, as advancing the frontiers of knowledge, and also impressed upon him the importance of abstract thought or the generalizing power of the human mind. In short, before he ever began his formal education at Harvard, Peirce had already acquired the roots of a scientific philosophy, a view of things based on precise logical reasoning and experiment and tending to speculation on general laws.

After his graduation from Harvard in 1859, he took a position as physicist with the United States Coast and Geodetic Survey, the only post that he held for any appreciable length of time during his life. He returned to Harvard, and in 1862 received a master's degree. A year later he obtained the first Sc.B. degree in chemistry that Harvard ever offered. Throughout the remainder of his long life he wrote scholarly articles, delivered occasional lectures at Harvard and Johns Hopkins, and worked on the formulation of his scientific philosophy. Although his talents and original philosophic mind were recognized by William James and a few others, he remained, practically speaking, a philosophic recluse up to the time of his death in 1914. Not until after 1930, when his collected papers were published by Harvard University, did Peirce receive anything like worldwide attention and prominence for his major philosophic ideas.

Peirce's philosophic debut began with an oration he delivered in 1863 on *The Place of Our Age in the History of Civilization*. Here he argued for the need of a scientific orientation toward philosophy that would overcome the deficiencies of idealism on the one hand and materialism on the other. According to Peirce, materialism and idealism both err but in opposite ways:

> Materialism fails on the side of incompleteness. Idealism always presents a systematic totality, but it must always have some vagueness and thus lead to error.[2] . . . But if materialism without idealism is blind, idealism without materialism is void.[3]

The real advance of knowledge depends upon both scientific practice and speculative ideas. Idealism does not subject its theories to scientific tests, and materialism does not augment its practice with meaningful theories. It is Peirce's view that good theories lead to the discovery of new facts, and that there is no other way to find out whether they are good than to trace the consequences of ideas in practice. Philosophy, especially metaphysics, must become scientific, making its ideas logically rigorous and open to definite testing in terms of predictable consequences. But it cannot do this by giving up speculation, reasoning, or the framing of abstract theories. Somehow, science and speculation must come together if philosophy and knowledge are to make any advance.

The problem of how to unite science and philosophy was one of Peirce's major concerns. To solve this problem, he believed that proper methods had to be discovered that would (1) give meaning to philosophical ideas in experimental terms and (2) organize and extend these ideas and inferences to new facts. Traditional philosophy, Peirce found, was seriously lacking in such methods. Traditional metaphysics and logic offered only closed or sterile theories of meaning, truth, and the universe. In short, traditional philosophy could not really teach us anything new. With its closed systems of absolute truths, it blocked the road to genuine inquiry rather than making some advance in inquiry itself.

The overhaul of traditional philosophy was the ambitious task that Peirce set for himself. Unlike previous American thinkers he could not accept an already worked out philosophical framework. As a consequence, his studies and writings were pioneering efforts. In metaphysics he proposed an evolutionary view of the universe when evolution was a novel idea. In logic he formulated mathematical logic and initiated scientific reforms of logic which only recently have come to be widely appreciated. His concepts of language, signs, and meaning were also a good many years ahead of their time. It is no wonder, then, that his pragmatism was ignored or that, when first noticed, it was largely misunderstood. Pragmatism itself was a pioneering method based on other pioneering ideas.

Peirce's pragmatism is the central part of his attempt to make traditional philosophy scientific. But to revise traditional philosophy, as Peirce intended, is no simple matter; it required on his part major revisions in logic and metaphysics and thereby implied basic changes in the purposes of philosophy. In discussing the roots of his pragmatism, Peirce makes special mention of his philosophical conversations with Chauncey Wright, William James, and others while he was a member of the Metaphysical Club, which met in Cambridge in the early 1870's. He draws particular attention to the definition of *belief* which emerged from these discussions—that upon which a man is prepared to act. With this definition in mind, Peirce asserts that pragmatism is but a corollary. When we locate the meaning of a belief in terms of action or the actions it leads to, we have its pragmatic meaning, since we have defined its meaning in terms of practical consequences. Peirce formulated his pragmatic method in his early essay (1878), *How to Make Our Ideas Clear*. Here his purpose was to offer a fruitful method of determining the meaning of any concept, for example, hardness or weight. He claimed that the whole conception of a quality such as hardness lies in its conceived effects. In other words, in order to determine what a concept means, we must examine its future consequences. These consequences Peirce called "practical consequences" in order to emphasize the connection between thought and action. To conceive or think what a thing is, is to think or conceive of what it can do or how it functions. Pragmatically, for example, force is what force does. To look for sensible effects, therefore, is the only scientific way to find out what any concept means.

The simplicity of Peirce's pragmatic method is misleading. On the face of it, it merely claims that a thing is what it does. The real importance of Peirce's method, however, lies in its implications. These implications Peirce never tired of tracing. In fact, the major portion of his life was spent working out the implications of and justification for his pragmatism. He came to see that, since every thought or concept is a sign, his pragmatism implied a theory of signs to which he subsequently gave extensive attention. He also claimed that his pragmatic method cut across the problem of the nature of universals insofar as it required him to adopt the realist's view that the world has real, objectively discoverable general traits. Further, his exploration of the implications of his pragmatism suggested the need to formulate a third kind of logical reasoning in addition to the traditional dichotomy of deduction and induction.

Pragmatism, Peirce claimed, essentially involved the logic of what he called "abduction," which is the kind of tentative reasoning, for example, that a physician uses in trying to diagnose a disease. All logical thinking is a form of self-control where the mind follows a certain order of ideas to fulfill some purpose. In abduction the purpose is to draw a tentative conclusion with the aid of a general rule in order to explain a particular observed fact. Peirce strongly insisted that his pragmatism was essentially a logical doctrine. His ideas about logic, however, were based on radical departures from traditional logic, and Peirce continually met disappointments in trying to explain his philosophy of pragmatism to his contemporaries.

It is often said that, although Charles Peirce invented pragmatism, it was William James who made it famous. While this is basically true, it is also true that William James in his own pragmatism neglected much of the logical and metaphysical force of Peirce's doctrine. Peirce was so disturbed about the way in which his original idea of pragmatism was being used by James and others that he coined the term "pragmaticism" to mark off his own doctrine from others that were similar but still very different.

Originally Peirce derived the name "pragmatism" from a careful study of the German philosopher Immanuel Kant. But unlike Emerson, who borrowed the term "transcendental" from Kant, Peirce did not misconceive what he had borrowed. Kant had given the name "pragmatic beliefs" to a certain class of hypothetical beliefs that involve the adoption of a probable means for attaining a certain end. He had in mind such useful but only probable beliefs as a physician might have in prescribing a medicine to cure an illness.[4] However, while Kant admitted that such pragmatic, or useful, beliefs are appropriate in medicine or its like, he did not consider them appropriate for philosophy.

Peirce, on the other hand, was most interested in making philosophy testable in a scientific or experimental manner. He, therefore, adopted the term "pragmatic" to designate a philosophy that looked to practical consequences or experimental results as a test of the meaning and validity of its ideas. But the greatness of Peirce's achievement lies in his careful tracing of the logical and metaphysical implications of this initial idea.

As the founder of pragmatism, Peirce represents a significant new force and direction in American philosophy. His pragmatism is not only important in the narrow sense of being a new technical method for determining the meaning of intellectual concepts, but in the broader sense of representing a new attitude toward philosophical activity. Peirce's pragmatism calls for a genuine inquisitive approach toward all philosophic problems; pragmatism does not allow philosophy conclusions arrived at in advance of inquiry itself. If pragmatism stands for the view that all rational ideas must be tested in terms of their future consequences, then philosophy itself must bring its conceptions to the test of practice. Philosophy cannot block the way to inquiry, but must treat all its ideas as tentative hypotheses which are to be tested. Pragmatism, as an experimental approach toward philosophical inquiry, must be logical, or self-consistent. In order to be logical it must leave room for the possibility of error, which means that it must begin with the serious desire to find the truth rather than the ulterior purpose of merely wishing to make use of truth to defend or secure some special absolute value. Like the scientific method, Peirce's pragmatism advocates a value-free attitude toward philosophy. The pragmatic philosopher searching for the truth cannot restrict his inquiry to conform with religious, social, poetic, or any other ulterior ends. In this sense pragmatism demands free and continual inquiry into all the discoverable consequences of ideas.

SCIENTIFIC METHOD AND FALLIBILISM   In a series of articles which he wrote after the Civil War for *The Journal of Speculative Philosophy* and the *Popular Science Monthly*, Peirce formulated a good number of carefully argued criticisms of unscientific conclusions and methods used in philosophy. The numerous unscientific claims made in the name of philosophy and the lack of any experimental methods of backing up these claims indicated to Peirce the need of carefully working out exactly what the scientific method really is, and what advantages are to be found in it for philosophy. What he found so disturbing in many traditional philosophic positions was the manner in which each claimed for itself an absolute infallibility or certainty of apprehension. He was also disturbed by the impurity of philosophical methods—the ulterior purposes which entered into supposed investigations of the truth, unstated biases for orthodox dogmas and edifying morality. Peirce tried to expose these disturbing features in his earliest philosophical articles.

The St. Louis idealists who founded *The Journal of Speculative Philosophy*, in which Peirce published his first philosophical criticisms, had sympathies and connections with Emerson and the movement of transcendentalism in New England. As romantic idealists, they were concerned with establishing absolute or higher spiritual truths within the mind itself, whether by intuition or by pure *a priori* reason. This type of philosophy not only made great claims for philosophy and the powers of the mind but attempted to do this by bypassing scientific or experimental methods as such.

Peirce called into question the claims of any intuitive powers in man and likewise the view that the mind is self-contained or introspective. In his essay *Some Consequences of Four Incapacities*, published in 1868, he asserts:

1. We have no power of introspection, but all knowledge of the internal world is derived by hypothetical reasoning from our knowledge of external facts.
2. We have no power of intuition, but every cognition is determined logically by previous cognitions.
3. We have no power of thinking without signs.
4. We have no conception of the absolutely incognizable.[5]

The view that the mind was capable of true intuitions independent of anything other than itself was held by the French philosopher Descartes, and it is he whom Peirce cites by way of criticism. Although Peirce does not mention Emerson by name, it is also Emerson's view of the mind as in touch with ultimate truth through its intuitions which is being criticized by implication. Peirce argues that if an intuition is a direct, self-contained type of awareness, then how can we ever know that we have such intuitions? Can we know by intuition that we have intuitions? This leads to an infinite regress, and is purely subjective. It is a notorious fact that many a truth that seems intuitive or self-evident to one person does not seem so to someone else. Nothing is really evidence for itself, and an intuition or a self-contained awareness is really like a premiss that is not itself a conclusion, a cognition undetermined by any previous cognition. But, Peirce argued, there cannot be any cognition undetermined by any previous cognition. All thought involves interpretation or representation of something by something, and all thought is continuous. No thought or awareness interprets itself; any thought is either interpreted by some other thought, or interprets some other thought. According to Peirce, all thought worthy of the name is in terms of signs. A sign is simply "something which stands to somebody for something in some respect or capacity." But no sign can literally be what it signifies. If a cloud is a sign of rain, the cloud is not identical with the rain, but rather indicates it. The word *rain* is a sign of rain, but certainly it is not identical with the rain itself. Similarly, no thought can be literally what it signifies. Peirce's doctrine of thought-signs is set in sharp contrast to all intuitive views of the mind.

Ideas for Peirce are complex and dynamic rather than simple or static. Every thought or idea is triadic: it means *something* to *somebody* in *some way*. First a thought or idea must refer to some object. A thought or idea of a tree, for example, must actually refer to a tree as its object. Second, this object must mean something to some person or to some mind; and third, this object must mean something to a person or mind in some way or other. In other words, ideas or thoughts require (1) an object for interpretation, (2) an interpreter of the object, and (3) the actual interpretation of the object.

Instead of being self-enclosed, every thought is essentially capable of evoking an endless series of further thoughts. "Ideas tend to spread continuously and to affect certain others which stand to them in a peculiar relation of affectability. In this spreading they lose intensity, and especially the power of affecting others, but gain generality and become welded with other ideas." [6] Peirce's notion of the spreading of ideas may be likened to the consequences of throwing a stone into a pool of water. Just as the ripples of water produce further circles of ripples which are wider and less intense, so thoughts tend to spread. Ideas have effects on other ideas, since for Peirce there can be no idea without consequences.

He maintains that all ideas have essentially three characteristics. (1) Every idea has its own intrinsic *quality* or feeling. (2) But ideas also have an ability to affect other ideas; they possess an *energy*. (3) Finally, any idea has a tendency to bring along other ideas with it; it has *generality*. Just as thoughts show these triadic features, so, Peirce points out, all signs can be divided into three main kinds: icons, indices, and symbols. An *icon* is a sign that resembles its object. A picture of a tree would be an icon. An *index* is a sign that does not resemble its object, but causally points to it or is a symptom of it. A bullet hole would be an index of a gunshot, because it is a result of a gunshot. Finally, a *symbol* neither resembles its object nor is causally or physically connected with it; rather, a symbol depends upon adopting a rule of usage or assumption regarding what it refers to or means. The word "tree" is a symbol. Words, sentences, concepts, and arguments are symbols: their significance depends upon the assumption of general rules which indicate what they shall mean.

From his doctrine of thought-signs, Peirce moves on to several conclusions which are basic to his philosophy. First, since all thinking involves signs or ideas which have a representative function, we cannot meaningfully speak of "absolute things in themselves" apart from their relation to signs or representation by the mind. To talk of knowing something as it is in itself, independent of any consequences for our actual or possible experience, is to talk of nothing at all. For example, to talk about the essence of force as something apart from any of the conceived consequences that might appear in experience is to talk about nothing real.

Second, although no reality can be granted apart from that which can be represented by some sign or idea, things exist independently of the mind's thinking of them. "That is, there is no thing which is in itself in the sense of not being relative to the mind, though things which are relative to the mind doubtless are, apart from that relation." [7]

The reference and existence of ideas or thoughts must be distinguished from one another. Peirce holds that no thought or sign can be identical in existence with that to which it refers. If it were, the idea would lose its entire representative function. Therefore, although all ideas are mental in their existence, they are not necessarily mental in their reference or pointing function. No thought or idea refers to itself, and the doctrine of intuitive awareness which claims that thoughts can directly embody their objects rests on confusing a sign with the thing signified.

Peirce's arguments here are not merely destructive of intuitive views of consciousness, such as that of Emerson, but of nominalism and subjective idealism as well. Peirce's criticisms imply a strong realism, holding (1) that thoughts or ideas refer to real existence outside the mind and (2) that there are real general existences outside the mind. A whole community of investigators is required for objectively testing the truth of any idea, and such elaborate procedure would make no sense if truth were enclosed within the individual consciousness. Also, no representation or concept is absolutely determinate; no conception or idea determines any absolute individuality without room for further determinateness. Every idea or genuine representation has some degree of generality to it, from which Peirce concludes that nominalism must be false and that reality has indeed real general features. In fact, it is only by neglecting the realistic orientation of the scientific method that one would be led astray into taking the position that only individual minds and their ideas exist. The whole point of the use of the scientific method is to come to know things as they really are, that is, independent of what you or I merely think or believe them to be. The scientific method must be impersonal and objective and can never block the way to further inquiry. Any view of the nature of the mind itself or its claims to knowledge must be subject to experimental testing. The superiority of the scientific method over all others, according to Peirce, is not that its methodology guarantees that it will always arrive at true conclusions, but rather that the scientific method is not an exception to its own use and that in always looking for its own errors, it does not block, but in fact opens, the way to further inquiry.

In 1877 Peirce published an article called "The Fixation of Belief" for *Popular Science Monthly*. In this early essay, he attempted to formulate the main characteristics of the scientific method and indicate its relation to alternative methods of fixing or arriving at beliefs. Here we find some of Peirce's most characteristic ideas: (1) the necessity of a carefully worked out theory of leading principles with which we can reason or carry on inquiry, and (2) the necessity of a (pragmatic) concept of belief so that genuine beliefs may be purposefully related to actions or practical consequences. Peirce distinguishes between belief and doubt by asserting that belief involves a rule or habit upon which one is prepared to act, whereas doubt involves no such rule of action. Doubt, however, implies an unsatisfactory feeling or uneasiness which may initiate inquiry. To begin an inquiry one must have a real or genuine doubt, not merely a pretended one. The only purpose of inquiry, then, is the resolution of doubt or the settlement of opinion. It will be noted that although they are differently related to action, both doubt and belief are given a pragmatic analysis by Peirce. Genuine doubt is an impulse to the doing of something, it is the "immediate motive for the struggle to attain belief." Genuine belief is the end or purpose of inquiry as well as a rule or habit upon which one is prepared to act.

Peirce notes that opinions may be settled in a variety of ways. The simplest way to fix a belief seems to be by sheer tenacity. The method of tenacity, as Peirce calls it, holds on to a belief by refusing to look at alternatives. This may be compared with the ostrich sticking its head in the sand. The trouble with such a method is that it contains no way of determining whether it is in error, or, for that matter, whether it has a hold on any truth. It is also met with any number of inconveniences, and, as Peirce suggests, man's social impulse is against it. Therefore, another method may be preferred which fixes beliefs with the power of authority, making individuals conform unanimously to one belief or opinion.

This method, which Peirce calls the method of authority, at least has the advantage of bringing some order into men's beliefs, making them all agree upon the same opinion. However, the method of mere authority has the disadvantage of making men intellectual slaves, since the power of authority cannot be questioned. The power of authority cannot make any mistakes, or at least none can be detected through its use, since it is the only authority. That this method may have a great use in regulating the lives of men Peirce does not deny. He does deny that the method of mere authority is good for arriving at the truth. Because it cannot be questioned, except by stepping outside its own framework, it provides only an arbitrary regulation of opinion, and offers no self-corrective method for settling opinions.

If coercion cannot be counted upon as a rational method of settling opinion, perhaps the *a priori* method will work since its conclusions will always be found to be agreeable with reason. Here at least one does not hide in the sand or fall down beneath some overpowering authority. The *a priori* method permits the individual to adopt those ideas which he believes as the result of reason, e.g., $2 + 3 = 5$. However, careful reflection on this method will reveal that sometimes men reason correctly and sometimes they do not. This method may therefore not only lead to fallacious results, but there is no guarantee that it will be in agreement with facts or experience. Pure reason may be in agreement with the facts, but there is no way that this can be discovered by the method itself.

Peirce concludes that the methods of tenacity, authority, and *a priori* reasoning are unsatisfactory as far as the genuine settlement of opinion is concerned. Each in its own way allows for no method of correcting its own errors, and hence has no objective test of truth or agreement with the facts. In contrast, the scientific or experimental method of settling opinion treats all its conclusions as tentative hypotheses. Contrary to all the other methods, *fallibilism* (the possibility of error in the genuine pursuit of factual truth) is part of the very procedure of experimental inquiry as such. Genuine inquiry starts with the purpose of finding out what the truth really is and freely admits that any specific attempt in this direction may be in error. Therefore, the only way to look for truth is to be constantly on the lookout for error. The scientific or experimental method does not tenaciously cling to any belief to the exclusion of any other, does not submit unquestioningly to the power of some arbitrary authority, and does not rely upon mere *a priori* reason without the benefit of testing its conclusions in experience.

In his later writing, Peirce came to regard fallibilism as synonymous with the procedures of all fruitful inquiry. Fallibilism exposes several important sources of the blocking of inquiry. Absolute certainty, absolute precision, absolute universality, self-evident truths, even the inexplicable or the absolutely unknowable all fall down under the scrutiny of fallibilism.

If genuine inquiry involves the pursuit of realities or facts, then absolute certainty is out of the question. Neither experience nor reason can show any fact that can be known with absolute certainty. The more evidence that comes in to support any genuine fact, the more there is still to come. No one observation in science is ever sufficient to establish a fact, and all that further observation can do is to increase the probability that it is true. All reasoning that applies to facts depends upon our samples or selections, and we can never be certain that the part that we have not sampled is like the part that we have. Absolute exactness is also out of the question since our samples are always finite and our measurements accordingly limited, thus always capable of further refinement. Further, absolute universality cannot be claimed for any scientific conclusion, since such a claim would imply that all future possibilities were already taken into consideration; but this is impossible, since they have not yet occurred.

Self-evident truths are inconsistent with the scientific method since self-evidence is a purely subjective criterion. Scientific results must be objective and public, that is, open to an indefinitely large community of investigators. No truth is evidence for itself, according to Peirce, but must be supported by independent evidence.

The claim that something is essentially unknowable or not explainable at all—or not explainable further—is inconsistent with genuine science. The limits of scientific knowledge cannot be set out in advance of the use of its methods without blocking the way to inquiry. All that science can say is that such and such has not yet been explained, or that something is not yet known.

Finally, the scientific method cannot investigate anything apart from its implications, effects, or consequences in experience. The scientific method can have nothing to do with things independent of all else, things in themselves. This last point brings to light the pragmatic aspect of the scientific method. The scientific or experimental method involves the *operational* study of phenomena. In science assumptions are made and operations performed in order that predictable consequences may be observed. To suggest that there is an objective, self-corrective method of studying anything apart from its consequences, as a thing isolated in itself, is to suggest something purely illogical.

Peirce claimed that his doctrine of fallibilism kept the purity of the scientific method intact. The purity of the scientific method does not at all mean that it is removed from the entanglement of facts, but simply that it has no ulterior purpose as the goal of its inquiries—not even the laudable humanitarian purpose of making the world a better place to live in. To require the scientific method to arrive at results which are useful to man in some special sense would be to subvert its impersonal character. This does not mean that scientific results cannot be useful to man, but only that the truth of beliefs must not be confused with the question of their usefulness. Peirce believed that the human usefulness of scientific ideas could best be preserved if science were allowed to pursue its investigations without any distractions concerning the human applications of its hypotheses. It is precisely on this point that Peirce's pragmatism and the pragmatism of William James diverge.

It is important to see the relation between Peirce's pragmatism and his idea of scientific method. The purpose of the scientific method is to fallibilistically and impersonally inquire into and settle the truth of opinions. The purpose of the pragmatic method, on the other hand, is simply to determine the meaning of intellectual concepts experimentally. Pragmatism and science are similar as methods, since both are experimental, fallible, and impersonal. But they differ in their purposes—science pursuing the question of the truth of ideas, and pragmatism pursuing the question of the meaning of ideas. Since they differ in purpose but agree in method, they can and must be useful to each other. The scientific method must be the key to unraveling the truth of general ideas in experimental terms. The pragmatic method, in turn, must give meaning to all concepts used in science, since only a pragmatic account of meaning insists on testing meaning by predictable consequences. Thus, Peirce adopts the view that philosophy itself must become scientific and correct for error if it is to make any progress or arrive at the truth. "In those sciences of measurement which are the least subject to error—metrology, geodesy, and metrical astronomy—no man of self-respect ever now states his result without affixing to it its *probable error;* and if this practice is not followed in other sciences [philosophy] it is because in those the probable errors are too vast to be estimated." [8]

PRAGMATISM AND MEANING   William James gave full credit to Peirce for originating pragmatism:

> [Pragmatism] was first introduced into philosophy by Mr. Charles Peirce in 1878. In an article entitled "How to Make Our Ideas Clear" in the *Popular Science Monthly* for January of that year Mr. Peirce, after pointing out that our beliefs are really rules for action, said that, to develop a thought's meaning, we need only determine what conduct it is fitted to produce: that conduct is for us its sole significance.[9]

At the outset it is important to see that Peirce's pragmatism involves a new philosophic method or approach to problems rather than a philosophical doctrine about the makeup of the universe or the nature of reality. Pragmatism is not a world-view or outlook on a par with materialism and idealism. Instead of being a theory or hypothesis about the makeup of reality, pragmatism is a method of determining the *meaning* of any rational concept or hypothesis and its admissibility to rank as a hypothesis in the first place.

Before any hypothesis can be tested to determine its truth or falsity, we must first understand what that hypothesis means. Testing the truth or falsity of an idea is dependent upon what meaning is given to the idea, since if it is given one meaning the hypothesis may turn out to be true, and if it is given another meaning the idea may turn out to be false. However, if the idea is not given a clear meaning or is in fact meaningless, then its truth or falsity cannot really be decided. A theory or test of meaning, therefore, is a logical prerequisite for the adequate application of the scientific method. If the scientific method is to pursue the truth of any hypothesis, then first it should be decided that the hypothesis is genuine (not a pseudo-hypothesis, i.e., untestable), and *second* it should be known exactly what the hypothesis means. Peirce's pragmatic method was intended to supply these two needs—that of determining the legitimacy of any hypothesis to serve as a hypothesis, and that of clarifying the meaning of a rational concept or hypothesis.

One of the striking features of Peirce's pragmatism is the modern ring to his whole approach. His essay of 1878 in which he calls for a proper method or theory of *meaning* for philosophical investigation was far in advance of his own times and more in line with twentieth-century developments in British and American philosophy which are characterized by a strong emphasis on theories of meaning and language. This fact to some extent explains why Peirce's pragmatic theory of meaning has had a greater impact and has received more attention in recent years than it ever did during his lifetime. Peirce's contention was that unless philosophy pays careful attention to the question of the meaning of its ideas, its answer to a problem will collapse like a house of cards.

The need for a new and carefully formulated theory of meaning can be seen by attending to some of the traditional philosophic conceptions of meaning. In *How to Make Our Ideas Clear* Peirce subjects a number of proposed tests of meaning to sharp criticism. To clarify the meaning of an idea, it had been proposed that we become familiar with the idea in such a way that it will be recognized whenever it is met with and that no other idea will be mistaken for it. This familiarity is to be attained purely by the mind's own power of rational inspection. However, Peirce argues that this method of intellectual familiarity is subjective, that it does not distinguish in any objective way between those ideas that only *seem* to be clearly apprehended and those that *really are*. Obviously, we can think that an idea is clearly apprehended when in fact it is not. Another test may therefore be proposed as a method of clarifying ideas: the method of arriving at a general definition of the concept in question. This apparently has the advantage of overcoming the subjectivity of mere familiarity, but only offers an abstract objectivity. As Peirce observes, "Nothing new can ever be learned by analyzing definitions." [10] Testing an idea for clarity only in the abstract carries with it no guarantee of factual objectivity. Peirce admits that familiarity with a notion is the first step toward clarity and definition is the second. But the process must be carried further; the third and real step toward the clarification of ideas must be *experimental* in terms of finding the anticipated consequences of any concept in experience or fact.

Peirce's pragmatism consequently provides a hypothetical rule for clarifying the meaning of intellectual concepts. He is careful to point out that pragmatism does not pretend to offer a method for determining the meaning of all signs or ideas, but only for those upon which reasoning may turn. That is, pragmatism is intended to clarify the meaning of general terms or ideas such as hardness, weight, force, and reality. It is just such *general* terms or universals, as they have been called, that philosophy is concerned with. All genuine reasoning, according to Peirce, requires the use of general ideas, since there can be no sound pattern of reasoning without a leading principle. A leading principle is that rule by which we draw a conclusion from its premises, and as such it must, as a leading principle, be capable of generalization or application to other cases.

For example, if we reason that since Socrates is a man, and since all men are mortal, it therefore follows that Socrates is mortal, we have used the general rule that if S is M, and if all M are L, then S is L. To be a valid pattern of reasoning, such a rule must apply not just to one man, Socrates, but to other individual cases as well. It is important then to see the logical or general character of Peirce's pragmatic method. In the first place, the pragmatic rule applies only to determining the meaning of general ideas, and not to singular or unique ones. Secondly, the pragmatic method applies only to what Peirce calls the "rational purport" of an idea, only to the logically predictable consequences that can *repeatedly* be found in experience. The pragmatic method must look to repeatable or general consequences, otherwise it would not be *experimental*. To suggest that any experimental results are not repeatable would be to say that the same experimental operations could not be used over and over again to obtain the same results, which would mean that the experiment had failed. Experimental results must be general in the sense that other repetitions of the same experience must produce the same result.

Peirce formulated his pragmatic rule in several ways. Perhaps the best formulation is as follows:

Now this sort of consideration, namely, that certain lines of conduct will entail certain kinds of inevitable experiences is what is called a "practical consideration." Hence is justified the maxim, belief in which constitutes pragmatism; namely, *In order to ascertain the meaning of an intellectual conception one should consider what practical consequences might conceivably result by necessity from the truth of that conception; and the sum of these consequences will constitute the entire meaning of the conception.*[11]

Peirce's notion of practical consequences or consideration is central to his pragmatic rule. His rule calls for locating the practical consequences of an idea in order to determine the meaning of that idea. However, he does not mean by practical consequences simply those that are useful to man or those that have an economic value. Rather, by practical consequences he means experimental consequences, those consequences that can repeatedly be found to result or follow from deliberately controlled actions or experimental operations.

Peirce's practical consequences are those that can be predicted to follow as the result of performing some operation. His pragmatic rule therefore is (1) hypothetical, (2) operational, (3) predictive, and (4) observational. To say it is hypothetical means that it is asserted in the form of a conditional proposition: if A then B. To say that it is operational means that the A part or antecedent of the conditional involves a purposefully controlled action or the doing of something to obtain a certain result. To say that it is predictive means that the B part or consequent of the conditional is anticipated to follow as an inevitable result of the A part or the operation performed. Finally, to say that Peirce's pragmatic rule is observational means that one must actually refer to experience or observation to determine whether the predicted results actually occur.

How to Make Our Ideas Clear gives a number of illustrations of Peirce's pragmatic rule to show how it works. Suppose we wanted to make clear what it means to call a thing *hard*, or to determine what *hardness* means. Pragmatism stipulates that we should consider what practical consequences follow. But follow from what? The answer would be to consider what practical consequences follow from deliberately or intentionally devised and controlled experimental operations. For example, we might try to scratch or crush an object believed to be hard anticipating that if it is hard then it should resist most or many attempts at scratching or crushing it. Notice, however, that the point of the pragmatic method is not to prove that a particular substance or object is hard or soft, heavy or light, or something else. Rather, the point of the pragmatic method is to clarify what the concept *hard* (or some other concept) means. To explain the meaning of the concept hard, one would have to specify what predictable results necessarily follow from certain operations specifically designed to produce those results time and time again. The sum of these predictable results will then constitute the entire meaning of the general concept.

It will be noticed, however, that no experimental results are final and that the number of practical consequences will have to be indefinite. This shows the intimate manner in which Peirce's pragmatism is connected with his fallibilism. Fallibilism asserts that absolute exactness or precision is not to be expected in using the scientific or experimental method. Pragmatism confirms fallibilism by always allowing for the possibility of further refinement of meaning. In other words, Peirce's pragmatism does not pretend to offer a rule for determining *the final* and absolutely exact meaning of any concept; it offers rather an experimental rule for determining the meaning of any concept, subject to further improvement by continued use of the same method. Peirce held, in fact, that no general concept was absolutely precise, or rather that no general concept could be *made* absolutely precise, since absolute precision would mean that all future experimental results were taken into consideration, which is impossible.

Peirce also believed that the pragmatic method could be applied to the general concept of reality. This idea has been given various interpretations by philosophers—one might say, too many different meanings. The question is, what meaning will stand up under experimental testing? Unless the concept of reality is brought to a pragmatic test, it will only be given a verbal meaning. That is, we may call reality mental, material, this, or that, but we will never know whether we are asserting the same thing by using different words, or asserting different things by using the same words unless we examine practical consequences.

We might begin with the familiar expectation that if something is real, then it is opposed to that which is only fictional or imaginary. Here we have one test at least; if something is real we could not simply wish it or think it away. However, it will be noticed that our thoughts or wishes are themselves real as actual thoughts or wishes, and therefore a further test is needed. If something is really thought or wished, *that fact* does not depend upon what you or I or anybody thinks about it. Thus we may get closer to a clear conception of what reality means by defining it as "that whose characters are independent of what anybody may think them to be." [12] Nothing is made real by virtue of the fact that it is thought about. First, if it were, realities could be manufactured at will, and then anything and everything would be real, thus making the concept superfluous. Second, thoughts themselves are not made real by virtue of the fact that they are thought about, since according to Peirce no thought thinks about itself.

Pragmatism is fundamentally a method of determining the meaning of certain signs, and all thoughts are signs or mental representations; but it is essential for pragmatism that no sign be confused with what it signifies. If a thought is a sign, then the existence of the thought or sign itself is one thing and its meaning or reference another. To give a pragmatic meaning to the concept reality, we would have to go beyond the prior stipulation (that reality means that whose characters are independent of what anybody may think them to be) and add, "The opinion which is fated to be ultimately agreed to by all who investigate, is what we mean by the truth, and the object represented in this opinion is real." [13]

In other words, the pragmatic or experimental meaning of the concept reality would have to stand up under the continuing investigation of an indefinite community of investigators. This fact, according to Peirce, would have to be included in the very meaning of the concept reality. The meaning of the concept reality, like any other concept determined by the pragmatic method, must tell us how we arrived at that concept, and, further, the meaning arrived at and the method of arrival must be consistent with one another. This is exactly what Peirce maintained as the logically consistent character of the pragmatic theory of meaning: that pragmatism tells us what a concept means by spelling out the operations or what we have to do to test any concept experimentally, and that these same operations with their predictable consequences are included in that concept's meaning; in fact, they constitute all the meaning that any concept can have.

REALISM AND LOGICAL REASONING   Throughout his scientific philosophy or pragmatism Peirce strove to combat what he considered to be the serious errors of subjectivism and nominalism. Subjectivism is the view that reality and truth are determined by the mind or by what is thought, and nominalism is the view that only individuals are real and that general words or concepts are mere names of convenience and do not in fact refer to general traits of reality. Peirce believed these views to be fundamentally wrong and opposed to the requirements of logic and the scientific method. Subjectivism is inadequate since it would confuse the logical with the merely psychological. Validity or truth in reasoning must be factual or objectively discoverable or it would depend on human bias or opinion. A conclusion in logic is valid not simply because we think it is or wish it to be, but rather because it in fact follows from its premises. Sometimes we reason correctly, sometimes we do not, and the whole point of logic is to analyze and evaluate our reasoning in terms of proper norms or standards. But the only norms or standards that logic deals with are impersonal or scientific, that is, those that are free of personal feeling or subjective bias.

Peirce claims, too, that nominalism is out of place in logic. Nominalism denies that ideas can be abstract and general, but this is exactly what all logical principles have to be. All reasoning assumes that particular cases fall under some general rule. But no general rule is ever exhausted by particular cases since for any particular case we can always anticipate another. Every logical inference is both general and abstract in the sense that no mere particular or concrete cases can ever exhaust its meaning. For example, if we infer from All A is B and All B is C that therefore All A is C, then we are assuming that *whenever* these premises are true the conclusion will also be true. Unless the general rule here really holds indefinitely, the inference is invalid. Fallacies in reasoning show exactly this point, since a fallacy is reasoning that breaks down or does not generally hold. For example, consider the false conversion: Some A is not B, therefore, some B is not A. This holds for Mexicans and engineers, but it does not hold for fish and trout. Logic requires real general principles that can never be exhausted by any limited number of particular or individual cases.

The scientific method or any scientific approach to philosophy must assume a realistic attitude toward the questions of reality and truth:

> Such is the method of science. Its fundamental hypothesis, restated in more familiar language, is this: There are Real things, whose characters are entirely independent of our opinions about them; those Reals affect our senses according to regular laws, and, though our sensations are as different as are our relations to the objects, yet, by taking advantage of the laws of perception, we can ascertain by reasoning how things really and truly are; and any man, if he

have sufficient experience and he reason enough about it, will be led to the one True conclusion.[14]

The scientific method must assume that there is an independently existing world, or body of real facts, that is discoverable by the continued use of objective and self-corrective methods of investigation. Hence, a pragmatic or laboratory philosophy can never be *a priori* or intuitive; it must be realistic and public. It must look for independent evidence in support of any hypothesis and it must subject each hypothesis to the repeated or continued verification of a whole community of investigators. To establish that any hypothesis is true, what must be shown is not that some mind can think that it is true, but rather that the anticipated consequences of that hypothesis can repeatedly be found in experience by *all* persons who would seriously investigate it.

Peirce's realism actually has two sides. On the one hand "realism" signifies a belief in the reality of things independent of the *fact* that they are thought about. On the other hand it signifies a belief in the objective reality of general traits, habits, or laws. Peirce insisted that these two forms of realism belong together and are equally essential for a pragmatic and scientific philosophy. Nominalism, in taking the opposite view that only individuals exist, holds that general concepts or words like "hard," "round," or "triangle" are *mere names* for collections of individuals. Nominalism cannot grant an objective reality for anything general. For example, the nominalist would say that this or that individual man exists, but man in general has no objective existence. He would also take the position that all ideas are individual or particular, and that the mind cannot frame an idea of anything purely general, such as man, triangle, or horse, but that the meaning of such ideas must be found in the various particular cases of men, triangles, or horses.

Peirce's pragmatic method rules out any nominalistic interpretation. If only individuals existed, we could not find any practical consequences of an hypothesis, since only repeatable consequences are experimentally significant or testable. For example, to give pragmatic meaning to the concept "acid," it may be assumed that if we place blue litmus paper in what we take to be acid, then we can anticipate that the blue litmus paper will turn red. However, here the experimental operation and its predicted consequence must be repeatable, and thus constitute a general law. A certain (general) kind of operation must inevitably entail a certain (general) kind of result. Unless the objective reality of generals is allowed, any scientific or experimental approach to both the meaning and truth of hypotheses would be paralyzed. Speaking of his own brand of realism, Peirce asserts:

> It is plain that this view of reality is inevitably realistic, because general conceptions enter into all judgments, and therefore, into true opinions. Consequently, a thing in the general is as real as in the concrete. It is perfectly true that all white things have whiteness in them, for that is only saying, in another form of words, that all white things are white; but since it is true that real things possess whiteness, whiteness is real.[15]

Peirce even goes to the extent of arguing that pure or absolute individuals cannot exist at all. The nominalist, in claiming that all existence is individual, holds a doctrine that conflicts both with logic and with the facts:

> The absolute individual cannot only not be realized in sense or thought, but cannot exist, properly speaking. For whatever lasts for any time, however short, is capable of logical division, because in that time it will undergo some change in its relations. But what does not exist for any time, however short, does not exist at all. All, therefore, that we perceive or think, or that exists, is general. So far there is truth in the doctrine of scholastic realism.[16]

Peirce's realism applies to his whole pragmatic conception of knowledge. "If I *truly know* anything, that which I know must be real." [17] He gives the example of knowing that if one lets go of a stone it will fall to the ground. What does this simple illustration show? It shows (1) that knowing is a matter of inference, (2) that all knowledge requires real generals or universals, and (3) that knowledge of fact is pragmatic and involves the successful anticipation or prediction of experimental consequences.

First, all real knowing is inferential rather than intuitive. To know, for example, that the stone will fall is to draw a logical conclusion from premises. Here the premises would be the *general rule* that solid bodies fall in the absence of any upward force or pressure, together with the particular operation or result that the stone is dropped, from which the case is predicted that the stone will fall to the ground.

Second, all knowledge requires that general principles or universals are really operative in nature. In order to know by logical inference that this stone will fall, one must use the general rule that solid bodies fall in the absence of any upward force or pressure. One must assume that this general rule or others really exist; otherwise our knowledge of particular cases would be purely accidental or a matter of mere guesswork.

Third, our knowledge of facts is pragmatic. Knowledge is related to action, since knowledge is a form of true belief or successful anticipation of consequences. Belief itself, according to Peirce, is pragmatic insofar as it is a rule or habit upon which one is prepared to act. Knowledge is essentially pragmatic because when we *really* know or understand something, this means that we know or see that certain consequences or practical results logically follow from certain things we do or control. To return to our previous example: to know that the stone will fall is to know that if we deliberately do certain things (e.g., let go of the stone) in conjunction with the belief that real general laws or principles operate in the world, then certain practical consequences will inevitably follow (the stone will fall). Here again it should be noted that practical consequences refer to experimentally or operationally derived results.

We are now in a better position to see the logical element in Peirce's pragmatism. Peirce considered it the business of the logician to study and classify the various forms of argument or reasoning. The purpose of logical reasoning is "to find out from the consideration of what we already know, something else which we do not know. Consequently, reasoning is good if it be such as to give a true conclusion from true premises, and not otherwise. Thus, the question of validity is purely one of fact and not of thinking." [18] Logical conclusions are not correct simply because we think they are. If any logical reasoning is sound, this must be because a given conclusion is really the result of its premisses. The premisses will then stand as evidence for the conclusion in an objective way.

What are the possible ways in which premisses argue for a conclusion? What are the various types or classifications of logical reasoning? Peirce believed that all reasoning could be classified under three main types: deduction, induction, and abduction, which is sometimes called hypothesis. Deductive reasoning is exemplified by the following: if we know that all men are mortal, and that Socrates is a man, then we can deduce that Socrates is mortal. What makes this type of reasoning deductive? First of all, in truly deductive reasoning the conclusion *necessarily* follows from its premisses. That is, once they are accepted, the premisses provide decisive evidence for the conclusion. Deduction is not at all a question of probability. In a deduction, if the premisses are admitted, the question is *not* with what degree of probability does the conclusion follow, but rather, whether it follows or does not follow.

Deduction, according to Peirce, starts with a rule (All men are mortal), adds a case under the rule (Socrates is a man), and draws a particular conclusion which applies the rule to the case and states the result (Therefore, Socrates is mortal). However, Peirce asks himself, how is it that deductions can provide conclusions which are necessary? The answer is that deductions are only hypothetically necessary, or in their pure form involve drawing necessary conclusions from purely hypothetical premises. Peirce asserts that "it is impossible to reason necessarily concerning anything else than a pure hypothesis." [19] By a pure hypothesis he means one that is free of any factual content.

But are there any such fact-free hypotheses? Peirce claims there *are* and that mathematics deals with them all the time. Mathematics is a science which draws necessary conclusions from pure hypotheses. Therefore, every apodictic or necessary inference is, strictly speaking, mathematical. Every deduction, as a deduction, is a mathematical inference, not because every deduction deals with numbers, but because an inference can be necessary only if it follows the formal procedure of mathematics and treats its premises as pure hypotheses. If we return to our previous example, it can be seen that it is a deductive inference only if it can be formalized and freed of all factual content. This can be achieved by writing it mathematically, or purely in terms of symbols that refer to hypothetical states of affairs, as follows: in place of "All men are mortal" we write "All A is B," where A and B are any classes of anything; in place of "Socrates is a man" we write "S is an A," where S is anything falling under the hypothetical class A; and in place of "therefore, Socrates is a mortal" we write "therefore, S is B." Here we have shown that the inference in no way depends upon any fact about Socrates, men, or mortals; it is, rather, a purely hypothetical inference that is valid no matter what content is indicated.

Inductive reasoning is conspicuously different. It is exemplified by the following: if we know that A, B, C, etc. are crows, and further that A, B, C, etc. are black, we may then draw the inductive conclusion that all crows are black. What makes this type of reasoning inductive? First of all, inductions can only be probable; that is, if the premises are admitted in an inductive argument, the conclusion is never necessary, but only follows with a degree of probability. In an inductive argument, the premises never provide conclusive evidence for accepting the conclusion, but only provide some or a certain degree of assurance that it follows. In the example cited, we have only a certain number of cases observed where crows are black, but we draw the conclusion that they all are black. This means that our conclusion is far from necessary and only follows with a certain degree of assurance.

In an induction, according to Peirce, we reason from a case and a result (limited samples) to a general rule. Induction reasons from previously observed cases of a certain kind to new or future cases of a similar kind. Since induction depends upon limited sampling, it can never be apodictic. However, since induction is an important form of inference, and necessary for the growth of science, Peirce raises the question of its validity. What is the rational basis of inductive inference? Here Peirce refuses to accept either of two traditional solutions to this problem. One view attempted to base induction on deduction, and the other attempted to ground induction in the regularity of nature. Peirce argues that induction can never be reduced to deduction since a deductive conclusion must never go beyond its premisses, whereas an inductive inference goes well beyond its premisses with the assumption of an indefinitely long run. Further, induction cannot be validated by invoking the notion that nature is regular or orderly, since in certain respects it is *not*. Careful observation shows deviations from orderly laws which cannot simply be explained away. Induction can only be validated fallibilistically by showing that it never blocks the way to further inquiry because it is able to correct its mistakes. Whenever we form an induction we generalize on the basis of limited samples; but every general idea is vague in certain respects, and leaves certain facts undetermined. Induction is therefore justified because it is a positive furtherance to inquiry; we can know that it will generally work even though it may sometimes fail since its general validity always allows for error.

Abductive reasoning, according to Peirce, is the boldest of all types. For this reason it is sometimes called mere hypothesis, or a tentative explanation which may have to be abandoned. Abductive reasoning is exemplified by the following: if we know that a certain number of horses (A,B,C) are brown, and that all the horses from a nearby stable Z are brown, we may draw the abductive conclusion that these horses (A,B,C) are from that stable Z. What makes this type of reasoning abductive? First of all, abduction, like induction, is only probable; its conclusions cannot follow as a necessary consequence of its premisses. In an abduction the premisses are based on limited samplings and hence we *cannot* claim that they provide certain evidence for the conclusion. But abduction is even more precarious than induction since it does not argue from like to like or from similarities in the past to similarities in the future. Induction says that from a certain case or cases and from a certain result or results, a general rule follows about all those cases and results. Abduction, on the other hand, argues from a certain result (a certain number of horses (A,B,C) are brown) and claims that a certain rule (all horses from a certain stable Z are brown) applies to that result; so that a *new* case follows (that these horses (A,B,C) are from stable Z).

Abduction is therefore a more creative and bolder form of reasoning, and is needed by science in order to explain new facts or anticipate new discoveries. Since abduction is a synthetic form of inference, it cannot be validated *a priori* or deductively. However, according to Peirce, its rational basis can be found in induction and the doctrine of fallibilism. Abduction must be grounded in induction since every abduction assumes that a general law or rule can be found to explain a certain case or fact—but every general law or rule is itself an induction, or is derived by inductive reasoning. Also, since every abduction is only a probable explanation, it must be fallible and open to possible correction when necessary. Further, we can now understand what he meant when he said: "If you carefully consider the question of pragmatism you will see that it is nothing else than the question of the logic of abduction." [20]

Peirce maintained that science requires all these types of reasoning. Deduction is essential to all mathematics, induction is essential to deriving general rules or laws of nature, and abduction is needed to make new discoveries and anticipate new facts. However, Peirce claimed that abduction is also of special importance for pragmatism in that pragmatism is essentially the logic of abduction. Pragmatism, as a method of determining the meaning of any general concept, makes use of abductive reasoning since it draws a conclusion of a new case from a general rule together with a previous result. Pragmatism involves hypothetical or abductive reasoning precisely because it asserts that giving meaning to a concept depends upon the operation of applying a general rule to an observed result.

To illustrate, if we want to give meaning to the concept "hard" or explain what hardness means, then we have to find a rule and a result. The rule might be, if any substance is hard then it will not easily be scratched or crushed by many other substances. The observed result might be that when we try to scratch this or that substance believed to be hard, we find that we do not succeed. To say, then, that the meaning of a particular concept is explained by applying a general operational rule to certain known results, is to say that the explanation of a concept's meaning is hypothetically or abductively determined. To set out the pragmatic meaning of any concept, then, is to reason to a tentative conclusion.

Abduction, or pragmatism, therefore, does not claim that any hypothesis of what a concept means is final or absolutely correct, but only offers a tentative explanation. But pragmatism or abduction does insist upon experimental consequences. It does demand that any hypothesis must be, in principle, verifiable. "Any hypothesis, therefore, may be admissible, in the absence of any special reasons to the contrary, provided it be capable of experimental verification, and only insofar as it is capable of such verification." [21]

PHENOMENOLOGY, SCIENTIFIC METAPHYSICS, AND EVOLUTION   In addition to originating pragmatism as a logically rigorous and scientifically oriented method in philosophy; Peirce systematically developed the implications of his scientific philosophy into a highly speculative metaphysics—an evolutionary view of the universe. By combining his pragmatism with a theory of cosmic evolution, Peirce gave scope to his own philosophy, and provided the movement of American pragmatism with a highly original and pregnant vision of the universe. Although he never worked out a completed system of philosophy, he did formulate the outlines of a system as well as a great number of acute and interesting speculations. Peirce's educational background was well suited to his interest in combining scientific method and philosophic speculation. Not only did he possess experimental training and a first-hand acquaintance with science and mathematics, but at the same time he was extremely well read in the history of philosophical systems. Peirce was the first American philosopher to combine a mastery of scientific knowledge with an extensive understanding of the history and development of philosophic thought.

Peirce thought of philosophy as a positive science on a par with mathematics and physics. That is, the purpose of philosophy, as the purpose of science, was primarily theoretical—to acquire knowledge, to advance the frontiers of understanding. However, he distinguished among the sciences, dividing them into three basic classifications: mathematics, philosophy and ideoscopy (specialized factual science). Mathematics is the science which studies only what is logically possible, not actual states of affairs or facts. Mathematics is only concerned with deducible relationships between purely hypothetical or abstract objects. It accordingly makes no claim to offer information about observable facts, and hence does not depend upon experimental findings to validate its theories. Mathematics justifies all its results by reasoning alone, since it deals only with general abstract possibilities. However, it is precisely because of its general, abstract, and hypothetical nature that mathematics is applicable and necessary for all the other sciences. According to Peirce, every positive science must have a mathematical part since every science must specifically *use* that with which mathematics is concerned—patterns of deductive reasoning.

Ideoscopy and philosophy are differentiated from mathematics in that they are concerned with the factual world. They both depend upon observation, but in different ways. Ideoscopy encompasses the specialized factual sciences (physics, chemistry, biology, etc.), which require technical methods of observation (spectroscopes, microscopes, etc.) and detailed experimentation. Philosophy, on the other hand, although it too is concerned with the factual world and depends upon observation, does not depend on technical or specialized methods of observation and refined experimentation. Philosophy depends only upon observation that is available to common experience.

Peirce subdivides philosophy into three main branches: phenomenology, normative science, and metaphysics. Phenomenology is the basic descriptive study of all actual and possible phenomena that are and can be presented in experience. It attempts to describe and classify rather than to evaluate or speculate on all the different sorts of things that can be found in experience. Phenomenology comprises the observational or descriptive basis upon which the other two branches of philosophy (normative and metaphysical) are built. As the science of the data given in experience, it seeks to uncover the basic categories or classes of things that are universally or pervasively present in any experience. Peirce finds that there are only *three* basic kinds or categories of phenomena. These he calls Firstness, Secondness and Thirdness.

> My view is that there are three modes of being. I hold that we can directly observe them in elements of whatever is at any time before the mind in any way. They are the being of positive qualitative possibility, the being of actual fact, and the being of law that will govern facts in the future.[22]

If we carefully attend to experience or what is ever before the mind, we can always find three different sorts of things or phenomena. We can note the presence of bare or given qualities or feelings such as pleasures, colors, sounds, and smells. These qualities Peirce calls Firsts (First-ness) because they are single phenomena independent of anything else. Each quality is complete in itself—it just is what it is—red is red, sweet is sweet. Each is a free possibility of experience—free of time—since no quality is an event or an action, but a mere timeless quality that may be felt, remembered, or found. Moreover, we can note the actual existence of brute fact, such as the shock of electricity, the resistance of a wall, or any brute force or struggle. These actual events Peirce calls Seconds (Second-ness) because they are not mere single qualities, but actual two-term relationships of one thing happening to another. No event or real fact is ever complete or isolated, but always falls into relationships with other facts; it is affected by other things and also affects other things. Facts are entangled with other facts. They are not free of time, but are perfectly temporal, each occurring at a specific time and having a certain duration.

Finally, we can note the presence of continuity or law which is exem-plified by growth, logical thought, or anything that is continuous. These laws or habits Peirce calls Thirds (Thirdness) because they are neither bare qualities nor brute facts, but three-term phenomena always implying a connection between one phenomenon and another. No real habit or law is a mere quality, since qualities do not develop or grow, whereas habits or laws do. Also, "No collection of facts can constitute a law; for the law goes beyond any accomplished facts and determines how facts that *may be,* but *all* of which never can have happened, shall be charac-terized." [23] Laws cover the potential (Firstness) and the actual (Second-ness), and laws are general (Firstness) as well as particular (Secondness). Every real law makes reference to what will be, as well as to what ac-tually is. Every real law applies to repeatable phenomena and is therefore general; it also applies to actual specific cases and is therefore particular. Peirce considers that thought itself is a good manifestation of Thirdness. All thoughts are thirds, since all thoughts are signs, and a sign is simply *something* which stands to *somebody* for *something* in some respect. Every thought or sign, then, can be analyzed into three elements. The three-fold character of thought-signs may be illustrated as follows: If a cloud is taken as a sign of rain, the cloud formation itself is the first element or sign, the anticipated rain is the second element or object re-ferred to by the sign, and the interpreter who takes the cloud to be a sign of rain is the third element.

Peirce saw an extensive application for his categories of Firstness, Secondness, and Thirdness. This is understandable because they are the most general features of all phenomena. They appear in the realm of logic as terms, propositions, and arguments. Terms are the elements of statements, since every statement can be broken up into its terms. "Socrates" is a term in the proposition "Socrates is a man." Terms such as "Socrates," "man," and "mortal" are single logical elements and are therefore *Firsts*. Propositions such as "Socrates is a man," and "All men are mortal"—dual logical phenomena implying that one term is asserted of a second term—are *Seconds*. Arguments, such as "All men are mortal, Socrates is a man, therefore Socrates is mortal" are *Thirds*; they are made up of terms (Firsts) and propositions (Seconds) but add a third phenomenon, an implication or logical connection between premisses and conclusion.

Peirce believed that his three categories also applied to three broad classifications of men. Artists, or men of feeling, are interested in the pure qualities of experience, and hence illustrate the category of Firstness. Practical men are interested in facts, in actual events and getting things done, and hence illustrate Secondness. Scientists, or men of thought, are interested in ideas, principles, or theories, and hence illustrate Thirdness. Also, Peirce believed that his categories illustrated three fundamental states of mind. Feeling is a First, choosing is a Second, and knowing is a Third. Feelings imply qualities or Firsts; choices imply goals or ends, doing one thing in relation to a second; knowing implies drawing an inference or seeing a *connection*, a Third, between two things.

After phenomenology, Peirce calls for normative science as the next major division of philosophy. Normative philosophy seeks to study phenomena in terms of certain norms. Normative philosophy itself is subdivided into three main branches: aesthetics, ethics, and logic. Aesthetics would seek to evaluate phenomena in terms of their qualities of aesthetic value or beauty. Ethics would seek to evaluate phenomena in terms of actions which are morally right or wrong. Logic would seek to evaluate phenomena in terms of inferences which are valid or invalid. Aesthetics, ethics, and logic are the three normative sciences which involve making value judgments of beauty, goodness, and validity respectively. Peirce's own work in normative philosophy, however, is virtually limited to his work in logic. He did very little work in aesthetics and ethics. In fact, Peirce was not convinced that philosophy could do very much in these areas. He allowed that the science of logic could make reasonable (provable) value judgments concerning the validity of inferences. However, he was skeptical that a science of aesthetics or ethics could make reasonable (provable) value judgments. Peirce asserted that there was room for doubt as to whether ethics and aesthetics were really normative branches of philosophy. He tended to assume that the fundamental questions of ethics and aesthetics—what is morally good or right and what is aesthetically beautiful—were actually pre-normative questions—questions decided not by philosophic thought, but by feeling, instinct, or custom. Since he accepted a neutral, disinterested, and value-free conception of scientific method, he regarded the important value questions of life as outside the range of philosophy.

> On vitally important topics reasoning is out of place. . . .[24] In regard to the greatest affairs of life, the wise man follows his heart and does not trust his head. This should be the method of every man, no matter how powerful his intellect.[25] Common sense, which is the resultant of the traditional experiences of mankind, witnesses unequivocally that the heart is more than the head, and is in fact everything in our highest concerns, thus agreeing with my unproved logical theorem.[26]

From this it is understandable why Peirce did not really develop a moral, social, political, or religious philosophy. In holding that the deepest concerns of man were not a function of reason or thought, he tended to view them as outside the legitimate domain of the scientific method. This point is of special importance for the later development of pragmatism and American philosophy, especially in the work of James and Dewey. As we shall see, James and Dewey will draw different conclusions for pragmatism on the whole question of the relation between intelligence or science on the one side and humanly important values on the other.

Peirce regarded metaphysics as the third main branch of philosophy after phenomenology and normative science. The task of metaphysics is the study of the most general features of reality. The special sciences or ideoscopy, as Peirce calls them, would study the particular features of reality, i.e., the chemical, biological, physical aspects of the real world. Metaphysics would confine itself to such speculations as can be based on unaided observation. However, to be legitimate, metaphysics would have to be scientific, and could not be based on ulterior purposes or preconceptions. In fact, Peirce considered that metaphysics was in a backward condition precisely because it was based on practical considerations. He identified theologians as the principal agents responsible for the lack of progress in metaphysics. To Peirce, theologians were not scientific men bent upon objectively searching for the truth, but practical men interested in using ideas as a guide to conduct or as a path to salvation and the absolute truth. The scientific man searches for a reasonable tentative hypothesis to explain the facts, while the practical man requires a fixed belief upon which he can act. No idea or principle is absolute for the scientific attitude, since the whole scientific method is based on the notion of fallibilism which tells us *never to block the way to further inquiry.* Theology, however, is primarily apologetic, not interested in further inquiry; it is rather concerned to seize upon and defend an all-important truth. Inquiry is only a means to an end for the practical man while the scientific man is never satisfied that everything has been perfectly explained.

For Peirce, philosophy is misconceived if it is construed as providing us with a way of life. To use philosophy to defend Calvinism as Edwards did, to defend democracy as Jefferson did, or to defend transcendentalism as Emerson did are three good examples of what Peirce considered bad use of philosophy or metaphysics. If metaphysics is a science of the most general features of reality, its conclusions must be based on observations and its arguments must be logical. It is a fundamental mistake of metaphysics to try to make the facts fit some preconceived plan. It is a mistake to consider any laws of the universe to be absolute. Determinism, materialism, and transcendentalism all conceive that there is an absolute truth which governs the world, and in this they are fundamentally mistaken according to Peirce. These theories are without a real concept of evolution and do not allow for fallibilism or the existence of real indeterminacy in the world; therefore they cannot explain how any laws of the universe have come to be. If nature has any laws (and Peirce believed that there was ample evidence that it does) then they must be accounted for. A scientific metaphysics which accepts a universe governed by laws must explain how laws themselves become realities; it cannot merely accept them as ultimate, unexplainable facts. Peirce thought this explanation could be accomplished with the concept of evolutionary law.

He attacks the notion of absolute determinism, the doctrine that every single fact in the universe is precisely determined by law. Jonathan Edwards had argued for a rigid determinism. His position was based on both the *a priori* thesis that events are inconceivable without their causes, and the religious thesis of predetermination, or God's foreknowledge of exactly what is to take place. Although Peirce does not attack Edwards by name, it is important to note that his criticism of determinism is one of the first carefully worked-out arguments against the *kind* of position that Edwards held. Peirce's arguments are quite acute and detailed. The

gist of his objections may be indicated as follows: Determinism is pur-
portedly a thesis about the facts of the empirical world which takes
science into consideration. However, it cannot be an empirical hypothesis
since no empirical hypothesis can be absolute, infallible, or exact. No
empirical proof can ever be given to show that all facts absolutely follow
a rigid law, since any law must be general, and hence, must leave some
facts undetermined. Careful observation shows us that more and more
deviations from any law are witnessed as our observations become more
precise. These observed deviations cannot be explained away simply as
errors of observation since they can be shown to exceed our antecedently
calculated probability of error.

The determinist who defends his position in the face of carefully
collected contrary facts is defending an *a priori* position, one that maintains itself on the basis of theory alone, independent of observation and
experience. Peirce argues that absolute determinism is not a necessary
postulate or assumption of scientific explanation. No assumption is required by science that cannot be tested for correction over a period of
time. Determinism, as an absolutely exact thesis about past, present, and
all future events, is not susceptible to correction in any way. Hence, the
assumption of absolute determinism cannot be certified by the progressive and self-corrective methods of science. Determinism cannot explain
how growth involves real diversity since it has to assume a universe which,
in principle, is already finished rather than evolving, and one whose
parts always fit some uniform whole. In effect determinism must deny
any real growth, chance, or diversity in the universe.

Real chance, or spontaneous, free possibility is a metaphysical First,
according to Peirce. Chance is therefore the First, most fundamental
feature of reality or the universe. Peirce believed that his doctrine of
chance as a metaphysical First could be sustained by observation and by
logic. "Try to verify any law of nature, and you will find that the more
precise your observations, the more certain they will be to show irregular
departures from the law." [27] Also, the logic of probability shows us that
chance occurrences can actually be calculated, and hence, must be real.
The chance of picking four consecutive aces from a deck of fifty-two
cards is very small indeed, but it can be calculated and does occur. What
this means is not that such a chance occurrence is absolutely fixed by
law, but rather that chance does not occur without some law and that
both chance and regular law are genuine features of the real world.

The doctrine of materialism, too, is attacked by Peirce as an example
of bad metaphysics. Jefferson had maintained a strong form of material-

ism, even though he never succeeded in formulating it in great detail. He believed that immaterial existences are mere nothings, and that all mental events could be explained in terms of certain material or physiological facts. Along with this, he also affirmed a natural religion of deism which asserted that a divine creator or architect had given laws of motion, rest, etc. to the natural world. Peirce attacks materialism because its metaphysics does not account for how certain portions of matter become aware of other portions of matter. Materialism reduces mind, thought, and feeling to matter or motions of matter, but leaves a gap between them that cannot be explained on materialist grounds alone.

Matter, according to Peirce, has a tendency to take on habits or laws, but so does mind or feeling. Matter is effete mind, or mind hidebound with habits. He claims a real continuity between them in terms of the notion of habit or evolutionary law. Matter and mind should not be explained away. Rather, mind should be considered a *First* and matter a *Second*, both being connected by the idea of real development or evolutionary law. Thought and physical motion are both subject to habits or patterns of regularity. Mind, as a *First*, suggests spontaneous action that is free, whereas matter, as a *Second*, suggests struggle or resisted action that is bound by certain conditions or limitations. But materialism if it assumes unchanging laws of nature which govern motion and matter is no more able than determinism to give a real explanation of these laws. Laws are not simply given, according to Peirce, but rather they develop or evolve, and it is the business of metaphysics to try to explain this continuity.

The doctrine of subjective idealism or transcendentalism as a possible metaphysics is attacked by Peirce. Emerson adopted a form of idealism, claiming that all things are subjectively grounded in the mind and that a higher fixed universal law explains all differences or opposites in the universe. Emerson also claimed a religious basis for his metaphysics insofar as every individual part of the universe was said to be actually divine when seen transcendentally, that is, in a mystical or unified manner. As Peirce views it, transcendentalism falsifies the nature of reality by making it a function of the structure of the mind, a structure which itself is not accounted for or explained. Since subjective idealism fails to interpret thoughts or ideas as signs it confuses the existence of thoughts with what is thought about. When thoughts are interpreted as signs, it is incorrect to say that reality is in the mind or present to the mind. Peirce asks, "Where is the real, the thing independent of how we think it to be found? There must be such a thing, for we find our opinions constrained; there is something, therefore, which influences our thoughts, and is not created by them." [28] Reality is both objective and intrinsically knowable. It is neither made by the mind (subjective) nor out of reach of the mind (unknowable). Reality is that which can be represented by signs or thoughts, but no existing sign or thought exhausts all that is real. Reality is that which all true opinions or representations would converge upon in the indefinitely long run of time.

Transcendentalism therefore fails to explain how the mind is related to the real, since it simply compresses them both into an empty unity. What is needed, according to Peirce, is the concept of evolutionary law. We have to explain how the real has come about, and further, how the mind develops or acquires a knowledge of this reality. But transcendentalism explains neither, since it has no theory of evolution. Because transcendentalism does not allow for an evolving reality, or the continuous spreading of thoughts in the form of signs, it is condemned to accept an absolute and unverifiable law of mind that governs all things. Consequently, it substitutes mystical intuition for the logical and self-correcting methods of science. It assumes that the universe is condemned to repeat the same fundamental law over and over again. It therefore explains away novelty and has no way of telling us anything definite about the shapes of things to come, since it simply asserts that things only repeat, in amazing ways, the way things have been.

Peirce consequently argues that the most general features of reality can only be accounted for by a vision of cosmic evolution. This means that there are no ultimates or unchanging absolutes, but rather that everything (whether laws, matter, or mind) in the real world is to be explained in terms of how it evolved. In the cosmological order, chance is *First*, force or struggle is *Second*, and evolutionary development is *Third*. Chance or spontaneity is First, since chance can develop out of chance itself. Free possibilities give rise to more possibilities. Struggle is Second, since in some way possibilities limit one another. Free or spontaneous phenomena tend to interfere with another's freedom so that contingent facts, lines of force or habits begin to emerge. When this happens, a Third has already intervened to make the First continuous with the Second. Evolutionary law admits both diversity or chance and regularity or law. Evolutionary law is Third, therefore, since the continuity between what is possible (chance) and what is actual (fact) must be taken into consideration.

Peirce rejects monism as well as dualism in metaphysics. Monism, whether it makes either mind or matter or *one* neutral stuff the essence of the whole universe, is unable to account for the diversity and the development of laws. Dualism, which separates reality into *two* ultimate irreducible compartments of mind, matter, etc., is unable to explain the gulf set up between its poles. A third principle is needed that makes room for cosmic evolution to show the connection between things. Peirce thinks this is provided by evolutionary law which admits both chance and law as real features of the world, and attempts to tie them together with a theory of continuous evolution. Evolution is a truly inclusive and scientific principle of explanation since it allows continuity in nature and fallibilism in our knowledge of nature. Fallibilism and continuity must be connected since

> The principle of continuity is the idea of fallibilism objectified. For fallibilism is the doctrine that our knowledge is never absolute but always swims, as it were, in a continuum of uncertainty and of indeterminacy. Now the doctrine of continuity is that all things so swim in continua.[29]

However, he argues that evolution itself must not be construed in a mechanical manner, as he says was done by the English philosopher Herbert Spencer. Peirce argues against any mechanical account of evolution by asserting

> the principle of evolution requires no extraneous cause, since the tendency to growth can be supposed itself to have grown from an infinitesimal germ accidentally started. Second, because law ought more than anything else to be supposed a result of evolution. Third, because exact law obviously never can produce heterogeneity out of homogeneity; and arbitrary heterogeneity is the feature of the universe the most manifest and characteristic.[30]

Peirce further speculated that a true account of cosmic evolution must include the notion of evolutionary love, since only a principle of love will foster the greatest diversity and growth, and at the same time strive for a harmony or continuity between things. Evolution by accidental variation or chance alone is insufficient, this being only an illustration of *Firstness.* Evolution by brute or mechanical necessity is also insufficient, this being only an illustration of *Secondness.* But evolution by creative love would be sufficient to account for the universe, since this implies real continuity and further growth; this is an illustration of Peirce's category of *Thirdness.*

Peirce's speculations did not stop here since he sought as many implications or extensions of his ideas as possible. If evolution is a hypothesis that includes scientific confirmation and cosmic love as well, then perhaps science can be wedded to religion. A religion based on love would never conflict with the scientific attitude if both are viewed as united through the bond of continuous evolution. The reality of God may even be given a pragmatic meaning, according to Peirce, if we grant that all of creation is of the nature of that which has to be continuously evolved. The concept of God, of course, will remain intellectually vague and fallible, since absolute precision is not to be looked for in any real concept. But this is counterbalanced by the fact that the belief in God is definite as an instinct or as a growing emotion. Theology, therefore, is wrong to pretend to rationalize the concept of God since, as a real concept it is based on instinct rather than reason, the heart, or love, rather than the head. But science and philosophy would be equally wrong to pretend to refute the reality of God, since that reality is necessitated by the whole evolutionary process which both science and philosophy must consider.

With these bold and speculative strokes, Peirce indicated the outlines of a cosmic theory of evolution, which he did not succeed in finishing. He did, however, make an original use of the evolutionary science of his day by applying it to a metaphysical system of the universe. He tended to think of metaphysics as architectonic, or analogous to architecture. It was to be a work of art, built up from foundations, and open to public inspection. To be scientific, metaphysics would have to be a cooperative effort of inquiry open to the continued testing and correction of a whole community of investigators. Metaphysics searches for the whole truth, for the whole of reality. To do this, it must follow the evolutionary process and consider not only that *things* change or evolve, but also that the laws or *principles* of things change. Only a continuing type of fallible inquiry could hope to grasp things as they really are, or as they are in the process of evolving. It is this vision of an evolving universe that charged the minds of James and Dewey and gave the movement of American pragmatism a wideness of scope equal to other great visions of man and the universe.

THE SIGNIFICANCE AND INFLUENCE OF PEIRCE   Charles Sanders Peirce, unlike Edwards, Jefferson, and Emerson, did not leave his mark on a large public, nor did he really represent any phase of American history. Edwards, Jefferson, and

Emerson made a definite impression on the times during which they lived. American Puritanism found in Edwards its leading light; the American Enlightenment found in Jefferson its principal architect; and American transcendentalism had in Emerson its best prophet. Compared with these men, Peirce was historically a recluse, recognized by only a few men during his lifetime. When he died in 1914 he was in a virtual state of poverty and generally unrecognized as a thinker of the first rank.

However, Peirce did leave a profound mark on a small number of other thinkers, including William James, Josiah Royce, and John Dewey. Peirce's influence on James is of special importance for the history of American philosophy. Within this influence we can trace the creation of American pragmatism. Peirce not only developed an original philosophic method, but imparted this method to James who in turn is chiefly responsible for making it famous. Although James must be credited with popularizing pragmatism, he always gave credit to Peirce for originating it. Josiah Royce, who called himself an "absolute pragmatist," was also greatly influenced by Peirce. In fact he asserted, "I now owe much more to our great and unduly neglected American logician, Mr. Charles Peirce, than I do to the common tradition of recent idealism. . . ." [31] Peirce is the first major American philosopher to influence *specifically* the philosophical development of subsequent major thinkers.

If Peirce had done nothing more than originate the method of pragmatism, his importance for the history of American philosophy would be secured, since, if any one movement of philosophic thinking were to be singled out in America as the most important, it would be pragmatism. However, Peirce's real significance cannot be confined to his having originated pragmatism and having influenced William James and John Dewey. Peirce's work in logic, the philosophy of science, and metaphysics is as original and philosophically important as his development of the pragmatic method. This fact has become quite apparent to students of philosophy since the publication of Peirce's *Collected Papers* during the 1930's. Peirce is today more widely studied by philosophers than ever before, and there are many who judge him the greatest and most original philosophic thinker to appear in America thus far.[32]

Even though his stature has grown and his work is more widely studied, Peirce cannot be regarded as a popular philosopher. He is still primarily a "philosopher's philosopher." This point is made quite evident by attending to Peirce's own conception of the function of philosophy, as well as by observing the style of his writing. Peirce regarded the function of philosophy as theoretical, its purpose being the pure search after truth. Consequently, he made great demands upon himself and any-one who desired to understand what philosophy really is. He believed that the ordinary man does not truly understand what science or a scientific philosophy is all about. The practical person considers science to be a collection of proven facts or conclusions, as well as a series of useful applications that make the world a better place in which to live. He does not see science as a living, growing inquiry into unsolved problems.

The real work of science—the logic of its reasonings and tentative hypotheses, its controlled observations, its continual corrections and re-examinations—can only be understood by adopting the scientific attitude and by engaging in searching inquiry. According to Peirce, the pursuit of science and scientific philosophy can only be appreciated by those rare individuals who really want to find out what the truth is. Any pre-conceptions as to what use it may have, or how congenial it may be to life, must be left behind. For Peirce science and philosophy must possess a pure integrity of purpose which can only be maintained by keeping them as free as possible from human biases. Peirce's conception that philosophy cannot solve vital human problems contrasts markedly with James' pragmatism and even with Dewey's. Despite the fact that Peirce was the founder of pragmatism, he did not subscribe to the kind of philosophy of action that is usually associated with the name. He be-lieved, of course, that thought must be related to action or to deliberately controlled operations, but for the *theoretical* purpose of clarifying the meaning of concepts, not for the human or moral purpose of improving the conditions of life.

Peirce's manner of writing is another indication of why he is not a popular philosopher. He often coins special terms to establish a particular distinction, and therefore is not easy to read. His coinage of the term "pragmaticism" is a good case in point. Years after he had originated the use of the term "pragmatism" to signify an experimental method of determining the meaning of concepts, he found William James and others using the same name for different purposes. When James broadened the pragmatic method to include a theory of truth, and gave pragmatism an application to the *areas* of personal experience and the vital problems of men, Peirce could not agree with him. As a consequence, Peirce coined the term "pragmaticism," a more cumbersome term that others would not be likely to use. He thereby emphasized that his intended method only applied to determining the rational purport of concepts, and not all the meanings—emotional, personal and otherwise—that might be asso-ciated with some other interpretation. In this way, Peirce sought to emphasize the logical and experimental character of his method, which implies that it must be freed from all subjective interpretations and sentiments.

Peirce's penchant for peculiar terminology can be seen by his frequent use of such terms as "tychism," "ideoscopy," and "phanerons." However, consistent with the pioneering character of his thought, his style of writing is also rather difficult. Peirce was always more interested in pushing his ideas further into new implications, and he did not polish his writings to make them read more easily. However, as a pioneer in the development of mathematical logic, Peirce's use of special symbols was fruitful. In his careful researches in logic, he made a number of important discoveries which again were not widely appreciated during his lifetime, but which subsequently have been recognized. He saw that logic had to be rigorously formalized to be free of psychological biases. For example, he noted that any logical implication is true if either its antecedent is false or its consequent is true. Although this equivalence may not seem psychologically true, it is nevertheless one of the definitions for implication used in many current logic texts.

Peirce's work in the philosophy of science, like his metaphysics, shows the unique way he combined logical precision with speculative scope. This union of analytic philosophy with a speculative metaphysics is puzzling to those who view philosophy as exclusively one or the other. Peirce is a difficult philosopher to characterize since he defies any narrow classification. Yet this does not imply that he is unable to draw careful distinctions. Peirce's value seems to lie in the fact that he cultivated the methods of logic and pragmatism to eliminate ambiguity and vagueness, but he also sought to build a metaphysical system to show that clarity is not enough for philosophy, that philosophy cannot stop short of the Herculean task of explaining the whole universe.

NOTES

1. Charles Sanders Peirce, in Charles Hartshorne and Paul Weiss, eds., *Collected Papers of Charles Sanders Peirce*, Vol. 6, p. 86, from "Scientific Metaphysics."
2. Charles Sanders Peirce, in Philip P. Wiener, ed., *Values in a Universe of Chance: Selected Writings of Charles S. Peirce*, p. 11.
3. *Ibid.*
4. "The physician must do something for a patient in danger, but does not know the nature of his illness. He observes the symptoms, and if he can find no more likely alternative, judges it to be a case of phthisis. Now even in his own estimation his belief is contingent only; another observer might perhaps come to a sounder conclusion. Such contingent belief, which yet forms the

ground for the actual employment of means to certain actions, I entitle *pragmatic belief." Immanuel Kant's Critique of Pure Reason,* trans. by Norman Kemp Smith (London: Macmillan, 1961), pp. 647–648.

5. *Collected Papers,* Vol. 5, Book II, Paper 2, p. 158.

6. *Collected Papers,* Vol. 6, p. 87, from "Scientific Metaphysics."

7. *Collected Papers,* Vol. 5, p. 186, from "Pragmatism and Pragmaticism."

8. *Collected Papers,* Vol. 1, p. x, from "Principles of Philosophy."

9. William James, *Pragmatism: A New Name for Some Old Ways of Thinking, Together with Four Related Essays Selected from The Meaning of Truth* (New York: Longmans, Green, 1907), p. 46.

10. *Collected Papers,* Vol. 5, p. 251, from "Pragmatism and Pragmaticism."

11. *Ibid.,* p. 6.

12. *Ibid.,* p. 266.

13. *Ibid.,* p. 268.

14. *Ibid.,* p. 243.

15. *Collected Papers,* Vol. 8, p. 18, from "Reviews, Correspondence and Bibliography."

16. *Collected Papers,* Vol. 3, p. 58, from "Exact Logic."

17. *Collected Papers,* Vol. 5, p. 64, from "Pragmatism and Pragmaticism."

18. *Ibid.,* p. 226.

19. *Collected Papers,* Vol. 4, p. 192, from "The Simplest Mathematics."

20. *Collected Papers,* Vol. 5, p. 121, from "Pragmatism and Pragmaticism."

21. *Ibid.,* p. 123.

22. *Collected Papers,* Vol. 1, p. 7, from "Principles of Philosophy."

23. *Ibid.,* p. 229.

24. *Ibid.,* p. 352.

25. *Ibid.*

26. *Ibid.,* p. 353.

27. *Collected Papers,* Vol. 6, pp. 36–37, from "Scientific Metaphysics."

28. *Collected Papers,* Vol. 8, p. 15, from "Reviews, Correspondence and Bibliography."

29. *Collected Papers,* Vol. 1, p. 70, from "Principles of Philosophy."

30. *Collected Papers,* Vol. 6, p. 15, from "Scientific Metaphysics."

31. Josiah Royce, *The Problem of Christianity,* Vol. I (New York: Macmillan, 1913), p. xi, from "Preface."

32. For recent interpretations of Peirce, see Richard J. Bernstein, ed., *Perspectives on Peirce: Critical Essays on Charles Sanders Peirce.*

QUESTIONS FOR DISCUSSION

1. How does Peirce's pragmatism offer a new method and approach for philosophy?

2. Why does Peirce emphasize the fact that his pragmatism is essentially a logical notion?

3. Can Peirce's view be justified that philosophy ought to become as scientific as possible?

4. Why does Peirce so strongly insist on the idea of fallibilism in philosophy?

5. What advantages does Peirce claim for determining the meaning of concepts pragmatically?

6. Why does Peirce insist that his pragmatism implies the truth of realism and the falseness of nominalism?

7. Why does Peirce think that the idea of evolution is so important for metaphysics?

8. What does Peirce mean by bad metaphysics? Are his criticisms of determinism, materialism, and transcendentalism sound?

9. To what extent are Peirce's metaphysical speculations consistent with his pragmatism?

10. Does the fact that Peirce's stature as a philosopher has increased with time indicate anything important about his philosophy?

SUGGESTED READINGS

A Definition of Pragmatic and Pragmatism. [In *Collected Papers of C. S. Peirce*, Vol. 5, Preface, pp. 1–9.]

Some Consequences of Four Incapacities. Peirce's arguments against intuitive knowledge. Why he says that we have no power of thinking without signs. Peirce distinguishes between a sign and the thing signified. [In *Collected Papers*, Vol. 5, Book II, pp. 156–189.]

Critical Review of Berkeley's Idealism. Peirce argues against idealism and nominalism. Peirce argues the case for his own realism. [In *Collected Papers*, Vol. 8, Book I, pp. 9–38.]

The Fixation of Belief. Peirce's conception of the scientific method in fixing beliefs and how he believes it superior to other methods. [In *Collected Papers*, Vol. 5, Book II, pp. 223–247.]

How to Make Our Ideas Clear. Peirce's formulation of the pragmatic theory or test of meaning. [In *Collected Papers*, Vol. 5, Book II, pp. 248–271.]

Deduction, Induction, and Hypothesis. Peirce's division of all reasoning into three main kinds. [In *Collected Papers*, Vol. 2, Book III, pp. 372–388.]

The Essence of Mathematics. Peirce distinguishes mathematics from logic. Look for his conception of mathematical logic. [In *Collected Papers*, Vol. 1, Book I, pp. 19–58.]

The Scientific Method and Fallibilism. Peirce considers ideas that block the way of inquiry. [In *Collected Papers*, Vol. 6, Book I, pp. 19–58.]

The Doctrine of Necessity Examined. Peirce's arguments against absolute determinism and for chance. [In *Collected Papers*, Vol. 6, Book I, pp. 28–45.]

The Backward State of Metaphysics. What Peirce means by metaphysics and what has held up its progress. [In *Collected Papers*, Vol. 6, Preface, pp. 1–7.]

The Categories: Firstness, Secondness, Thirdness. Peirce holds that there are three modes of being in general and what they are. [In *Collected Papers*, Vol. 1, Book III, pp. 148–180.]

Synechism, Fallibilism, and Evolution. What Peirce means by evolution and continuity, and why he believes that all laws of nature are results of evolution. [In *Collected Papers*, Vol. 6, Book II, pp. 169–173; Vol. 1, Book III, pp. 170–175; Vol. 1, Book III, p. 223; Vol. 6, Book I, p. 101.]

PRIMARY SOURCES

Charles Hartshorne and Paul Weiss, eds., Vols. 1–6; A. W. Burks, ed., Vols. 7–8; *Collected Papers of Charles Sanders Peirce* (Cambridge, Mass.: Harvard University Press, 1931–1958).

P. Wiener, ed., *Values in a Universe of Chance: Selected Writings of Charles S. Peirce* (New York: Anchor Books, 1958).

SECONDARY SOURCES

Richard J. Bernstein, ed., *Perspectives on Peirce: Critical Essays on Charles Sanders Peirce* (New Haven, Conn.: Yale University Press, 1958).

James K. Feibleman, *Peirce's Philosophy Interpreted as a System* (New Orleans, La.: Hauser Press, 1960).

W. B. Gallie, *Peirce and Pragmatism* (Baltimore: Penguin Books, 1952).

Thomas A. Goudge, *The Thought of C. S. Peirce* (Toronto: University of Toronto Press, 1950).

Thomas S. Knight, *Charles Peirce* (New York: Washington Square Press, 1961).

Edward C. Moore and Richard S. Robin, *Studies in the Philosophy of Charles Sanders Peirce*, Second Series (Cambridge, Mass.: Harvard University Press, 1964).

Murray G. Murphey, *The Development of Peirce's Philosophy* (Cambridge, Mass.: Harvard University Press, 1961).

Manley Thompson, *The Pragmatic Philosophy of C. S. Peirce* (Chicago: University of Chicago Press, 1953).

Philip Wiener and Frederic H. Young, eds., *Studies in the Philosophy of Charles Sanders Peirce*, First Series (Cambridge, Mass.: Harvard University Press, 1964).

5 *William James*

Pragmatism and Psychology

William James (1842–1910), more than anyone else, is responsible for making pragmatism world famous. Largely through his efforts it came to be identified as America's first original contribution to the mainstream of Western philosophical thought. By the early part of the nineteenth century James' pragmatism had gathered adherents and audiences in England, Germany, France, and Italy, as well as in the United States. With the publication of his *Pragmatism* in 1907 and *The Meaning of Truth* in 1909, the pragmatic movement was launched as one of the leading tendencies in twentieth-century philosophy. The prominence of pragmatism is due in large part to James, not Peirce, even though James gave full credit to Peirce for originating the pragmatic method. James was a fundamentally different kind of man than Peirce, and the radical way in which he changed or humanized the original conception of pragmatism is more important than the fact that he borrowed the idea from Peirce. However, in order to see how James developed his version out of Peirce's, it is necessary to understand certain things about James' life, background, and varied interests. This understanding is vital to the comprehension of James' philosophy precisely because he made pragmatism into a life-philosophy, a philosophy centered in the most important concerns of human beings. James' pragmatism is fundamentally a philosophy of action. It deals with those topics of vital importance to human beings which Peirce had ruled out of bounds for philosophy.

William James was born in New York City in 1842, the son of Henry

James, Sr., who was a well-to-do, highly cultured, and creative thinker in his own right. Henry James, Sr., was the head of a friendly and intellectually stimulating household. He allowed his children the widest possible freedom and individuality, and at the same time he gave them a lasting appreciation of ideas and a sense of their vital importance. William James, consequently, possessed a number of unusual advantages. The individual members of his family were not only wealthy and in touch with the best culture of the day, but were also persons of rare sensitivity, and articulate and talented in the things of the mind. The James family was humanistic in the real sense of the word, finding human nature not only fascinating to know and to explore, but, equally important, to cultivate and develop. James' father made a lifetime study of man and religion. He became absorbed in a most individualistic mystical interpretation of existence. His writings and personality bear the stamp of an unusually creative and critical mind. He enjoyed the friendship of such men as Emerson and Thoreau, yet he did not hesitate to criticize what he took to be the extravagances and errors of Emerson and New England transcendentalism. James' brother, Henry, also possessed an unusually creative and probing mind. Famous in his own right as a novelist, Henry James' works reveal a minute and artful study of the psychological shades of human character. More reserved and cautious than either his father or brother, he nevertheless displayed a keen and penetrating concern for the makeup of human nature.

It is, therefore, quite true to say that William James first developed his strong sense of individualism and his vital concern for the meaning of human existence from within his own family circle. The James family was a rich educational source, free and creative to the core. However, just because it was free and stimulating, it did not offer final answers for anyone as sensitive and restless as William James. The problems of religion, psychology, ethics and society—in short the problems of man in the face of the universe—were anything but a closed book for the young James. His whole life may be viewed in its successive stages as both an educational experience and a creative effort to work out tentative answers to all of life's most important concerns. Every major phase of James' life was not a dabbling in religion, art, medicine, psychology, or philosophy, but rather, a serious and creative attempt to do justice to the *whole* of experience while paying careful attention to the vital parts.

His early formal education was irregular—caught on the run, so to speak, in schools and from tutors in England, France, Switzerland, Germany, and America. Finally, he entered the Harvard Medical School in 1864 and there received his M.D. in 1869. Less interested in the practice of medicine than in the functioning of the human body, he then began to teach anatomy and physiology at Harvard. By 1875 his interests had turned more to the problems of psychology and the functions of the human mind. It was also about this time that he joined Peirce, Chauncey Wright, Oliver Wendell Holmes, Jr., and others in the Metaphysical Club for philosophical discussions on scientific method, religion, and evolution. Thus James came under the influence of Peirce's earliest formulations of the pragmatic method. Empirical by nature and training, James caught the importance of Peirce's theory of testing the meaning of ideas in terms of anticipated consequences.

During the late 1870's, James was teaching both psychology and philosophy at Harvard. It is important to note the manner in which his interests and creative talents combined psychology with philosophy. In 1878 he began writing his famous *Principles of Psychology* which is noteworthy for its pioneering studies in modern psychology as well as for its excursions into philosophy. When he finally published it in 1890 he was already a Professor of Philosophy at Harvard and the author of such philosophical essays as *The Sentiment of Rationality* and *The Dilemma of Determinism*. These essays, as well as many portions of the *Principles*, reflect the sense in which James found psychology necessary to philosophy, and philosophy as inevitable to any real probing in psychology. *The Sentiment of Rationality*, written in 1879, conveys in its title the psychological bent of James' philosophy. For James the philosopher's primary quest—the quest for rationality or the understanding of the unity of things—is based on a living, human feeling. Rationality, when it is seen for what it really is, is not a static, abstract, or impersonal vision, but a vital human sentiment concretely embodied in real life situations.

The Dilemma of Determinism, written in 1884, shows his sensitivity to the moral and metaphysical aspects of the problem of free will. Here we are at the crossroads of philosophy and psychology. There is no better point to show the connection between them than the question of the freedom of the will. James saw that psychology certainly could not prove the will to be free, since psychology must always look for causes and explain things in terms of what determines them. Hence psychology must always look for determinism and by so doing can never locate any "free" choice. But psychology can never refute free will either, since determinism is a working hypothesis behind all science and hence is part of the scientific faith. To believe that causes can determine things is the faith of science. To believe that by an effort of his will man can initiate and control his own acts is the faith of morality and common sense. Psychology can pose the problem of freedom but cannot resolve it. Morality and common sense demand it but cannot demonstrate it either. Demanding freedom or requiring it, so James contends, although necessary to the very existence of freedom, is not equivalent to understanding exactly what it is or what justification there can be for believing in it.

Here is where a philosophy is required that will see the *whole puzzle,* face it squarely, and not deny any of the concrete facts. Such a philosophy will certainly need to borrow from psychology, since the problem is based in part at least on the facts of man's actual experience. But such a philosophy will have to go beyond psychology and address itself to the moral, human, and even metaphysical sides of the problem. Only a philosophy, according to James, takes in the full sweep of man's ultimate problems, since only a philosophy expresses one's basic orientation to the meaning of things. Philosophy has the patience and courage to work continually at a problem when common sense and even science have long since set it aside or given it up. This is just the point that reveals the intimate connection between James' own life and his philosophy. His human concerns and pursuit of the science of psychology carried him into philosophy *precisely* because they left him with more questions to resolve. But what is more important is the *kind* of philosophy into which he was led. James came to realize that the only kind of philosophy that could honestly stand up to real problems of real men was a philosophy always on the move, a philosophy in the process of evolving, a philosophy of action, a philosophy of the concrete particular—in short, pragmatism.

The psychological character of James' pragmatism may be seen in many ways, all of which present a striking contrast to Peirce's pragmatism. First, it should be noted how James' approach to the study of psychology reinforces his conception of philosophy itself. He attacks the older rationalistic conceptions of psychology in the same way that he attacks rationalistic philosophies. Rationalistic psychologies falsely conceive the mind or soul as a pure, separate entity and do not conceive it as functionally related to natural facts or the body. James' *new* approach in psychology was to call for the treatment of psychology as a natural science based on empirical evidence or careful observation. But to James this naturalistic approach to the mind meant that the mind is to be studied functionally in terms of how it works and how it becomes adapted to the environment in which it lives. This involves the acceptance of the evolutionary hypothesis "that mental life is primarily teleological;

that is to say, that our various ways of feeling and thinking have grown to be what they are because of their utility in shaping our *reactions* on the outer world." [1] This means that the human mind cannot be understood as cut off from the natural world, but rather must be understood dynamically as both affected by it and reacting to it. The mind is anything but self-enclosed. It is not a mere passive observer or knower, nor a purely theoretical instrument. It is primarily a practical instrument engaged in action. Thinking, willing, choosing, desiring, believing, feeling, sensing—all the mental functions—are basically activities or forms of *doing something*. The right way to study the mind is to study how it operates. James' view might properly be called "pragmatic psychology."

His pioneering work in psychology produced, in 1890, the book entitled *The Principles of Psychology*, which is an attempt to have psychology study the mind not from some remote or theoretical point of view, but in terms of action or the practical results that the mind actually accomplishes. James' *Principles* was such a success that two years after its publication he brought out an abridgment called *Psychology: The Briefer Course*. This work was widely circulated and used as a text in college courses. James' pragmatic philosophy was already contained, in germ at least, in these psychological studies. Further, he stressed the educational and human value of all his psychological ideas, thus making the study of the mind relevant to the practical needs of life.

During the 1890's he published a number of other works which indicate the pragmatic and psychological focus of his thought. *The Will to Believe*, published in 1896, clearly shows the humanistic character of his thought. He is in agreement with Peirce that *belief* must be understood in terms of *action*. Belief is pragmatic for both Peirce and James insofar as it represents an idea upon which one is prepared to act. But whereas Peirce limited his pragmatism to those practical results that were scientific, experimental, and objective, James broadened the whole idea of pragmatism to apply to those practical results that were religious, moral, and personal. Peirce refused to allow his pragmatism or scientific philosophy to meddle in questions on vitally important topics, such as value questions in religion, morality, or personal life. But this is just where James' pragmatism finds its real focus, in deciding questions that are not mere theoretical puzzles, but real-life problems that make a personal and practical difference to men. It is interesting to note that *The Will to Believe*, wherein James calls for a philosophy that will be useful in deciding moral questions, is dedicated to Charles Sanders Peirce.

James' position is that beliefs are not only rules of action, or ideas upon which we are prepared to act, but that certain beliefs are useful in making things happen, in making certain things true.

> The desire for a certain kind of truth here brings about that special truth's existence; and so it is in innumerable cases of other sorts. Who gains promotions, boons, appointments, but the man in whose life they are seen to play the part of live hypotheses, who discounts them, sacrifices other things for their sake before they have come, and takes risks for them in advance. His faith acts on the powers above him as a claim, and creates its own verification.[2]

This, the heart of his pragmatism, is at the same time a radical departure from Peirce. James' pragmatism is voluntaristic; it stresses the importance of effort and voluntary decision in making certain things come about. He asserts, "There are, then, cases where a fact cannot come at all unless a preliminary faith exists in its coming."[3] Moral questions and religious beliefs are such that they cannot be solved purely intellectually or in a theoretical way. But they can be solved pragmatically. It is not simply that human beings cannot always wait for outside evidence or proof, but that unless man makes an effort to have these things he will never have them at all. Take the case of moral values such as justice or courage. Should one act justly? Should one be courageous? Are these things really good or true values? According to James, man's intellect alone is powerless to decide. There are no completely satisfactory intellectual proofs for these values. But there are practical answers, and pragmatism shows us a way of dealing with such matters. Are these questions such that they can be affected by a personal conviction that they can be and will be of some human good? In short, can we make these values worthwhile by acting on them, by participating in an effort to put them into operation? James concludes that we can and that we *must* in order to have such values at all. Pragmatism is a practical philosophy because it gives man's desires, hopes, and beliefs some control over his actions, some part to play in his future. In this way it looks to the future for its verifications. It does not passively wait for things to come true; rather, it believes in helping to make them come about.

James' pragmatism, then, is in a certain way anti-intellectual, while Peirce's is not. Peirce insisted on the rigorous use of logic and scientific objectivity in his pragmatic method. James, on the other hand, insists on faith and personal conviction. Peirce limited his pragmatism to a theory of *meaning* alone, whereas James insists that it must also give us a way of deciding the *truth* of questions. But most important of all, Peirce insisted on limiting pragmatism to determining only the rational or conceptual meaning of ideas, whereas James takes it out into life itself and makes it applicable to the personal sphere and the whole area of human values in religion and morality.

The sense in which he broadened pragmatism is much more significant than the fact that he derived it from Peirce. But what is also important, and what has to be included in the description of James' contribution to the pragmatic philosophy, is the way he popularized it and made it available to a significantly wide audience. William James wrote as he spoke; his style of writing may itself be described as pragmatic. He believed in bringing his ideas out into the open and in reaching the personal interests of men. He therefore strove to relate his philosophy to living situations. In short, he tried to convert his readers and audiences to pragmatism simply because he believed in its wide-scale usefulness. After he delivered his California lecture "Philosophical Conceptions and Practical Results" in 1898, he wrote his famous *Pragmatism* in 1907 and *The Meaning of Truth* in 1909, both of which were originally delivered in lecture form. In these works especially, he succeeded in giving full formulation to his humanistic pragmatism and at the same time helped to make it more widely known and popular than any other American philosophy. By the early part of the twentieth century, pragmatism, largely due to the personality and talent of William James, had become world-famous. In 1902 he published *The Varieties of Religious Experience*, which established itself as a classic psychological and philosophical study of religion. In 1909, just before he died, he published *A Pluralistic Universe* which, together with *Essays in Radical Empiricism* (published posthumously), shows the complete way in which James blended his psychology with his philosophy on the more difficult subjects of epistemology and metaphysics.

William James was a radical empiricist, or a pragmatic empiricist. His personality and human concerns demanded a kind of philosophy that would do justice to man's deepest feelings in religion, morality, and human affairs. But he also demanded that any philosophy worthy of the name must face the facts squarely and not paint a veneer over them. He was suspicious of all systems of philosophy that were purely intellectual or claimed to be absolute and completely objective. The only philosophy that he could endorse was one that frankly admitted its human basis and was based on the personal sentiments and convictions of the philosopher himself. Such a philosophy would have to be unfinished and could never be absolute, since so long as man is living he points to some future and is incomplete himself. But such a philosophy would also have to help man to adjust to life and give him an optimistic hope for all his vital concerns. Such is James' pragmatism, a humanistic faith that combines the psychological with the philosophical for the sake of practical consequences.

MELIORISM AND THE MEANING OF TRUTH   In contrast to Peirce's pragmatism which had developed out of his studies of logic and scientific method, James' pragmatism grew out of his studies of psychology and vital human concerns. A psychological and characteristically human orientation so dominates his thought that his very conception of philosophy may be characterized as always applied and never purely theoretical. Therefore, although pragmatism signifies a looking toward purposes, consequences, or practical results for both Peirce and James, the results looked for by these two philosophers are quite different. The principal difference here is that Peirce viewed pragmatism as a means of continuously furthering inquiry into conceptual meaning and never blocking the way to better understanding. For Peirce, the purpose of pragmatism and its practical results are conceived logically, scientifically, and philosophically in terms of *intellectual* improvement (enhancing our ideas of things). For James the purpose of pragmatism and its practical results are conceived morally, spiritually, and individually in terms of human improvement (enhancing our ideas as well as our lives).

The pragmatic question for James is, What discoverable difference or differences does an idea make for you or me in our real-life encounters? To have truth value for human beings an idea must be useful for some *definite* life purpose. Concrete and life-enhancing purposes are required by James. These two characteristics of James' pragmatism—concreteness and life enhancement—must be kept in mind as marking its central focus. In fact, they mark off what James meant by practical results— those that are specific or particular rather than merely general, and those that are helpful in getting us over the hurdles of life by enriching and enlarging our life.

To see how James developed his broader and more personal brand of pragmatism it is necessary to understand what he meant by meliorism, the pragmatic function of mediating between what he called "tender-minded" and "tough-minded" tendencies in philosophic thinking. Philosophers, however great or small, are first of all human beings. No matter how abstract, refined, or careful a philosopher is in his system, he cannot escape expressing his own personality in all that he writes or thinks. Every philosophy, whatever else it may be, is basically an individual or personal interpretation. A philosopher cannot escape his own temperament because this is what makes him a real person. No two philosophers, no two human beings are going to see things in exactly the same way. This is because no two life situations are exactly alike and because things are continually changing. However, James holds that this point should not be taken as it is by some (the rationalists) as discrediting philosophy from the start. In addition to being fallible, every philosopher is essentially a living, breathing individual who sees things in terms of his own needs and psychological makeup. To begin any genuine philosophy, therefore, it should never be pretended that man can transcend these needs by intellectual abstraction. Rather, these psychological roots of all thinking should be squarely faced and used to make an honest life-philosophy.

James finds that there are two main types of philosophical temperaments. He terms these tough-minded and the tender-minded. The tough-minded attitude expresses itself in the empirical approach of always looking for facts. The tougher this philosophy becomes, the more heavily it relies on only those facts that can be definitely perceived by the senses. It tends therefore to be materialistic, finding itself at home with material things and skeptical of mere abstractions or of any immaterial things. Tough-minded empiricism only admits atomic facts, and has an inherent distrust of any principles or *a priori* reasons beyond them. The tough-minded attitude in philosophy is further characterized by a piecemeal and pluralistic approach to things. It finds many parts rather than any single unifying whole. Finally, it tends to be irreligious and pessimistic. The tough-minded philosopher is more prone to smash values and ideals than to construct any. He tends to be fatalistic, offering no hope for man in the face of the brutal facts of animal existence and cold nature. Few philosophies are tough in the nth degree according to James, but the empirical tendency, if unchecked, is always in the direction of the most brutal form of materialism and pessimism.

In contrast to the tough-minded attitude is the tender-minded. This temperament expresses itself in the rational approach, always looking for reasons and principles. It finds thought and intellectual efforts more complete, systematic, and consistent than reliance on the senses or anything else. It therefore finds abstractions and immaterial existences wherever the mind goes, and hence tends to be idealistic rather than materialistic.

Because of the mind's power to frame and comprehend ideals, the tender-minded philosopher has no trouble locating eternal and absolute values. His ideals are not based on the transitory reports of experience or the changing sensory world, but abstractly and *a priori* they completely transcend it for all eternity. As a consequence the idealistic or tender-minded philosopher tends to be optimistic and religious. His ideals, which he locates by reasoning, imply that things are harmonious and that man's greatest hopes will not be dashed. The more tender-minded he becomes, the more unity he sees, and the more monistic he becomes. Plurality is only complexity in need of rational ordering to the tender-minded philosopher. He tends also to believe in the freedom of the will and comes out against fatalism as an irrational position. Finally, the tender-minded temperament implies a refusal to be skeptical. This attitude finds much to believe in, in a positive and absolute sense. It is therefore dogmatic. There are very few purely tender-minded philosophers; but if the rationalistic tendency goes unchecked it always pushes in the direction of the most abstract form of idealism and optimism.

James looked upon the tough-minded and tender-minded temperaments in philosophy as the two most prominent. The tough-minded variety was embodied in his own day by the English philosopher Herbert Spencer, who advocated a tough-minded "survival of the fittest" type of evolutionary philosophy which acquired its widest audience and most supporters in America. He found the tender-minded tendency embodied in the works of his philosophic colleague at Harvard University, Josiah Royce, as well as in the efforts of the New England transcendentalists. James saw, too, that the tough-minded and tender-minded philosophies had opposite faults. He could not accept either type as it stood, but he found that he could accept certain parts of each. Reduced to its simplest terms, the problem was a pragmatic one. The tough-minded temperament was on the right track insofar as it was empirical or based on definite facts. However, it was unable to offer us any real values; it could not support religion, and therefore dashed some of man's greatest needs. The tender-minded temperament was on the side of religion and did offer men lofty values and hopes, but it was not mindful of the facts. The pragmatic question here is, Can we have a kind of philosophic attitude that will mediate between these two extremes; can we have a philosophy that is based on definite facts and that will offer us significant life-values and hopes?

Pragmatism, according to James, meets these two basic demands of human nature and philosophy. It is essentially melioristic in offering us

a way of mediating between the tough-minded and tender-minded attitudes. That is, pragmatism is broad enough in its approach to be both
tough and tender. However, it must be kept in mind that pragmatism is
essentially a method or approach to problems, and does not therefore
stand for any final answers. This may readily be seen by noting how James
thinks that pragmatism can mediate between the tough and tender tendencies. First, pragmatism sides with the empirical method of looking for the
facts. However, it allows more possibilities and a greater richness in facts
than the narrow-minded and older forms of empiricism allowed. "Pragmatism represents a perfectly familiar attitude in philosophy, the empiricist
attitude, but it represents it, as it seems to me, both in a more radical and
in a less objectionable form than it has ever yet assumed." [4] In other words,
it does not reduce all ideas to mere sensations; nor does it try to build up
all complex ideas by mere association. Because it is radically empirical and
not based on mere sensations, it is not materialistic. However, because
pragmatism is radically empirical it cannot accept abstract and static
spiritual objects *a priori* or on mere tender-minded grounds. It can allow
spiritual and religious realms of existence only as they can function in
men's lives.

But this is exactly the fact pragmatism uncovers: religious and spiritual
matters do operate in the lives of men, not as static or abstract principles
as the tender-minded rationalist supposes, but functionally or dynamically.
Pragmatism can be religious and factual at the same time because it interprets religious ideas or beliefs voluntaristically, as purposes or aspirations
that actually operate and enhance human existence. It is not pessimistic.
It offers man a piecemeal type of optimism. It cannot guarantee that the
future will be better than the past or present, but it encourages the hope
that by effort and faith the future may be made better. In this regard,
pragmatism is essentially pluralistic, and has faith in the freedom of man's
will. It refuses to picture a block-universe or a closed and determined
world, but rather it sees things as in process. It can accept a plurality of
things rather than a simple unity, insofar as these many parts are also
viewed as changing and as related to the individual needs of men. Finally,
it can accept skepticism as a worthwhile method, but not a doctrine.
Pragmatism neither doubts for doubt's sake nor believes in purely dogmatic
terms. Both believing and doubting on particular occasions may have
their purpose in human life.

Pragmatism as meliorism means that opposites or extremes are looked
at in terms of their practical consequences. That is, the method of pragmatism is to pose the question, What specific difference does it make to

you or to me whether this or that idea is true? It is a method of *setting up* and *working out basic life problems* which are also philosophic problems. It always tries to bring philosophy down to specific situations, and to find a philosophic meaning for all of life's most pressing concerns. James was always fond of saying that the most important things about a human being were not particular facts about him, but rather the way these facts fit together to make a complete person. This constitutes *that person's* philosophy of life no matter how thoroughly it is actually thought out. James grants that each person has a philosophy of his own which determines how he will live his life. However, he offers pragmatism not merely as *his* particular philosophy of life, but as a method with possibilities and applications for others. He holds that the validity of pragmatism as a philosophy for man cannot be worked out in advance of applying it. He cannot offer anyone an already finished system, but pragmatism as meliorism can be taken with a risk and used to find its practical consequences.

One principal advantage of pragmatism is its ability to cut through endless entanglements with words in philosophical controversies. Pragmatism cannot accept any purely verbal solution to problems. To say, for example, that ether puts you to sleep because it has the dormative essence in it does not really explain anything but merely gives a name to cover our ignorance of the real facts. Consider the problem of materialism versus spiritualism. The problem has long been debated in philosophy and in life as to whether purely material forces or spiritual ones explain the universe. The materialist wants to account for everything in terms of matter and motion, while the spiritualist wants to account for matter and motion themselves. But James contends that no adequate solution to this problem can be found until we ask what practical difference is involved in these two conceptions for our personal lives. There can be no point to the problem or the resolution of it until we demand and look for practical consequences. This means we must look to the future, since without a future there can be no practical consequences. Looking at the controversy of materialism versus spiritualism in terms of the future, James finds a significant difference. Materialism offers man no hope, only a dead universe of mechanical repetitions. But spiritualism offers man hope that his most cherished aspirations and values may count for something and that they may be fulfilled. This does not mean that spiritualism, or a pragmatic belief in it, is proven or verified—only that it *may be*—and further, that man may by taking a risk help bring about this verification, at least in part.

In sharp contrast to Peirce, James' pragmatism is nominalistic. What counts most in the pragmatic test of ideas for James is their particular meaning. James' nominalism is derived from his humanism or explicit individualism. It is quite clear that he looks upon the problem of universals not as a logical or scientific problem but rather as a human one. He therefore finds universals empty unless they are viewed as shorthand or summaries of particulars. General concepts for James are only pragmatically meaningful if they bear upon our experiences. The pragmatic test itself implies testing our general ideas to see what particular meanings they may have. To explain or test general ideas only by other general ideas is unsatisfactory, and may end in purely verbal solutions to problems.

James succeeded in popularizing pragmatism largely through his theory of the pragmatic meaning of truth. Running through his whole account of pragmatism is a strong and persistent notion of truth. This part of James' pragmatism immediately attracted great attention, calling forth many strong criticisms as well as enthusiastic endorsements. After he published his *Pragmatism* in 1907, *The Meaning of Truth* was issued as a sequel in 1909. The remarkable feature of these works was the diversity of their appeal and recognition. They not only occasioned responses from the general reading public and from people with no special interest in philosophy, but they also reached the ears of learned philosophers. For the first time, an American philosopher succeeded in eliciting serious attention from European thinkers.

James' account of truth may clearly be seen as melioristic, mediating between what may be termed correspondence and coherence. One of the traditional conceptions of truth held that it signifies the agreement of our ideas with reality. James can, of course, accept this correspondence, but only in part. He finds that while it is quite correct to say true ideas must *somehow* agree with reality, they cannot all be literal copies of reality. If true ideas are those which agree with reality, it must first be granted that reality signifies "the facts" in a radically empirical sense. Experience must be open to allow change, and must be rich enough to contain dynamic relations and functional growth. In short, correspondence is not a sufficiently dynamic concept to explain what truth is. What, for example, does our idea of force or electricity correspond to? What do these ideas copy? Here is where we need a more dynamic account of what truth is. Such an idea must be functional and explain how our true ideas work. James thinks this is conveyed by the idea of "agreeable leading." True ideas not only agree with the facts, but they work by *leading* us to them. Thus they have a certain coherence and tie the various parts of our experience together.

Mere coherence, however, does not explain the meaning of truth, since it too is static rather than dynamic. Pragmatism refuses to see truth as a static, colorless term, but rather insists that truth must be conceived (1) dynamically, as something which happens to ideas and (2) humanistically, as having some value or good in the way it functions in our lives. Truth is process for James, a process of validation or verification for our ideas, which are simply instruments in this process. If a theory or idea is true, this means that it works or is a good means of leading us toward the facts. A false idea is simply a bad instrument that does not work or does not lead us to the facts. As a consequence, James holds that truth is one type of good. An idea could never be true if it were not good for something. Truth is not the only kind of good, however, since many other things are good as well, but truth is one very important good. James refuses to separate truth and value, but insists that if truth has any pragmatic meaning, it must be of some human value. Purely rationalistic conceptions of truth he finds defective, because they merely present us with an abstract, colorless definition that has no relevance or personal meaning for our lives.

Pragmatism holds that truth must not be merely functional or useful but that it must have concrete uses as well. Therefore, truth "is simply a collective name for verification-processes, just as health, wealth, strength, etc. are names for other processes connected with life, and also pursued because it pays to pursue them." [5] True ideas are cognitively useful insofar as they "lead us into useful verbal and conceptual quarters as well as directly up to useful sensible termini." [6] The melioristic character of James' theory of truth appears here in its comprehensive character of being useful and covering all our true ideas, however commonplace or special, however directly or indirectly verified they may be. All true ideas have in common their usefulness in getting us at their facts. Either precise truths or approximate ones have the pragmatic character of "agreeable leading." Even abstract ideas or principles are pragmatically true, if they are true at all. Abstract and mathematical truths have a double utility insofar as they (1) lead us into better intellectual and conceptual arrangements of our own ideas and (2) lead us to concrete applications. For example, the truth that $2 + 2 = 4$ has an abstract or conceptual usefulness in arranging our purely mental ideas into a consistent and useful way of thinking. But this abstract truth also has true or useful applications to things in the world: buying and selling, keeping accounts, etc. We can go so far as to say that our ideas are true because they are useful, and that they are useful because they are true. If truth is pragmatically defined, then ideas are obviously true because they are cognitively and humanly useful. But in the long run this means that the only ideas which are *really* useful to man are those that lead us to realities—in short, true ideas.

In his *Pragmatism* James included a whole chapter on "Pragmatism's Conception of Truth." This occasioned so much comment that in his sequel, *The Meaning of Truth,* he included an entire section entitled "The Pragmatist's Account of Truth and Its Misunderstanders." Here he took up what he considered to be at least eight different misconceptions of his doctrine. It is important to see that, generally, these misconceptions fail to take note of the broadness of James' whole theory. One criticism, for example, suggests that pragmatism only explains how truth is arrived at, but not what it really is. This misses the point that pragmatism explains *both* by virtue of the fact that it makes truth dynamic and functional. Therefore, an idea's being true and an idea's functioning to enable us to arrive at the truth are inseparable. We can never tell someone what truth is without spelling out how it is arrived at, since the very essence of any true idea's usefulness is its enabling us to arrive at the facts or reality.

Another criticism is that pragmatism ignores the theoretic interest because it is primarily an appeal to action. It should be clear from what has already been stated that James' pragmatism includes the theoretic interest as one of man's important life concerns. James contends that pragmatism is broad enough to allow ideas and theories to work cognitively as well as to have other uses in our lives. Ideas can be useful in giving us a better understanding of things and in helping us to live better. In fact his pragmatism calls for a broad interpretation of the word "action" so that thoughts and ideas, as well as building and making things, are interpreted as forms of action. It is contrary to James' whole purpose to assume that thought and action are separate things or that thought is to be measured only in terms of the grossest or most obviously useful types of action. He replied quite strongly to the criticism of some who asserted that pragmatism is nothing more than the American policy of reducing everything to profit or money-making.

We may note here that the word "pragmatic" has been used to refer to mere expediency as well as ruthless or vulgar success. However, these meanings clearly do not express James' basic teachings, and it is to James' credit that he pointed this out time and time again. It is well known that false ideas may be expedient for certain desired results. Telling lies or deliberately misleading people may at times indeed be financially rewarding or expedient for some personal gain. However, this does not mean that a lie or a deception is pragmatically true. To be pragmatically true an idea must be *cognitively useful*, it must lead us to the facts. A lie or deception may be useful in arriving at certain results, but it is not useful in representing the facts. Pragmatic truthfulness, therefore, cannot be reduced to mere expediency, since to be pragmatically true an idea must function specifically to allow us to discover reality.

HUMANISM AND THE MORAL LIFE   The constant note of humanism in William James' pragmatism signifies the impossibility of separating the real from the human factors in anything we can know. The point of the pragmatic theory of truth is that there is no meaning to truth apart from its human usefulness. However, this human usefulness includes science and the theoretic interest as well as other more obviously practical endeavors. James' humanism, therefore, is not hostile to science and to the search for objective truth. What James does oppose are those philosophies that would make science something either inhuman or superhuman. Science must be admitted as a human attempt to unlock in piecemeal fashion the secrets of the universe. The more exact or abstract it becomes, the better it may be able to explain things or predict future consequences. However, it must always be remembered that some human interest selects the facts to be observed and suggests a hypothesis into which they may be arranged. Science must correct its errors, but it can never do this by trying to eliminate the human orientation or interpretations involved in its workings. Some interpretations are more successful than others. Newton and Darwin surpassed the work of their predecessors in definite ways. However, at no time is it possible to frame a perspective which is absolute or completely independent of the human desire to know things.

James' pragmatism sees the progress of science to reside as much in its creative additions to knowledge as in its continual corrections for error. Therefore, truth when considered pragmatically or melioristically is created as well as it is discovered. To see truth as simply discovered is too one-sided. This view is merely passive and misses the functional character of truth-making. Truth is created in the sense that we must take the responsibility for selecting and arranging whatever facts are looked into. Truth is also created in the sense that man can help bring about certain truths by desiring them and by working toward their realization. But truth is also discovered; it is not merely a free creation of the human mind or will. True ideas must work; they must lead us to reality. James always insists that pragmatism requires the assumption of a real object of knowledge to be pursued. He argues that pragmatism involves the realistic postulate or assumption, but it does this in a *radical* way. The real cannot be separated from the human and both must be considered as in the making. Therefore, if true ideas are discoveries of the ways and workings of reality they must keep in touch with the changeable character of reality.

If the postulate of humanism is that the real and the human cannot be separated from one another, then not only do science and the pursuit of truth possess a human significance, but also humanity's concern with morality and religion must be in touch with reality. James' humanism not only implies that science and thought must always have some human value, but also involves the assumption that man's interest in values and ideals, especially in morals and religion, can only be explained and justified pragmatically.

Though a moral focus may be found in virtually all the writings of William James, two essays are of particular importance for an understanding of his moral philosophy: *The Moral Philosopher and the Moral Life* and *The Dilemma of Determinism*. These essays were originally delivered as lectures at Yale and Harvard, respectively. In style and content both essays show clearly the pragmatic and humanistic bent of James' mind. He poses theoretic dilemmas only to show that they cannot be solved on intellectual grounds alone, that only a pragmatic solution will work. He also addresses himself to moral problems of real men simply to show that pragmatism does indeed fulfill its promise of being a philosophy of action.

The first thing to grasp in moral philosophy is the volitional rather than the purely intellectual character of the whole enterprise. Whether we can and ought to have a moral outlook at all cannot be decided by pure reason or any mere disinterested analysis of the facts. No moral skeptic can be refuted by logic or by appeal to the facts if he has already decided against any moral viewpoint. A moral outlook can only exist if it is desired by someone. Morality stands on an initial faith in its possibility, and has pragmatic meaning only if this faith is made concrete and actively related to future, practical consequences. An abstract possibility is not enough for James, since this would be merely static and verbal, whereas morality, if it is demanded at all, must be related to action. Philosophers may try to establish the grounds of morality by purely abstract or rational principles and thereby set up an absolute, finished system. However, such an attempt must always fail to be convincing since it makes no room at all for faith, desire, or action—the very things in which our values and vital interests are centered. Rationalism and absolutism in ethics such as that of Royce imply that issues have *already* been decided, that the moral truth is already there and does not have to be demanded or made. Pragmatism, on the other hand, maintains that all truth, and hence moral truth, is something which comes into being and is essentially functional. No impersonal and static truth, moral or otherwise, can function in our lives.

James contends that there are three fundamentally different kinds of questions in ethics: the psychological, the metaphysical, and the casuistic. The psychological question asks about the origin of our moral notions, the metaphysical question asks for the meaning of these notions, and the casuistic question asks for a way of determining the right order of moral values. Here, it is James' contention that a humanistically oriented pragmatism is best suited to answer all three questions. It should be realized that moral values are not physical relations. Without sentient creatures who can feel differences between good and bad, moral values would not arise at all. Moral notions, then, depend for their origin upon the sensitivity of creatures who can respond with preferences, desires, or choices in the context of their environment. These preferences originate as specific responses to life situations and are eminently teleological. That is, they originate as means of adjusting the organism to life. Therefore, if moral ideas originate in particular life situations involving action, their meaning must be understood in pragmatic terms.

What is the meaning of any moral obligation, whether it be an obligation to keep promises or act honestly? What does it mean to say that any of these obligations are good or right? According to James, "*the essence of good is simply to satisfy demand.*" [7] Where there are no demands to keep promises or to act honestly, there cannot be any meaning for these obligations. But obligations form a plurality of demands that cannot be reduced to any abstract unity or single principle. No one demand can possibly rule over all of the others. Therefore, each genuine demand has its right to exist, however small that may be. Real moral obligations have their meaning in specific demands made by particular agents in concrete situations. James refuses to separate a demand from its validity. "Any desire is imperative to the extent of its amount; it makes itself valid by the fact that it exists at all." [8] However, it is a notorious fact that not all claims can be satisfied. The most complete ideal would be a mutually satisfactory world where every person's needs would be satisfied. But according to James, the world in which we live is not at all like that; rather, it is tragically practical; that is, when looked at in the concrete, "some part of the ideal has to be butchered." The task of the moral philosopher cannot be to ignore this fact of the conflict of interests.

The casuistic question of estimating the right way of grouping these various demands only begins to be meaningful when it is seen as a pragmatic problem—one to take action on always at some risk of failure, but also always with some hope of success. The real ethical ideal is therefore inclusiveness—attempting to satisfy as many demands as possible. However, this inclusiveness, if it is to remain concrete and actually include the individual demands of its members, can only be piecemeal and never absolutely complete. Ethics, like science, rests on a humanistic faith that man can make some headway, but this faith can never be rationally proved, and always implies something left unfinished. Ethics, therefore, can never be a closed book as long as life lasts. Its verdicts, when genuine, can never be more than fallible and limited. There is a certain blindness in human beings "with which we all are afflicted in regard to the feelings of creatures and people different from ourselves." [9] This affliction, when ignored, makes our moral judgments pieces of arbitrary legislation. However, when this blindness is faced honestly as indicating the very essence of the human condition, it may be used as an instrument of moral good—that of encouraging tolerance and understanding regarding others. James does not pretend this is easy since he holds that the very nature of moral problems does not allow them to wait for proof. Science can take its time in formulating its hypotheses and in checking them again and again. Scientific questions are not matters of life or death, nor are they directly addressed to our vital values. Moral matters, on the other hand, are directly involved with how we should act and live. Moral decisions cannot therefore be put off since the consequences are too great.

One of the most perplexing problems of man's moral life concerns the free-will controversy. The dilemma of determinism versus freedom is a good example of an issue that shows the intimate connection of philosophy and real life. It is James' pragmatic contention that no satisfactory solution to this problem can be found without seeing both sides—its philosophic side and its real-life aspect. To ignore the true philosophic character of the problem is to be left with either premature sentimentalism or despair. To uphold only an intellectualistic, philosophic perspective on the problem which ignores the concrete facts is to come away with only a verbal or empty resolution. Therefore, in posing the free-will problem as both a philosophic concern as well as a human problem, it is James' intention to cut through all mere verbiage and face the issue head-on. Is man's will rigidly determined or is it free; are man's actions the results of strict necessity or free choice? Both sides, the determinists and the indeterminists, admit that an action has been performed or a choice has been made by someone. The indeterminists assert that another action or a different choice could have occurred. The determinists say that no other act or choice could have occurred. Both parties cannot be right since they contradict each other. And it may seem that only an appeal to the facts or to science has to be made to decide which side is right. However, it is a fallacy to think that the facts or science can decide the question.

The gnawing aspect of this problem is that the way you look at it depends upon the way you view the whole universe. In short, the problem is really a philosophic one because it concerns how the facts ought to be conceived in a very basic way—so basic that the way of conceiving them affects the very manner in which one will live his life. Science cannot prove that a choice once made by a person could have been left undone, or that a different choice could have been made. No matter how much the indeterminist may want science to prove that the will is free, it will always remain beyond the pale of science to do this. "Only facts can be proved by other facts. With things that are possibilities and not facts, facts have no concern. If we have no other evidence than the evidence of existing facts, the possibility-question must remain a mystery never to be cleared up." [10] The same conclusion follows for the determinist. No matter how much he may want science to prove that the actual facts could not really have been otherwise, the proof is always beyond the range of science.

James contends that although the dilemma of determinism cannot be resolved by science, it nevertheless can be resolved by pragmatism. Pragmatism as a method of cutting through verbal entanglements and otherwise insoluble philosophic problems simply asks its specific question—what concrete life consequences or differences does it make if either determinism or indeterminism is true? James finds that, looked at in this way, the problem presents us with quite different alternatives as far as *action* is concerned. Determinism implies pessimism and despair as far as our future is concerned. It implies that since things cannot be otherwise, one must therefore simply resign himself to whatever occurs. It thus makes a shambles of our moral life by eliminating hope or regret. If things are absolutely determined, then there can be no point to regretting our mistakes or hoping to make any improvement on them. Determinism tells us, over and over again, that things will be the way they will be. But why should we adopt a belief in determinism if it cannot be proved and if its practical consequences are negative and even disastrous for one's life? James thinks that it is enough of a refutation of determinism that it leads to pessimism, is not proven by the facts, and is really based on emotions. One who decides to be a determinist possesses a tough-minded philosophical temperament.

However, indeterminism could simply mean the reverse of tough-minded determinism and could have results equally undesirable, according to James. A tender-minded indeterminism might simply mean subjectivism. The rejection of determinism may lead to the belief that what happens in the world is "subsidiary to what we think or feel about it." [11] This kind of romantic or sentimental belief in the freedom of the will is quite different from the pessimism of determinism, but for James it is morally no better. If we are allowed to have the freedom to make our moral values depend upon how we feel or think, then we are left with nothing but moral chaos. Subjectivism in ethics ignores the important fact that man's moral life requires behavior or action and cannot be defined merely in terms of feelings and thoughts. Hence, some reference to an objective factor in man's moral life is required if ethics is to be practical and not simply sentimental.

Pragmatism can provide us with an ethics that mediates between the extremes of tough-minded determinism and tender-minded indeterminism. After looking at the concrete consequences of pessimism and subjectivism, James finds that he cannot accept either alternative. His own moral philosophy thus is best seen as melioristic and as avoiding the other one-sided approaches. James' pragmatic theory of ethics avoids pessimism by a voluntaristic and piecemeal faith in an optimistic direction. It holds fast to a belief in the freedom of the will, not because this can be proved by science, but because this belief can be useful in action. Belief in the freedom of the will may help to bring about certain truths and goods that otherwise might not exist at all. Because pragmatism involves an appeal to action, it can accordingly overcome subjectivism. Human actions are public or objective, and not private or subjective like mere feelings or thoughts. James' view is that "conduct and not sensibility, is the ultimate fact for our recognition." [12] In other words, moral values must be linked with action if they are to fit any pragmatic test. Courage, for example, if it is to be really counted as a moral value, must somehow display itself in action, that is, its goodness is measured in terms of the kind of action it inspires or is fitted to produce. Even though moral values cannot be absolute, they can nevertheless be objective when fitted to conduct or action. In this sense, ethics will always be something better than arbitrary legislation, but will never be a closed book. This is exactly what humanism in the moral life signifies to James: the continued furtherance, however piecemeal, of useful and beneficial actions due to the efforts of separate individuals.

RELIGIOUS EXPERIENCE AND THE RIGHT   William James was the first phi-
TO BELIEVE   losopher to apply the methods
and results of modern psychology to the *study* of the nature and significance of religion. Prior to him no one had brought to religious inquiry the rare combination of the eye of a creative psychologist and the mind of a probing philosopher. This is exactly what makes James' *The Varieties of Religious Experience* such a unique and important work. It is a classic in both psychology and philosophy. The philosophic scope and attention to psychology contained in James' inquiries into religion may perhaps be better appreciated by contrast with the efforts of earlier American thinkers. Peirce's scientific orientation in philosophy required the drawing of a sharp line between the concerns of the scientific man, who seeks to find out the truth, and the concerns of the religious individual, who desires a fixed belief. The two concerns could not be brought together philosophically as Peirce saw it, and he believed that a religious or theological bias only produced bad metaphysics. Emerson, on the other hand, wove religion into all his themes and gave it an exalted position in life. However, he did this on an intuitive or poetic basis since his transcendentalism did not require any critical inquiry or proof. Jefferson was primarily concerned with the moral side of religion, with establishing the *freedom* of religion, rather than studying its nature or significance.

Finally, Jonathan Edwards had given careful attention to the nature of the religious affections and to the theological problems of the nature and validity of religion as such. However, in comparison with James, Edwards' concern with religion was narrow. While it is true that Edwards' inquiries are remarkable for their logical control of a difficult subject, they are all theologically enclosed within the firm acceptance of the Calvinist viewpoint. Edwards' works, therefore, reflect not a mind in search of the meaning of religion, but rather a mind in search of evidence and arguments to defend a particular outlook already taken to be true. There is nothing really open-minded about Edwards' probings of religion, nothing to suggest that he really wanted to find out what the truth is. In fact, when it comes to the question of a philosophy of religion, Edwards, Jefferson, and Emerson accepted more than they ever questioned in any philosophic way. On the other hand, the nature of James' whole approach to religion may be clearly revealed by asserting that he opened religion to philosophic and psychological inquiry in ways never before attempted. In short, he refused to be either tough or tender in approaching religion. Peirce was tough-minded in finding no room for religion via science or philosophy. Edwards, Jefferson, and Emerson were tender-minded in accepting some absolute in religion quite independently of sustained scientific or philosophic inquiry.

James contends that the study of religion will lead to nothing but confusion unless a very basic distinction is drawn at the outset between what may be termed the *descriptive* and the *evaluative* sides of the inquiry. Any thorough-going study of religion must concern itself both with *describing* what religious beliefs and practices are and *evaluating* their significance or validity. The descriptive side of the study of religion must remain neutral and be as pluralistic and psychological as possible. The descriptive aspect of the study cannot take sides, but must be radically empirical and study all the varieties of reported religious experiences, no matter how healthy or sick, exceptional or common, they may be. Such studies must be essentially psychological rather than sociological, since the institutional side of religion lives secondhand, as it were, upon tradition. The core of every religion is located in the lives of its individual founders. Therefore, James prefers to consult the records of individuals who profess a definite religious outlook, and of these he prefers to consult as many radically different kinds as possible to ensure that his study will not be too narrow.

It thus becomes apparent that one cannot expect to have a definitive or closed statement as to what religion really is. One of the conclusions of James' study is to point to the important fact of the essential diversity of religious experiences. What counts as religion must, in a certain sense, be left open, otherwise we simply would be imposing an arbitrary limit on the whole question. However, James is willing to allow a working definition which is extremely general, but which may be of some use in exploring such a wide and complex phenomenon. He says: *"Religion, therefore, as I now ask you arbitrarily to take it, shall mean for us the feelings, acts, and experiences of individual men in their solitude, so far as they apprehend themselves to stand in relation to whatever they may consider the divine."* [13] This is a neutral definition, and it merely opens the inquiry into exactly what religion is. The question remains whether anything which someone believes to be divine really is so. James considers this question of the truth of religious claims important, but it is his view that it cannot be properly answered without descriptive facts. Consequently, the greatest portions of *The Varieties of Religious Experience* are detailed descriptions of exceptional individual accounts of saintliness, conversion, mysticism, and morbid and healthy religious states. James' empirical approach is extremely liberal in allowing cases of religious experience from virtually all the major traditions of world-religions in order to present their claims and relate their own interpretations.

He finds, however, that the problem of evaluating the significance and validity of all these experiences and beliefs is an extremely difficult yet essential task. The science of psychology is helpful, but not sufficient to enable one to evaluate the truth of religion. For example, psychology may show that certain reported "visions" are due to epileptic attacks, that certain trances may be induced by drugs, or that morbid feelings of sin are connected with naturally and genetically explainable guilt-feelings, and so on. But psychology only touches the surface here, and nothing significant is proved without also considering the consequences of these experiences. In other words, James claims that it is a fallacy to explain experiences away by looking only at their origins. The only way to judge the significance of any experience is to look for its further results. In this way, he is able to find much significance and value in religious experiences by noting the good results that follow them. He therefore finds much to value in experiences of saintliness, conversion, or mysticism, when these experiences change the life of a person for the good and when their influence on countless others perpetuates these good works. Prayer, for example, cannot be explained without reference to future consequences; it may have value in relation to the burdens and catastrophes of life, where reason and science are ineffective.

But the fact that certain religious experiences and beliefs may have many worthwhile results for human life does not necessarily imply that they are valid or true in terms of their specific claims. It is a notorious fact that different religions present conflicting and even contradictory theological or philosophical claims for the truth of their doctrines, while their moral practices and results may agree in many ways. James finds that two principal justifications that have been offered for religious doctrines are the mystical and the rational. Mysticism essentially claims a knowledge of the reality and nature of the divine through the channel of a unique and ineffable union with this divine being. The experiences of the true mystic are said to be radically unlike any other more ordinary sensory, emotional, or conceptual state of consciousness. The mystic claims that his ideas of the existence and nature of his divine reality are true, yet they cannot be verified by anyone else or by any other method than by having the mystical experience itself. James does not doubt the sincerity of the mystic's convictions concerning his claim that he experiences a special truth which cannot be verified in any other way than by simply experiencing it. But he does believe that this claim to truth is only subjective and that as a private experience it does not establish any universal or objective validity. All we can say is that a profound and unusual experience may have occurred to a very devout individual, but this experience does not prove anything for us or for all men.

Rationalistic attempts to prove the validity of religious beliefs are based on an attempt to overcome the very weakness of any mystical or subjective approach. That is, the rationalist counts on the logic of his arguments and the universal and objective character of reason itself to establish religious truths. When reason shows us that $2 + 2 = 4$, this fact is proved for all men and can be verified over and over again. But reason has been used by theologians and philosophers in the hope of establishing —with certainty and finality—the existence of a supreme being. We have, for example, the ontological argument, which argues from God's essence to his existence; the cosmological argument, which argues for the need of a first cause behind all other causes and effects; and the argument from design, which argues for the need of a divine architect to explain the order in the world. James finds all rationalistic attempts to prove the truth of religious beliefs abstract and unsatisfactory. Such attributes as perfection, causal power, designer, applied to the divine being by the rationalists, are so abstract that they do not contain any particular meaning; they sidestep or overlook certain facts altogether, or they present us with such a vague conception of a deity that these arguments may be turned around to prove the very opposite of what is intended. For example, the argument from design, which has frequently been used to prove the existence of a divine being through the use of reason, only chooses those examples of design which fit its purpose, i.e., the eye is designed for sight, the heart for pumping blood, vegetation for giving food. However, according to this argument, earthquakes, floods, and disease could also be said to be designed to kill people and make them suffer. "It must not be forgotten that any form of disorder in the world might, by the design argument, suggest a God for just that kind of disorder." [14] The design argument tends to ignore the whole problem of evil because it is really based on a tender-minded attitude toward religion.

Rationalistic attempts to account for evil are either purely verbal or only succeed in wrapping a comforting mantle of abstract concepts over the hard facts of life. To argue that evil is nothing positive—only the absence of good, or like shadows in a painting necessary to enhance the beauty of the whole—is to use empty verbalisms that side-step the perplexing problems of real life. The rationalist, in short, is compelled to argue *a priori*, independently of the facts, and to force things to conform to his prearranged concepts. But, according to James, experience will never be adequately accounted for by concepts alone, as experience always overflows any neat concepts which are only shorthand or approximate renderings of the concrete particularity of things. In fact, he believes that mystical experiences and even the irrational experiences of many religious people, no matter how much they may fail to command universal and objective acceptance, have at least this negative value of pointing up the incompleteness and remoteness of those purely rationalistic or abstract depictions of the divine. The irrational in life and religion is a constant reminder of the need to consult experience or the facts and not whitewash them with vague formulas.

To understand how James attempted to solve the problem of evaluating the truth claims in religion, we must consider the whole problem of religious skepticism. James saw the problems posed by the skeptical disbelievers to be as formidable as those posed by the great variety of religions, by the mystics and the rationalists. In fact, James' own pragmatic account of religious truth only makes sense against the background of the possible claims against it in the name of religious skepticism. There are various forms of skepticism regarding religion, all the way from particular doubts of certain religious truths to the most sweeping and tough-minded variety which rejects religion *in toto* on the grounds of insufficient evidence. James, intent on facing the problem head-on, gives foremost attention to the most sweeping kind of skepticism. Quoting the nineteenth-century English mathematician W. K. Clifford, he states the skeptical position succinctly: "It is wrong always, everywhere, and for everyone, to believe anything on insufficient evidence." [15] This kind of skepticism had a certain currency in James' day and was related to the great advances made in science. It seemed to some that the real value of science was contained in the sufficient mounting of evidence with which it backed up its theories and thereby gained a certain integrity of belief. To believe anything in science, therefore, without sufficient evidence would be dishonest and scientifically wrong. Given also the fact that the sciences of James' day were intruding into areas previously claimed as the privileged domain of religion, it appeared to some that the scientific attitude must apply to test all beliefs, even religious ones.

The problem, then, as James saw it (because he was a man of science) was this: How can we defend the right to believe in religion when its evidence is always less than sufficient when judged in terms of science? He freely admitted that religious claims to truth are based on insufficient evidence if looked at in scientific terms. This admission follows from his refusal to accept the claims of mysticism and rationalism as valid criteria for proving religious truths. He sympathized with the efforts of mystics and rationalists in their tender-minded concern with religious truth, but his tough-minded nature would not allow him to accept their accounts of it. James faced the problem of religious truth pragmatically and melioristically by trying to mediate between the radical opposition of tender-minded and tough-minded views. He granted that if religious truths exist at all, then they cannot be absolute or final, but at best are insufficiently proved or open at the end. He also maintained that one has a right to believe in certain truths, including religious ones, even upon insufficient evidence. This does not contradict the scientific attitude, for science itself never has sufficient evidence to begin its inquiries; the sufficient evidence comes only after much laborious observing, experimenting, and reasoning. Scientific questions are also different in kind from religious ones in that they are theoretic and not basically vitally important. In science, James claims we can afford to be patient and run the risk of not immediately finding the truth in order to discover error and correct it. But in religion and life it is quite different. When it comes to fundamental interests, such as life or death, or being saved or losing salvation, we cannot afford a patient wait for sufficient evidence.

James holds that gaining truth and shunning error are two different imperatives. They are both important and ideally good. But in life our situations are much less than ideal—they are tragically practical. "Some part of the ideal has to be butchered." [16] On this note, he makes his pragmatic defense of the right to believe in religion. A genuine religious belief for James must have the following three characteristics (remembering that a belief is an idea upon which one is prepared to act): it must be living, forced, and momentous. A religious belief or choice cannot be dead, but must present the individual with an option that makes sense to him or interests him in a vital way. A religious choice must also be forced in the sense that it presents the individual with an either-or proposition—either follow this truth or go without it. There can be no middle ground between these two. The reason for this is the third characteristic, that the choice must be momentous and not trivial; the alternatives of following this truth or going without it must make a sizable difference in pragmatic terms. The person's whole life must be radically affected by this choice.

Given these three characteristics of a real religious choice, James contends that pragmatism is able to offer a justification for the right to believe in religion. Pragmatism here asserts that the truth of a religious belief can only be discovered by looking to future, practical (concrete) consequences and that religious beliefs must be functional or useful in bringing about certain truths that otherwise will not come. James does not claim to have proved that any religious beliefs are true, but only that a belief in their eventual truth is pragmatically justified. The case of religious salvation, for example, pragmatically calls for a conviction or belief on the religious person's part, without which any eventual salvation could not be accomplished. This means that unless one believes in his own salvation he can never be saved. But belief in one's eventual salvation may also be instrumental in bringing that truth into existence. James, as he often said, only wants to give religion a fighting chance. In fact, to give it more than this would not only bring it into conflict with science, but would make faith or individual initiative unnecessary.

James realized that his earlier work, *The Will to Believe*, gave many people the wrong impression. It received considerable attention and awakened many persons to the importance of its questions, but it actually misled certain individuals into thinking that James had proved religion true once and for all. No wonder, then, that he later admitted he should have called his work *The Right to Believe*. James wanted least of all to allow that any belief could be made true simply by wanting it to be true. This would have contradicted his whole pragmatic approach by making truth merely subjective and even allowing it to be final or absolute, if some one happened to want that. James therefore defends man's right to believe in religion in the same way that he defends the freedom of the will. Both freedom and religion depend upon *acting on faith*. For this reason they can never reside in complacency or finality. Man cannot sit back and hope to be saved or free. His only hope of salvation is to actively strive for deliverance. In this way religion is given a fighting chance; it is given the chance of shaping man's destiny. Religion is pragmatically true to this extent—man's belief in the divine can function in his life to bring about in piecemeal fashion a higher and richer moral order.

RADICAL EMPIRICISM AND PLURALISM   William James dedicated his famous *Pragmatism* to the memory of the great English empiricist, John Stuart Mill. James saw in Mill not only the value of grounding philosophy in empirical fact or experience, but also an openness of mind that would do justice to the needs of men and to the richness of experience. In fact, it was the empirical orientation of Peirce's pragmatism that first attracted James to the pragmatic method as a means of solving philosophical disputes. Peirce required that ideas be tested in terms of their consequences in experience. Where there is no detectable difference between two ideas there can be no difference of meaning. As we saw previously, however, James broadened Peirce's original conception of pragmatism by making it applicable to all of man's experiences and life concerns. He agreed with Peirce that pragmatism was a method only, and not itself a world-outlook or a doctrine concerning the make-up of the whole universe. But because James saw pragmatism as applicable to all human concerns, he was led to develop the kind of world-outlook which pragmatism seemed to him to lead to. Since it was basically an empirical or factual method, this indicated a world-outlook that would first of all have to be some form of empiricism. But it could not just be any form of empiricism, since pragmatism for James signifies a dynamic or functional conception of truth which the older and narrower forms of empiricism fail to provide. If pragmatism is to be empirical, therefore, it must lead to a radically dynamic kind of empiricism. Radical empiricism is the name James gave to his world-outlook, which he sought to work out in piecemeal fashion in his later years.

His *Essays in Radical Empiricism, A Pluralistic Universe,* and *Some Problems of Philosophy* give expression to his growing concern with the metaphysical and epistemological implications of his pragmatism. Pragmatism, he saw, gave one a way of setting up philosophical problems and working out sensible solutions to them. But this was not enough for James since he recognized that his pragmatic solutions bore certain relations to one another, that the basic questions which pragmatism considers suggest a certain view of the universe. This view is nothing less than a metaphysics which James came to see as an attempt to reach clarification on points where common sense and ordinary thinking are unaware of the need of any more clarity. These questions, though they may be helped by science, are too general and fundamental to be solved by science alone. What is experience? What is knowledge? What is the difference between mind and matter? Is the world one or many? These questions are so fundamental that any genuine answers to them must involve making all our assumptions regarding their solution as explicit as possible. What is needed here is a comprehensive view of basic things that states its reasons carefully and ties its various parts together.

The traditional systems of philosophy did attempt to give us a comprehensive view of basics. They also gave elaborate reasons for their views and tied everything rather neatly together. However, the more they gave reasons and the more they tied things together, the more unempirical and unsatisfactory they became. The great philosophic systems, according to James, sooner or later make experience evaporate; in its place they offer us an abstract, static, and monistic conception where all the concrete particulars of change, plurality, and life are gone. The intellectualist fallacy in philosophy must be avoided, since it confuses concepts or abstract ideas with the reality it presumably is studying. Concepts, no less than percepts, are working parts of our experience. And if concepts are to give us knowledge, they must stay within our range of experience, not falsely attempt to go outside or beyond it and see all things as absolutely one. Monism, or the view that everything fits into a single, fixed whole, is completely unempirical. Empiricism, especially radical empiricism, is essentially pluralistic, since it leaves the doors of experience open for novelty and change.

James thought philosophy needed a metaphysics that would be faithful to experience. Such a metaphysics would have to be based on a theory of knowledge that refuses to substitute static concepts for the changes taking place in the real world. James believed that his own functional psychology could assist us to understand what thinking, perception, consciousness, conception, etc., really are. Theory of knowledge would have to be connected with psychology and profit from its findings. Radical empiricism was just such a philosophic outlook. In the preface to *The Meaning of Truth* he gave a very succinct formulation of his theory of radical empiricism. "Radical empiricism consists first of a postulate, next of a statement of fact, and finally of a generalized conclusion." [17] The postulate states "that the only things that shall be debatable among philosophers shall be things definable in terms drawn from experience." [18] The statement of fact asserts "that the relations between things, conjunctive as well as disjunctive, are just as much matters of direct particular experience, neither more so nor less so than the things themselves." [19] Finally, the generalized conclusion states "that therefore the parts of experience hold together from next to next by relations that are themselves parts of experience. The directly apprehended universe needs, in short, no extraneous trans-empirical connective support, but possesses in its own right a concatenated or continuous structure." [20]

Here James states his world-outlook as a philosophy of experience *par excellence*. If we want to know what reality is or what the make-up of the universe is, not only do we have to consult experience, but we have to *keep on* consulting experience. We must look down into and out into experience. The postulate behind his radical empiricism is also an integral part of his pragmatic method, since that method is empirical insofar as it requires that any practical consequences must be detectable within our experience. The postulate of radical empiricism is also an integral part of James' humanism, which requires that man can debate questions in a meaningful way only if those questions bear upon his experiences. The so-called "matter of fact" in this radical empiricism is nothing more than a result of the Jamesian psychology, which finds that the connections and relations between things are just as much a part of our experience as are the things themselves.

If I experience one rock as heavier than another, for example, the felt relation of "heavier than" is just as much a part of experience as is the perception of either rock. If I experience heat as causing wax to melt, the relation of causation is just as much a part of my experience as heating, wax, and melting. The experienced causation is not something that merely exists in my mind, nor is it an abstract relation, *a priori* and outside of experience, but is part of experience itself. Analysis or abstract thought may play tricks on us here and make us believe that relations, functions, change, or continuous motion cannot really be found. Analysis tends to break up experience into discrete and static parts, and cannot really find any flux or continuity. What intellectual analysis with its abstract concepts breaks up, it can never get back together again. It is therefore forced into a static picture of unity which loses all touch with the dynamic, flowing plurality of things. The classic example of this is found in Zeno's famous paradoxes of motion. When Zeno analyzed motion and plurality he found that they evaporated when he analyzed them into parts. For example, he argued that if a horse is to run the distance AB it must first cover half that distance, and before it can cover that half, it must cover one quarter of the distance, and so on to infinity. This means that when we analyze the distance to be covered we can break it up into an infinity of points; but obviously no horse could actually traverse an infinity of points in a finite time. Intellectual analysis, therefore, with its static, discontinuous concepts, leaves us with no real motion. The cure for this dilemma is to realize exactly how we have falsified the facts by painting a mere abstract picture over them.

It must be realized that our concepts tend to become fixed in their meanings insofar as we use them to mean only certain things and not others. They are therefore shorthand approximations, rather than exact copies, of bundles of facts. It is practical for concepts to become fixed; for example, the concept running can never mean standing still, or the concept hard can never mean soft. Useful concepts must possess a fixity of meaning; otherwise we fall into contradiction and confusion. However, the experiences and facts these concepts may apply to are quite different. Perception tells us that a man can be running and then can be standing still, or that a piece of wax can be hard and then soft. In other words, perceived particulars of our experience are not static, as the meaning of our concepts may be. Further, experience is continuous, as any simple motion of the hand or change of speed can indicate. However, when we analyze these simple motions and changes we tend to break them up into discrete, disconnected parts. We thereby lose the motion because we break up experience by using concepts which are themselves discrete. But this only means that we have projected discontinuity into experience from our concepts; it does not mean that we have actually found things to be discrete.

Radical empiricism, therefore, insists that philosophy must be brought back into experience, and that experience itself must be understood to include relations and functions rather than disjointed facts. The rationalists are the ones who point up the weakness of the older, narrower empiricism as merely giving us a jumble of atomic, isolated facts. The rationalists thus assume that the only way to make our understanding of things orderly and meaningful is to go away from experience and perception and locate some *a priori* principles that will put things together. James contends that this method of rationalism—going away from or beyond experience—is false. Instead, we should locate order or meaning within experience itself. In fact, James' humanism insists that we are unable to do more than this, since he defies the rationalists to separate the real from the human in any meaningful way. Experience is all we have to work with, and if we develop a truly philosophical account of experience, then we will see that experience is not simply chaotic or a jumble of meaningless facts. Radical empiricism asks us to look for order and connection as well as separateness, but its basic postulate is that these must be located within experience.

In his celebrated essay entitled *Does Consciousness Exist?* James applies his theory of radical empiricism to the age-old problem of the difference between mind and matter or ideas and things. He attacks the notion that there is a gulf between the mental world and the physical world. He tries to show that the assumption that consciousness is a different kind of stuff than material things is false. What is consciousness? James asks. In his psychological investigations he found that there are four main aspects of consciousness; it is (1) changing, (2) selective, in attending to certain things and not to others, (3) continuous, and (4) personal, in that each state is part of some personal experience. In other words, consciousness is not a thing or a stuff, but a *stream* that continues or flows. "Consciousness, then, does not appear to itself chopped up in bits. Such words as 'chain' or 'train' do not describe it fitly as it presents itself in the first instance. It is nothing jointed; it flows. A 'river' or a 'stream' are the metaphors by which it is most naturally described." [21] However, this means that its borders have fringes and are not sharply defined. We are conscious of some things but ignore others; we pass into and out of consciousness without being able to fix the transition with precision. In order to explain this philosophically, James postulated a notion of pure experience,[22] which means undifferentiated raw experience.

Pure experience is simply our field of awareness which eventually receives either an objective or subjective interpretation. The original field of awareness is neutral; it is neither subjective nor objective, as when we stare into space without attending to anything in particular. We may become conscious, however, and attend to something in particular, a snowstorm, for example. But if we become self-conscious, we may attend to our perception of the snowstorm. What is the difference between the two? What is the difference between the snowstorm out there and someone's perception of that storm which is not out there, but private? What is the pragmatic difference between the two? They are *functionally* different, or fall into different relations or contexts. The snowstorm may be called an object of consciousness, and the perception of it may be called the subject. Consciousness has duplicity, but not in terms of two different stuffs, one mental and the other material. Rather, the duplicity has only to do with the different relations and functions into which it falls. Consciousness requires a subject and an object, but the pragmatic difference between the one and the other still falls within experience.

If we are conscious of a wall, for example, the object *wall* falls within our experience; we can touch it and see it. Our *being conscious* of the wall, as distinct from the wall that we are conscious of, also falls within experience, but this experience is private. From this, James concludes that consciousness (mind) is not a different kind of substance or stuff from material things. Both mental and material existences are experiential, but they function differently in our experiences. Thoughts or mental existences function in their context, and external objects or physical existences function in their context. The only detectable differences between the mental and the physical are those that show up in experience, in the various functions and contexts wherein they work. I can sit in a chair, but I cannot sit in my thought or idea of a chair; I can think of a chair that has been destroyed by fire, but I cannot sit in such a chair. These differences and others like them are pragmatic meanings that show up in experience. To talk about a mental essence or substance as distinct from a physical essence or substance, neither of which can be located in experience, is completely unverifiable and unnecessary.

James' radical empiricism thus leads to a world-view of pure experience that becomes differentiated in an unlimited variety of ways. No matter how high or how deep is our philosophical quest, we always remain within the shifting field of experience. James finds flux and plurality everywhere in the richness and diversity of experience. Experience contains more individual things than we can count. We can never know the limits of possible experience since we can never get beyond it to look back and draw a limit or a curtain. Experiences may envelop one another, as one conscious state may include another, and therefore our conscious life may be part of a vaster consciousness and *that* of still another. Neither our consciousness, which is selective, nor our knowledge, which is fallible and finite, can possibly exhaust all there is in the field of experience. Philosophers have tried to enclose the universe in a schema of knowledge only to fail, only to leave many things out. Knowledge, when defined pragmatically, must be understood in a practical way as one part of experience leading us to another part. Knowledge must be selective to be true, and it can only represent a part of a vaster plurality of things still left to be known. In his last writings[23] James came to see the universe as a field of experience that continually undergoes creative evolution. This carried his radical empiricism to the full extent of allowing both meaningful arrangement of parts and an unforeseeable flux of novelty. Pluralism and empiricism, when pushed to the extreme, could mean nothing less than this for him: a universe of diverse particularity ceaselessly on the move to newer and more enriching arrangements or experiences.

THE SIGNIFICANCE AND INFLUENCE OF JAMES   The creative accomplishments and fame of William James brought American philosophy and psychology to the attention of the whole world. His books and lectures not only received recognition from learned, intellectual circles abroad, but they reached and affected a wide popular audience. His works in both psychology and philosophy have become classics. It is James who is first thought of when pragmatism is mentioned as an American philosophy. It was James who broadened pragmatism into something more than a theory of meaning and made it a theory of truth, religion, and a whole philosophy of life. However, his significance cannot be measured merely in terms of his thought and writings. He is also remarkable as a man of forceful character and personality. His life and career embody the way in which he lived his humanistic and pragmatic philosophy. His contacts with people and the friendships he made were as pluralistic and humanistic as his philosophy. He cultivated the personal and intellectual friendship of many of the greatest minds of his day.

James encouraged and helped the work of fellow philosophers even when these philosophers developed rival philosophies. For many years, he tried to gain recognition for Peirce as a man of philosophic importance. He even tried to secure an academic position for Peirce at Harvard at a time when few other people had any idea of Peirce's talents. He also encouraged and helped his friend Josiah Royce, even though they were on opposite sides of many basic philosophic questions. James did secure an academic post at Harvard for Royce, and he encouraged him to develop his philosophy, even though Royce stood for rationalism and the absolute, the two ideas James fought most vigorously. This tells us something most important about James and his philosophy. He was fundamentally a humanist; he loved to see each human effort sprout and grow—the greater the variety, the better. He kept on the warmest and friendliest terms with men whose ideas he nevertheless attacked. He encouraged Santayana in his graduate work at Harvard only to have Santayana join the faculty there and develop a rival philosophy. In fact, it is largely due to the efforts of William James that around the turn of the century Harvard had perhaps the finest and most diversified faculty of philosophy in the world. James, Royce, and Santayana were together in Harvard's philosophy department, but they were in opposition in their basic ideas. James the pragmatist, Royce the idealist, and Santayana the naturalist joined with one another to philosophize in stimulating disagreement. The fact that James was in large measure personally responsible for their all being there is a lasting tribute to his sound judgment and liberal personality.

He also encouraged and influenced the work of John Dewey. Actually, it is largely through James' impact on and relation to John Dewey that the movement of American pragmatism gathered momentum and continued to grow throughout the present century. Dewey not only accepted James' broader conception of pragmatism in many ways, but he carried it farther, and in his own right deeply affected both the intellectual world and popular audiences throughout this century.

By the early twentieth century James had profoundly impressed the intellectual climate of his time. Groups of pragmatists sprouted up in England, Italy, France, and America.[24] The French philosopher Henri Bergson, who welcomed James' ideas, wrote a preface for the French translation of James' *Pragmatism* in 1909. In England the philosophers Bertrand Russell and G. E. Moore published strong critical analyses of James' ideas. However, the sense in which James awakened followers and critics alike is only a superficial indication of his importance and significance. His real importance has to be located in his original and fruitful ideas. The rare combination of psychologist-philosopher marks the vantage point from which one can begin to locate and assess his significance. His pragmatism must be seen as balanced between the extreme types of temperament, the tough and the tender. This in itself implies a rich pluralism, another cardinal point in James' outlook, since the possible ways of balancing the tough and the tender attitudes are really unlimited. James' humanistic approach is distinctive in its claim that no real philosophic outlook can be based on pure abstract thought or intellectual matters alone. His fellow pragmatist John Dewey points this up as follows: "William James took into account those motives of instinctive sympathy which play a greater role in our choice of a philosophic system than do formal reasonings; and he thought that we should be rendering a service to the cause of philosophic sincerity if we openly recognize the motives which inspire us." [25]

Next, it should be observed that James' call for a human philosophy, a voluntaristic outlook, suggests a philosophy of continual application and use for human life. If, as he says, truth has to be created as well as discovered, then there is much to look forward to in philosophy, morality, and religion. According to Dewey, "William James accomplished a new advance in Pragmatism by his theory of the will to believe, or, as he himself later called it, the right to believe. The discovery of the fundamental consequences of one or another belief has without fail a certain influence on that belief itself." [26]

James is also an important influence on and forerunner of twentieth-century existentialism. His refusal to separate psychology and philosophy places him in direct line with many contemporary existentialists who believe as James did that man can only be understood by probing the concrete relations between commitment and action, between man's making decisions and his acting upon them.[27] Finally, since James originated a radical empiricism, philosophy and man are able to find much more in experience than many others even hope for. But radical empiricism also suggests that man's search for truth and meaning must look for verification; it must be mindful of those tests of fact which give reality to our philosophy and life.

NOTES

1. William James, *Psychology* (American Science Series, Briefer Course), (New York: Henry Holt, 1907), p. 4, from "Introductory."

2. William James, *The Will to Believe and Other Essays in Popular Philosophy and Human Immortality*, p. 24, from "The Will to Believe."

3. *Ibid.*, p. 25.

4. William James, *Pragmatism: A New Name for Some Old Ways of Thinking*, p. 51, from "What Pragmatism Means."

5. *Ibid.*, p. 218, from "Pragmatism's Conception of Truth."

6. *Ibid.*, p. 215.

7. James, *The Will to Believe and Other Essays in Popular Philosophy*, p. 201, from "The Moral Philosopher and the Moral Life."

8. *Ibid.*, p. 195.

9. William James, in R. B. Perry, ed., *Essays on Faith and Morals* (Cleveland, Ohio: Meridian, 1962), p. 259, from "On a Certain Blindness in Human Beings."

10. James, *The Will to Believe and Other Essays in Popular Philosophy*, p. 152, from "The Dilemma of Determinism."

11. *Ibid.*, p. 165.

12. *Ibid.*, p. 174.

13. William James, *The Varieties of Religious Experience*, pp. 31–32, from Lecture 2, "Circumscription of the Topic."

14. *Ibid.*, p. 428, from Lecture 18, "Philosophy."

15. James, *The Will to Believe and Other Essays in Popular Philosophy*, p. 8, from "The Will to Believe."

16. *Ibid.*, p. 203, from "The Moral Philosopher and the Moral Life."

17. James, *Pragmatism: A New Name for Some Old Ways of Thinking*, p. 310, from "Author's Preface to the Meaning of Truth."

18. *Ibid.*

19. *Ibid.*

20. *Ibid.*, pp. 310–311.

21. James, *Psychology* (American Science Series, Briefer Course), p. 159.

22. See William James, *Essays in Radical Empiricism and a Pluralistic Universe*, Vol. I, "A World of Pure Experience."

23. See William James, *Some Problems of Philosophy*.

24. See Ralph Barton Perry, *The Thought and Character of William James* (Cambridge, Mass.: Harvard University Press, 1948), Ch. 34.

25. John Dewey, *Philosophy and Civilization* (New York: Capricorn, 1963), p. 21, from "The Development of American Pragmatism."

26. *Ibid.*, p. 21.

27. See Rollo May, "The Emergence of Existential Psychology," in Rollo May, ed., *Existential Psychology* (New York: Random House, 1961).

QUESTIONS FOR DISCUSSION

1. In what ways did James broaden and humanize Peirce's original conception of pragmatism?

2. Why does James think that psychology has much to offer philosophy?

3. Why does James believe that the best conception of truth is the pragmatic?

4. How can moral values be understood pragmatically according to James? Can freedom of the will be justified pragmatically?

5. Is it legitimate to defend religion on pragmatic grounds as James does?

6. Is James' radical empiricism superior to older forms of empiricism?

7. To what extent is James successful in steering a middle course between tender-minded rationalism and tough-minded materialism in his philosophy?

8. How should we judge James' contribution to the development of American philosophical thought? How significant are his achievements?

SUGGESTED READINGS

The Present Dilemma in Philosophy. James' breakdown of philosophies into the two temperaments—tough-minded and tender-minded. [In James, *Pragmatism: A New Name for Some Old Ways of Thinking*, Section I, pp. 3–39.]

What Pragmatism Means. James defines pragmatism as a method for settling philosophical disputes. [In James, *Pragmatism*, Lecture II, pp. 43–81.]

Pragmatism's Conception of Truth. Note the difference between James' pragmatic theory of truth and Peirce's pragmatic theory of meaning. [In James, *Pragmatism*, Lecture VI, pp. 197–236.]

The Pragmatic Account of Truth and Its Misunderstanders. James handles eight different objections to his pragmatic theory of truth. [In Kallen, ed., *The Philosophy of William James*, pp. 172–196.]

Pragmatism and Humanism. Why James holds that pragmatism is basically a humanistic philosophy. See also *Humanism and Truth*. [In James, *Pragmatism*, pp. 239–270; pp. 369–419.]

The Will to Believe. James argues that pragmatism justifies a right to believe in religion. [In James, *The Will to Believe and Other Essays in Popular Philosophy*, pp. 1–31.]

Conclusions on Varieties of Religious Experience. James reinterprets religion by taking it out into experience—and by taking experience itself out of certain traditional restrictions placed on it. [In James, *The Varieties of Religious Experience*, Lecture 20, pp. 475–509.]

A World of Pure Experience. James defines his radical empiricism, establishes "relations" within experience. [In James, *Essays in Radical Empiricism and a Pluralistic Universe*, pp. 39–91.]

Does Consciousness Exist? James provides for consciousness functionally within experience. [In James, *Essays in Radical Empiricism and a Pluralistic Universe*, pp. 1–38.]

Monistic Idealism. James argues against monism, especially that of Royce. Look for James' own adherence to pluralism. [In James, *Essays in Radical Empiricism and a Pluralistic Universe*, Vol. II, pp. 43–82.]

The Moral Philosopher and the Moral Life. James' humanistic conception of basic values. [In James, *The Will to Believe and Other Essays on Popular Philosophy*, pp. 184–215.]

The Dilemma of Determinism. James argues for freedom of the will. [In James, *The Will to Believe and Other Essays on Popular Philosophy*, pp. 145–183.]

PRIMARY SOURCES

William James, *Essays in Radical Empiricism and a Pluralistic Universe* (New York: Longmans, Green, 1958).

——, *Pragmatism: A New Name for Some Old Ways of Thinking, Together with Four Related Essays from the Meaning of Truth* (New York: Longmans, Green, 1959).

——, *Some Problems of Philosophy* (New York: Longmans, Green, 1948).

——, *The Varieties of Religious Experience* (New York: Mentor Books, 1958).

——, *The Will to Believe and Other Essays in Popular Philosophy and Human Immortality* (New York: Dover, 1956).

Horace M. Kallen, ed., *The Philosophy of William James* (New York: Modern Library).

SECONDARY SOURCES

Edward C. Moore, *William James* (New York: Washington Square Press, 1965).

Lloyd Morris, *William James: The Message of a Modern Mind* (New York: Scribner's, 1950).

Ralph Barton Perry, *In the Spirit of William James* (Bloomington: Indiana University Press, 1958).

——, *The Thought and Character of William James*, Briefer Version (New York: Harper Torchbooks, 1964).

6 Josiah Royce

Idealism and Loyalty

Josiah Royce (1855–1916) is the greatest systematic idealist philosopher that America has produced. Unlike Edwards and Emerson, Royce did not merely make excursions into idealism or make use of idealistic principles; he constructed an elaborate system of philosophical idealism through which he sought to explain the nature of the universe and man's proper destiny therein. Royce philosophized in the "grand manner" of traditional system-building and complex argumentation, and must be considered one of the most learned of American philosophers. He viewed philosophy the same way that he fervently practiced it and wrote it—as exacting, demanding, and of the utmost importance. Like Peirce, whom he much admired, Royce believed that philosophy required the most rigorous and careful logical thought. With James, whom he also greatly admired, he shared the opinion that philosophy was something practical, having application to the concrete problems of men.

Royce thought of himself as an "absolute pragmatist." By this he meant that ideas are not only plans of action or expressions of purpose, as the pragmatists hold, but they must also be *true* in a fundamental sense in order to guide action or define purpose. Royce required concrete ideas and absolute ideals; he refused to regard them as static. Ideas are expressions of purpose or plans of action as well as mental representations of things. "Every idea is as much a volitional process as it is an intellectual process." [1] The concept of loyalty is an example. Loyalty is both practical and ideal, something concrete as well as absolute. On the one hand,

159

loyalty is *"the willing and practical and thoroughgoing devotion of a person to a cause . . . ,"* [2] and on the other hand it is a universal principle, *"so be loyal to your own cause as thereby to serve the advancement of the cause of universal loyalty."* [3] As a practical as well as a universal principle, loyalty is "an absolute moral principle, a guide for all action." [4] Royce's basic idealism is therefore absolute as well as pragmatic. It requires philosophy to search for and find practical ideals as well as unified or absolute ends. Throughout all his major works, Royce tried to prove the adequacy of idealism as the only kind of philosophy that can give us absolute as well as practical answers.

Josiah Royce was born in Grass Valley, California, in 1855. After receiving his B.A. degree from the University of California in 1875, he traveled to Germany for graduate study where he came into direct contact with German idealistic philosophers. Upon his return to America he entered Johns Hopkins, where he received his doctorate in philosophy in 1878. At Johns Hopkins, Royce attended lectures by William James, who was Visiting Professor there in 1876. He continued his friendship with James, and in 1882 he received an appointment as Instructor in Philosophy at Harvard, largely due to James' influence. Royce was promoted to Assistant Professor of Philosophy at Harvard in 1885 and in the same year published his first major philosophic work, *The Religious Aspect of Philosophy*. In 1892 he became Professor of the History of Philosophy at Harvard and published *The Spirit of Modern Philosophy*. He remained as Professor of Philosophy at Harvard for the rest of his life and continued to teach and publish major works in philosophy. In 1899–1900 he was invited by the University of Aberdeen to deliver the Gifford Lectures, which were subsequently published in the two-volume work *The World and the Individual*. In 1906 he lectured at Johns Hopkins on modern idealism.[5] In 1908 he published the major formulation of his moral philosophy in *The Philosophy of Loyalty*. From 1912 until the time of his death, he continued to write and publish major works in the philosophy of religion and social philosophy: *The Sources of Religious Insight* (1912), *The Problem of Christianity* (1913), *The Hope of the Great Community* (1916).

Royce was the first American philosopher to construct a full-fledged system of philosophy. Peirce developed the outlines for a system, but his efforts were essentially unfinished. James, in his later years, also worked out the outlines of a metaphysics, but this too was largely uncompleted. In fact, James attacked system-building in philosophy as artificial. Royce, on the other hand, made long and careful studies of philosophical systems, especially those of the German philosophers Kant and Hegel. Through these studies he came to see the virtues as well as the problems of system-building. The goal of any philosophic system is to unify our thoughts and experiences. Without a system our ideas would be disorganized and even contradictory. Everyone interprets the world or his existence in terms of his own ideas. The meaning, the truth, or the value of anything is not furnished already made. What the outside world is, what man is, what has happened, what is happening, and what will happen all require interpretation. Philosophy itself is a systematic effort to become fully conscious that all existence must be interpreted in order to have meaning and to be known. "The principal task of the philosopher is one, not of perception, not of conception, but of interpretation." [6]

Perceptions, concepts, and thoughts have no meaning or significance apart from how they are interpreted. A real concept has a specific meaning; it involves an idea with a purpose behind it. When we attempt to discover the meaning of our concepts, we are in reality giving them an interpretation. However, existence not only calls for interpretation, it also calls, according to Royce, for an infinite community of interpretation. No limited or finite interpretation can reveal the whole meaning, truth, or value of anything. No person can find the meaning of his own life in terms of any limited present idea. The meaning of a person's life can only be discovered by interpreting his past life and his future as a unified whole. But this requires a series of different interpretations that make sense when taken all together. In other words, the true meaning of an individual's life requires the assumption of a complete or ideal interpretation of that life. This ideal interpretation would have to contain all the parts of that life and their relations to other things in the proper order.

Royce contends, however, that this ideal interpretation can be no mere ideal, it must also be real. Every interpretation implies some interpreter; it is a contradiction to talk of an interpretation without a mind to do the interpreting. Every limited or finite interpretation not only implies a person or an individual to do the interpreting, but also an absolute mind that interprets the whole or makes the incomplete *actually complete*. One of Royce's most persistent lines of argument is that the part implies the whole, part of the truth implies the whole truth. However, this whole truth is neither a mere abstraction nor a mere intellectual construction.

Royce agrees with James that concepts or general ideas leave out many facts. For example, the abstract concepts of man and horse do not tell us everything about all men and all horses. Man's experiences, as well as his concepts, do not give him the whole truth. But Royce argues that the whole truth in all its detail and significance must exist, otherwise we could not know that our various individual ideas only give us *part* of the truth. Absolute idealism, or the view that the complete truth about the universe must exist in a mind that interprets or knows that truth, is a logical necessity according to Royce. Man, he admits, does not know *what* the absolute truth is in all its detail and significance; but man can be certain *that* absolute truth exists. The function of philosophy is to demonstrate and interpret this basic insight. Royce claims that philosophical idealism has always held the insight that the absolute truth exists and is known by omniscience or an absolute mind.

However, the older forms of philosophical idealism did not always interpret this insight correctly, and no philosophy has interpreted it completely. The proper interpretation of the insight of absolute idealism requires not only the careful use of logical thought, but continued references to experience. The proper task for philosophy, according to Royce, is to give theoretical as well as practical meaning to the "absolute." Theoretically, philosophy is expected to give cogent arguments in proof of the idealist's thesis that all existence is mental. Practically, it is expected to show that there is a true and absolute moral standard as a guide to action, and that there is a true or certain religion which fulfills man's destiny and hopes. The philosophy of idealism and the philosophy of loyalty meet one another in the notion of the absolute or infinite. Idealism shows that the world "is such stuff as ideas are made of." [7] Idealism, of course, admits facts, but "facts must be facts for somebody and can't be facts for nobody." [8] We cannot so much as mention or think of any facts which are not interpreted by a mind. However, idealism also shows that reality extends far beyond anyone's private consciousness, and that reality is, in fact, infinite. According to Royce, every fact that we can mention or think of implies a system of interpretation that must extend to infinity. For example, if I consider the fact that it rained yesterday, I become an interpreter with an interpretation that is always open to further interpretation either by me or by someone else. *A priori*, or logically, there is no limit to the possible interpretations of any fact.

However, mere quantity of interpretation does not imply order or rational unity. Hence, Royce argues that philosophical idealism requires not only an infinity of interpreted facts, but that this infinite series must be well-ordered or rationally interpreted. The absolute truth about the world must contain an infinity of interpreted facts that are, at the same time, completely ordered or unified. This infinite truth, Royce claims, is indeed supernatural or superhuman in character since it goes completely beyond any empirical verification or human comprehension. However, he insists that this does not make the absolute irrational, or a mere superstitious belief. Here Royce claims that the developments of modern mathematics and logic can help us to see the reasonableness of an absolute truth. Modern mathematics has developed powerful and rigorous methods of dealing with such concepts as the infinite. Mathematical truths are clearly objective and rationally demonstrable. That $2 + 3 = 5$, or that the area of a circle is πr^2, certainly does not depend on a private opinion or judgment, but no empirical test can ever completely verify these truths. Yet, we can know for certain that $2 + 3 = 5$ or that every circle's area is given by the value πr^2. Mathematical truths imply an infinite series of well-ordered relations. Every mathematical fact fits into a larger, more comprehensive system which is actually infinite. But the part-whole relationship here is isomorphic and rational. The parts mirror the whole in also being infinite.

Thus Royce is not satisfied with a mere negative concept of the infinite as that which has no end; rather, he makes use of what he takes to be the positive idea of the infinite devised by modern mathematics. He quotes Dedekind's positive definition of the infinite. "A system S is called 'infinite' when it is similar to a constituent (or proper) part of itself; in the contrary case S is called a 'finite' system." [9] For example, all the whole numbers constitute an infinite system since they can be put into a one-to-one correspondence with a proper part, e.g., all the even numbers. Even numbers are a part of all the whole numbers; yet here the part mirrors the whole since there are an infinite number of even numbers to match the infinite number of whole numbers.

Royce argues that the same point applies to the whole of reality when it is idealistically conceived as a system of thoughts. "My own realm of thoughts, i.e., the totality S of all things that can be objects of my thought, is infinite." [10] If I take any one of my thoughts about something, my thought that the sky is blue for example, I find that I can further think about my thought that the sky is blue, and moreover, I can think about my having thought that thought, and so on to infinity. Royce's idealism, therefore, conceives the world as an infinite system of individual thoughts, each of which mirrors or implies the whole. His absolute is an infinite intelligence which contains or thinks an infinite number of individuals or individual thoughts. The relation between the absolute mind and other individuals is such that together they form a well-ordered system or community of interpretation. Individuals are neither swallowed up in the whole, nor can they exist without it. Each individual person or thought occupies a definite place in the larger, infinite system. The absolute would be incomplete and could not exist without each definite individual as a meaningful part of it.

Royce's form of idealism is more complete and more carefully argued than any of the earlier idealistic philosophies in America. For example, Royce agrees with Edwards and Emerson that all existence is mental in character, but he goes far beyond them in explaining what this means and how it can be justified. Royce judged that Edwards and Emerson were the greatest American thinkers prior to William James.[11] However, neither of them had a complete philosophic system as did Royce, who was a great student of the history of philosophy. In fact, he was the first important American philosopher who was specifically trained in philosophy and who took a Ph.D. degree in the subject. If Edwards' idealism is mainly theological in character, and if Emerson's is mainly poetic and mystical, then by contrast Royce's absolute idealism is typically philosophical. Royce not only believed that philosophy could throw light on all things, but he also fervently believed in the importance of philosophical inquiry. For him, philosophy was not simply a set of truths to be used to defend religion or make life more beautiful, it was primarily a study or a method of inquiry that required critical thinking.

The uniqueness of his philosophy can be seen by observing the way in which he sought to combine idealism with pragmatism. What he found lacking in pragmatism was its failure to provide any absolute truth. Pragmatism assumes the position of fallibilism, that no truths are absolutely certain. Royce could not accept this position, and was fond of turning fallibilism upon itself and asking whether it was certain that no truths are certain. He argued that fallibilism itself could not be really true if there were no absolute truth. But Royce found much that was worthwhile in pragmatism, especially in Peirce and James. Pragmatism was indeed better than the older forms of idealism in requiring that truths be brought to a test in terms of their consequences in experience. The older forms of idealism, Royce agreed, were too *a priori*, too far removed from experience and practical consequences.

Therefore, he continually tried to construct a better form of idealism, one that would do justice to the richness of experience, but one which still upheld the reality of the absolute truth. In his concept of loyalty, especially, he thought that he could show the correct intersection of idealism with pragmatism. The value of loyalty not only requires practical consequences, but it also requires absolute allegiance to a universal or infinite cause. Loyalty requires a community of individuals united in a common cause. "Loyalty to a community of interpretation enters into all other forms of loyalty." [12] Morality and religion, Royce held, not only require practical actions that further the cause of humanity, but they must be based on truth or faith in the absolute goodness of their respective causes. This is only possible under absolute idealism, which upholds the reality of absolute truth with definite application to experience.

Royce regarded all other philosophies as incomplete forms of idealism. He was fond of arguing over and over again how those who deny idealism, in reality, have to assert it.

> Let anybody tell you why he refuses to interpret his world in idealistic terms and he at once confesses his latent idealism; for he can express himself only by defining his ideal of scientific method, or by confessing his practical attitude toward the universe. In either case he defines his real world in terms of his ideal. [13]

DIALECTICAL REASON AND THE ABSOLUTE   To Royce the pervasiveness of idealism as the true philosophic outlook is bound up with our need to use ideals or postulates in anything we choose to do or think about. Man cannot live or think without making assumptions about himself and about the world in which he lives. When we assume that there is an external world, existing beyond or outside our mere thoughts, we posit a truth which is ideal in the sense that we can never prove it by experience alone. By using our experiences or by referring to them alone, we can never arrive at anything which is outside of them. Similarly, when we refer to the past or to the future we must make use of some ideal construction, since neither the past nor the future can be given to us in any present experience. The past is no more, the future is not yet, hence any knowledge or meaningful belief regarding them must make use of certain assumptions or postulates.

The question, then, is not whether philosophy and life must make use of assumptions or ideals, but whether these assumptions can be made rational and can be justified. We cannot think or live without assuming many things. The problem for philosophy is to find out what postulates or ideals we need to live by and think with. For example, we assume that individuals definitely exist and that each person is a unique individual. We assume that we can know ourselves and others as individuals. We act in accordance with the same assumptions—that as individuals we initiate actions and that other individuals respond to or are affected by our actions. But what exactly is a real or true individual, and how can we prove that any individual is unique? To answer these questions fully we require a true system which will place each individual in its proper context and define all the relations of that individual to everything in the system. In short, we can never experience all of the detail, parts, relations, or effects of any given individual. Even if we put our various experiences together, we still leave something undetermined. Neither can our concepts catch the individuality of things, since they are always general and leave out certain details. Nevertheless, we assume the reality of determinate or unique individuals. This can only mean that we do interpret the world as made up of individuals, but that an infinite system of concepts and experiences is required to make these individuals determinate.

If man cannot live or think without making certain assumptions that outrun his limited experiences, then how is this fact to be explained? This can only be explained according to Royce by reference to the *a priori*. "Every idealist must emphasize the fact that we cannot and do not move a step in our thinking without using the *a priori*." [14] We make *a priori* assumptions in all our dealings with the world insofar as we interpret things in terms of purpose, consistency, and unity. We assume *a priori* that no two individuals are exactly alike; we assume *a priori* that the past is gone and that it can never be exactly repeated; we assume *a priori* that the external world exists beyond our mere thoughts about it. We make these assumptions because it is consistent to do so. *A priori* postulates about the world interpret it as forming a coherent system even though we can experience only a small part of it. *A priori* postulates are logically consistent; they show things to us as reasonable; and they must be distinguished from blind faith.

Reasonable postulates are not only self-consistent, they must be consistent with a larger system of things and must agree with more and more of the facts. Reasonable assumptions or postulates must be open to critical reflection and possible revision. Because man's ideas and experiences are limited rather than perfect, obstacles and conflicts will occur in theory as well as in practical affairs. Rational interpretations must therefore be open to logical as well as empirical tests. A synthetic method is needed which will show how difficulties can be surmounted, how problems can be solved. Traditionally, from the time of Socrates, idealists have made use of the so-called dialectical method to solve their problems. Royce admits that the dialectical method has meant different things to different philosophers and that it has not always been used correctly or wisely. He also claims that though this is the only rational method of solving problems, it nevertheless requires revision and is not automatic.

What is dialectical reason, and why does Royce believe that it is the proper method for solving not only philosophical problems, but human problems as well? Dialectical reason is simply the triadic process of critical interpretation used to overcome pairs of oppositions in theory and in practical life. It is a universal method in the sense that it can be applied to all meaningful problems. But it is a rational or *a priori* method in the sense that it always seeks a unification where there is disparity, a consistency where there is contradiction. Dialectical reason assumes that controversies are not final or incurable, but that a higher order or unity can be found beyond apparent conflicts. Dialectical reason holds that when two scientific theories, or two different moral ideals, or even two entire philosophies of life collide with one another, there is a higher or an absolute truth that can be found to resolve the conflict. The dialectical method as viewed by Royce assumes that there are *degrees of truth* and that different, even opposing, viewpoints can be reconciled if we find the way in which each opposing viewpoint interprets part of the whole truth.

For instance, consider the simple example of a stick of wood which feels straight but looks bent when it is immersed in water. Here we have a conflict between two perceptions. If we name the first perception the *thesis* (the stick feels straight), and the second perception the *antithesis* (the stick looks bent), then we require a *synthesis* (third view) which explains from a more complete point of view how this apparent contradiction is overcome. The dialectical triad of thesis, antithesis, and synthesis always requires reference to experience or facts, but even this simple illustration shows that mere facts or sense perceptions are insufficient to arrive at a complete synthesis or solution. Theories or rational interpretations are required in order to state the proper arrangement, including the assumptions and implications, of all the facts involved. To arrive at a genuine synthesis the facts must be linked together. But the one way to show the linkage of facts with consistency and completeness is by logical or *a priori* reason.

As a rational or *a priori* method for philosophy, dialectical reason must be able to justify itself; that is, the validity of this method and whatever it postulates must be demonstrated. Royce insists that nothing belongs in philosophy if it is incapable of being proved or justified. Consequently, he offers a number of demonstrations to show the validity of dialectical reason and the validity of the "absolute," or the absolute truth, which that method always postulates.

Since the dialectical method welcomes conflicts, it would naturally welcome objections to its own use. As a rational method of overcoming oppositions it would have to be able to meet any objections to its use. For example, "James, in common with many empiricists, also opposes experience in general to all processes of reasoning, and asserts that the latter never teach us anything novel." [15] Royce thinks that this objection is basically false and that it can even be turned against itself. He claims that it is surely false to say that reason never teaches us anything new. For example, if a certain doctor (Smith) tells us that the first patient he ever had was bitten by a dog, and if another man (Jones) later tells us that he was the very first patient that same doctor (Smith) ever treated, then we know without asking that Jones was bitten by a dog. This is a new fact which we learn by putting the other two facts together. We learn it by reasoning. Royce contends that reasoning is not at all opposed to experience, but rather that all genuine facts must be reasonable and that all genuine reasoning must agree with the facts.

Royce asks, How can William James or any empiricist claim to know for certain that experience is opposed to reason or that reason teaches us nothing new? Because empiricists admit that experience or empirical evidence is fallible and hence never certain, these claims must be derived independently of experience, or *a priori*. But the empiricist contradicts himself for he must reason with the facts to claim that reason provides us with no new facts at all. The empiricist flatly condemns the *a priori* as empty of factual information. But how does he do this? If he condemns it conclusively, if he claims that *a priori* reason is absolutely empty of any fact, then he contradicts himself by using an *a priori* principle to deny *a priori* principles. Royce asserts, "I am very willing, then, to hear people condemn the *a priori*; for I notice that they do so upon *a priori* grounds." [16] We can know *a priori* that 2 + 3 make 5 or that all bachelors are unmarried, since the *a priori* only means the consistent carrying out of purposes. We cannot know *a priori*, or any other way, that 2 + 3 make 6, or that all bachelors are married, since these assertions or judgments are inconsistent. They are false because they defeat their own purposes. Every idea or judgment is in reality a plan of action.

Royce is in agreement with the pragmatists here. But he goes beyond the pragmatists in claiming that ideas have both an *internal* and *external* meaning which, taken together, call for or imply an *absolute* frame of reference. The internal meaning of an idea is its aim or purpose, or what it intends to convey. For example, the internal meaning of "triangle" would be a three-sided enclosed plane figure. The external meaning of an idea would be the objects or applications of that idea. In our present example the external meaning of triangle would be all triangles: right triangles, isosceles triangles, scalene triangles, etc. Internal meaning, as the expressed purpose of an idea *a priori* or logically, implies external meaning as that which fulfills the idea's purpose. In other words, Royce claims that internal and external meaning cannot be separated. For example, even a false idea $(2 + 2 = 7)$ must have an internal and external meaning, although they are inconsistent with one another. If our purpose or intention is to have $2 + 2 = 7$, we find that this purpose is not and cannot be fulfilled. A true idea, on the other hand, involves an internal and external meaning which are consistent with one another. If an idea or thought is true, this means that its purpose is in fact fulfilled.

However, Royce further insists that no finite or relative frame of reference will suffice as a test or standard of truth. If any idea is true, this means that it must be a consistent part of the whole or absolute truth. A true idea is one whose purpose is completely fulfilled; but nothing short of an infinite or absolute system of ideas will be sufficient to prove that any idea's purpose is *completely* fulfilled. William James, in his pragmatic theory of truth, had argued that truth means "agreeable leading" or "practical success." Royce argues that this is insufficient. He is willing to admit that truth must be practical in fulfilling purposes or leading us to the facts. He also agrees that ideas must *work* in order to be true. But he adds that ideas must *really* work to be true; they cannot merely happen to work.

We must go further than the pragmatists, then, and ask, How is it that true ideas work, and what guarantees that they will always work? Dialectical reason shows that any mere human test or test from experience will always fail. A true idea must really work or always work, but pragmatism has no test for the absolute or the eternal and in this it fails to give a complete account of truth. Truth must be eternal and absolute as well as practical in order to be consistent and complete. In other words, truth must have *a priori* dimensions as well as *a posteriori* or *factual* ones. The *eternal*, the *infinite*, the *absolute* are all *a priori* dimensions of truth in that they are not themselves testable in terms of finite, temporal workings or practical success; but any temporal workings or practical success must be consistent with and tested by them as the only complete and ultimate ground of truth. Thus pragmatism is turned around and made to stand on the absolute. This is Royce's absolute pragmatism.

Another objection to the use of dialectical reason comes from mysticism and those who claim that intuition, and not logical reasoning, is the proper way to find truth, especially the truths of religion. Intuitive insight is opposed to reason by certain mystics and romanticists. However, if we raise the question as to how we know that any intuitive insight is true or valid, it then becomes obvious that we must have some way of proving these insights. But we cannot use intuition to prove an intuition since intuitions may conflict or even be contradictory. Suppose someone claims that he knows not by reason but by intuition alone that all squares are really round. Or suppose that someone claims he intuitively knows that intuition does not exist. If intuitive insight is opposed to reason, it would defeat its own purposes since it would end up in contradictions. The only kind of insight that will endure is rational insight, which signifies that many things are viewed with unity and consistency. Insight, therefore, is not opposed to reason. It is the perfection of it.

But the real test of any dialectical use of reason is, according to Royce, whether it can be used to explain the most important things. Even if we grant that reason can be used in science, mathematics, and everyday things, the question remains whether reason can illuminate metaphysical issues. Can reason tell us what the ultimate nature of reality is, can it tell us whether the human soul is immortal, or whether God exists, or whether any absolute truths or moral values exist? Serious reflection on these questions reveals a great number of obstacles to their being proven true by reason. Many opposing viewpoints exist in the history of thought on each of these fundamental questions. To simplify the problem we may say that everything hinges on whether anything ultimate can be proved or known at all. Empiricism and pragmatism, for example, cannot locate any absolutes, so they tend to deny them altogether. James and Peirce deny that an absolute can have any pragmatic consequences or real meaning. Other thinkers, including the philosopher Kant, allow that an absolute exists but deny that we can know it or prove its existence.

Royce delighted in using dialectical arguments to demonstrate the existence of the absolute. He was confident that he could show that its existence is implied in either denying it altogether or in denying that we can know it. Perhaps his most famous proof is the argument starting from the possibility of error. The gist of this argument can be put as follows. If we admit, as will even the worst skeptic, that error is possible, then we must also admit the actual existence of those conditions under which error occurs. Unless we admit that the conditions of error are real, error would turn out to be only an empty possibility. What then are the conditions of error? What is an error? It is a mistaken thought or judgment, "but mere disagreement of a thought with any random object does not make the thought erroneous. The judgment must disagree with its chosen object." [17] Our thoughts must have a purpose or must intend to judge something in order to be in error. A thought or judgment which did not intend to refer to anything could be neither true nor false. A necessary condition of error, therefore, is that our thoughts or judgments have a purpose or intend to refer to some object.

A second necessary condition is that an erroneous thought must fail to be true to its intentions; it must fail to refer correctly to that which it intends to represent. But now the question is, How can we know that any judgment fails to achieve its purpose? According to Royce, we can only know this if there exists a *higher* thought or judgment that does achieve the purpose which the erroneous judgment misses, and which also correctly judges the erroneous thought as having missed that purpose. Royce defines an error as "an incomplete thought, that to a higher thought, which includes it and its intended object, is known as having failed in the purpose that it more or less clearly had, and that is fully realized in this higher thought." [18] The possibility of error requires the existence of a more inclusive thought which shows any error to be a thought that is incomplete or does not fully achieve its aim. But since we cannot place any limit on the number of possible errors or possible degrees of error, we not only require a higher or more inclusive thought to account for error, we require an absolute or infinitely extensive thought. We can easily conceive a series of errors that runs to infinity by merely adding numbers as follows: $2 + 2 = 5$, $2 + 2 = 6$, $2 + 2 = 7$, etc. There is no limit to the number of possible errors concerning the simple sum of $2 + 2$. But remembering what was previously said, it then follows that this is only possible under the condition that a higher and equally infinite thought exists to explain the unlimited possibility of error.

Dialectical reason is thus able to show the necessity of an absolute or infinite thought by starting with the possibility of error. This of course involves an *a priori* proof, since no absolute can be found in mere experience or sense perception. The absolute can also be dialectically demonstrated by trying to deny it. If we claim that there is no absolute truth, our claim cannot be absolutely true, and therefore it may be false. If our claim may be false, then is it absolutely true that it may be false or only probably true? In this way we get pushed back into an infinite regress of mere probabilities where we cannot be absolutely sure that anything is really probable. Royce was fond of meeting the fallibilism of the pragmatists with the question, Can we be absolutely certain that nothing is absolutely certain?

Dialectical reason, therefore, is not only able to prove the existence of the absolute, but it is also able to establish a metaphysics that agrees with experience. If we ask what is the ultimate nature of reality and the ultimate destiny of man we find that these questions can only be answered in terms of absolute idealism. The ultimate nature of reality must be consistent with the whole or absolute truth about it. It is contradictory to say that something can be real, but that it is not true that it is real. However, apart from thought there can be no truth. It is inconsistent to say that something is true but that no mind or thought understands it or apprehends it to be true. For example, it is contradictory to say that it is true that matter exists independently of any mind's apprehension of matter. If matter truly exists, certain judgments concerning it are also true. But ideas and judgments themselves are products of mind. The reality of matter can only be proved by establishing the truth of definite *ideas* or judgments concerning it, e.g., that water boils at 100° centigrade, that all bodies fall with an acceleration due to gravity.

The idealist does not deny that matter exists; what he does deny is that matter can be without mind, or that matter is an unknowable substance opposed to mind. Matter can only be known in terms of ideas a mind has of its color, size, motion, and other properties. It is contradictory to say that matter or anything else is real but unknowable, because such a statement would mean that it is not known by the absolute truth or infinite mind. Materialism is therefore a false philosophy since it is incomplete and inconsistent. It is incomplete because it is unable to reduce mind to matter or explain how any unthinking matter can know anything at all. It is inconsistent because it falsely regards its idea of matter as something different from an idea.

Absolute idealism, in maintaining that reality forms an infinite system of truth which is mental or spiritual in quality, is also able to furnish an explanation of man's destiny. It can treat each individual person as an integral part of an eternal spiritual existence. It therefore should be able to justify an absolute moral and religious interpretation of existence. Royce's moral and religious philosophy is not a mere extension of his total system; rather, it shows in a practical way the meaning of the absolute and the significance of reason in all important walks of life. In a similar way, Royce's metaphysical concern with the question of reality is not an abstract, intellectual exercise remote from practical life. Royce's absolute, as a primary metaphysical principle, must not be thought of as a static and empty abstraction. The absolute is a single unity, but it is also a rich plurality. The absolute is not a simple unity but a complex one, having an infinity of parts which mirror the infinity of the whole. The absolute is not a static abstraction since it contains dynamically changing parts. But these parts are living conscious thoughts, and the absolute itself is an infinitely developed consciousness. It is absolute activity and not passivity—activity of struggle in the achievement of rational purpose on an infinite scale.

MORALITY AND THE STRUGGLE WITH EVIL Royce agreed with Peirce that philosophy must be kept at the level of rational inquiry, that every philosophic idea or concept must satisfy the most exacting tests of logical thought. Philosophy cannot abandon logic for the sake of poetic insight, practical success, or even religious faith. In this sense, Royce stands with Peirce as one of the first great American thinkers to defend the integrity and high intellectual standards of philosophical study. But Royce also agreed with James that philosophy must have practical application, that it must bear upon the real concerns of human life. Philosophy cannot be a mere intellectual exercise or academic pursuit, but must provide us with a way of life, a rational guide to conduct. In this sense Royce is, with James, one of the first American thinkers to defend the practical importance of philosophical thinking for morality and religion.

The moral philosophy of Josiah Royce is a good illustration of his absolute pragmatism, or his attempt to show that human conduct or practical action is susceptible to guidance and explanation through the use of logic. In his first major philosophic work, *The Religious Aspect of Philosophy*, Royce considered both the theoretical and practical sides of morality. He was concerned with the questions, How can we really know what is morally good? and How can this good be put into practice? His later works indicate his untiring attention to the difficult problems of stating the moral principle with exactness and giving it full application to the details of experience. He desired to show that although genuine morality cannot be derived from experience, it must nevertheless pertain to experience. Real morality, like genuine truth, must be eternal, must be of absolute value. Yet a true morality cannot be simply "up in the clouds," it must give us duties and values that work in our temporal life.

Throughout his major works Royce resisted the charge made by James that idealism can give us only a tender-minded moral outlook. Royce thought it necessary for idealism to face up to the difficult problem of evil in the world. Philosophy, if it is true to life, can neither give blind acceptance to evil nor simply explain it away by painting a veneer of abstract reasoning over it. Philosophy must contend with the problem of evil by understanding its innermost nature. Any moral or religious philosophy would be incomplete and even dishonest if it did not tackle this problem.

Royce's complete moral philosophy cannot be found in any single volume. However, *The Philosophy of Loyalty*, published in 1908, contains the most complete formulation of his view. In earlier works he showed that the problems of morality are essentially dialectical in character, that moral perplexities grow out of conflicts in thinking and living, and that a resolution or synthesis can be attained only by rational methods. Conflicts of interest, warring demands, and even indecision based on uncertainty of what is really good beset the human condition. As a consequence, any moral philosophy that does not expose and explain all the difficulties that lie in man's attempt to find and live the moral life will be superficial and inadequate.

It is essential to the systematic makeup of Royce's moral philosophy that it carefully consider a long line of objections to a morality based on reason. Foremost among these are the problems of skepticism and evil. Moral or religious skepticism may, in fact, be based on an inability to account for the great evil and suffering in the world. The good may seem to suffer along with, or even instead of, the bad. In *The Problem of Job*, Royce cites the ancient biblical story as a definite instance of a profound moral perplexity. Job suffers terrible pains and hardships, yet he is a good man. The apparent injustice of Job's suffering raises the question whether there is any moral order at all, or whether man is not the victim of unlucky fate or accidents over which he has no power. If we look to experience and survey the lot of mankind, there is ample evidence to suggest the pessimistic conclusion that man is born to suffer and then to die. What then are we to say about moral pessimism and skepticism?

Royce admits that if our moral outlook is based on experience alone, there can be no real answer to the skeptic or pessimist. The fact that things have been bad or that interests and values conflict does not, of course, prove that they must continue the same way. But if we appeal only to finite experiences, there can be no guarantee of any victory over evil. The piecemeal optimism of William James comes to just this: although it seems to give a fighting chance to victory over evil, it really does not do so; this victory could only be partial at best. James' piecemeal progress is only a compromise with pessimism and is, therefore, no real victory over it. Man's moral aspirations can be as easily dashed by compromising them as by aiming them too high. According to Royce, the mystic gives himself (and us) false hopes by his too lofty aspirations. The mystic requires a world where evil and suffering do not really occur; they are merely illusions for him. The mystical view of swallowing up evil, or having it evaporate in the unity of being, is simply a confusion. We cannot deny evil and suffering if we want to be complete and honest in our moral outlook.

However, it is also false to make a compromise with any form of pessimism. Mystical optimism is unsatisfactory because it is unreasoned, uncritical, and unmindful of the facts. Piecemeal optimism is unsatisfactory because it is mindful of the facts alone and accepts a compromise without thinking carefully about the principles or assumptions implicated in the facts. We must always remember, according to Royce, that whenever we come to a conclusion or make a judgment we have made assumptions or have interpreted certain postulates. Every interpretation involving assumptions logically extends beyond any finite experience. For example, if we draw the conclusion of the pessimist and despair of finding any real good in life, we have necessarily drawn a conclusion which no finite experience, however large, can justify. The pessimist must come to his conclusion *a priori* if he wants to stand by it at all. But the same principle holds if we take the position of piecemeal optimism, which is actually a compromise between the best and the worst. If we draw the conclusion of James' piecemeal optimism, and hope to find only an incomplete good in the moral life, then again we have drawn a conclusion which cannot ever be justified by finite experience. Like the pessimist, James must come to his conclusion *a priori* if he wants to uphold it.

Royce maintains that we cannot avoid the *a priori* in coming to any conclusion regarding morality. The philosophic problem is to see exactly how consistent our conclusions are with all the facts and with all the assumptions we have to make when we interpret them. It can then be shown that when we trace out the logical consequences of any of our interpretations of the problems of morality, we can only come to one rational conclusion which would be the absolute truth in morals. All roads must lead to the absolute, since, if we are consistent, we cannot help but see more and more of the infinite whole wherein all facts of the moral life are viewed in proper perspective.

Of all paths to the absolute moral truth, perhaps the most difficult and dramatic are those that start from either the problem of skepticism or the problem of evil. Skepticism arises in morals when we conclude that we cannot find any standard that will be everlastingly good and that will harmonize possible conflicts of values. But this means that the moral skeptic has tried to find the absolute moral truth, but thinks that he has failed. He also assumes that his failure is objective and not due to some personal defect. But already the contradiction begins to appear. The skeptic is safe from contradiction as long as he looks for the real or absolute truth and locates any failure in himself or in his apprehension of the absolute moral standard. But when the skeptic concludes that there is no way to harmonize ethical conflicts, no way to standardize moral conduct completely, he draws an absolute conclusion in defiance of the absolute moral truth. The skeptic comes to a final decision not because he has examined all the evidence or the whole logical range of his assumptions, but simply because he has given up any complete investigation of the matter. His conclusion is not really final, then, and the contradiction in his skepticism is that he comes to the absolute conclusion that no absolute truth is to be found in ethics. If he were consistent he would see that he already admits the absolute truth in his absolute denial.

The problem of evil, according to Royce, is both moral and religious. The struggle to understand and win out over evil pertains to man's relation to man, as well as to his relation to the universe and his destiny therein. Evil may include natural catastrophes such as disease or earthquakes that inflict untold suffering and death on human beings, or it may include malicious actions of men where many innocent persons become victims. The question is, Why should evil exist at all, and how can the existence of evil even be explained, let alone justified?

It is dishonesty or false philosophy to deny the existence of evil and suffering. Any philosophy that claims relevance to the facts cannot make this denial. And any philosophy that conceives reality in infinite terms must somehow make room for the bad as well as the good, for vice as well as virtue. It becomes apparent, according to Royce, that the more we try to define or conceive the good, the more definite would have to be our conception of what is bad. The man who truly understands what good is certainly must know what good is not. In terms of knowledge, our understanding of what is morally good would be empty if it contained no reference to facts of evil. "If moral evil were simply destroyed and wiped away from the external world, the knowledge of moral goodness would also be destroyed." [19] This means that the fact of moral evil is logically necessary for a knowledge of what is morally good. The same principle applies to fallacies in logic, or errors in regard to knowledge in general. If there were no fallacies in reasoning we would not understand what valid reasoning really is. Truth and error, good and bad, are correlative terms; we cannot understand the one without the other. However, even if we admit that moral evil is necessary in order to understand what the moral good is, what practical or specifically moral value can there be in moral evil? The fact that it has a logical or epistemological function does not prove that it has a moral function or that its existence can be morally justified.

Royce took this problem of the moral justification of evil seriously and gave his attention to its proper solution in many of his major works. First, it should be noted that moral truth, if there be any, cannot be separated from the whole or absolute truth. There can be no contradiction between truths, however difficult it may be to show how they are properly harmonized. Therefore, if there is such a thing as moral truth at all, and if a knowledge of moral evil is necessary for a knowledge of what is morally good, then in some way the existence of moral evil is necessary in order to have the true moral good. However, moral evil is itself not morally good. To assert that it is would be an absurd contradiction. What is morally good, according to Royce, is not evil itself, but the struggle to overcome it. It is morally good that evil should exist to be conquered. Courage, for example, would not exist as a moral virtue if there were no evil to overcome, no hardships and suffering to be conquered. This, according to Royce, is the only sense in which evil can be morally justified, as something over which it is good to win victory. The moral life of man cannot be likened to an ostrich sticking its head in the sand. Real virtue cannot be obtained without struggle and effort. Moral excellence only shows itself by its ability to face problems and deal with them courageously, instead of withdrawing from them.

However, all would be meaningless if evil could not be completely overcome. The struggle with evil takes on moral value only if the hope of complete victory can be rationally justified. Is there any logical guarantee that the struggle over evil to attain the complete moral good will meet with genuine success? Is there any absolute moral principle that is universally valid in theory and humanly possible in practice?

In *The Philosophy of Loyalty*, Royce attempted to prove that the supreme or universally valid principle of morality is what he called "loyalty to loyalty." He sought to show that all moral virtues—such as justice, honesty, and courage—were only particular forms of loyalty.

However, since not all forms of loyalty serve truly good causes (one can be loyal to a bad cause), only loyalty to loyalty itself could stand as the proper goal of all moral actions.

Royce found that loyalty is embodied in a great multitude of human actions. It can be found wherever someone is true to a cause: the soldier or plain citizen is loyal to his country, the parent is loyal to his family, the religious person is devoted to his religion, and even the criminal is faithful to his confederates. The existence and need for loyalty in humans is quite apparent, according to Royce. Loyalty is, therefore, a practical, social fact. It is practical because it definitely shows itself in action and requires action in order to exist. It is social because "if one is a loyal servant of a cause, one has at least possible fellow-servants." [20] Loyalty binds individuals together in a common cause.

Therefore, Royce argues that loyalty is impossible without self-control. The loyal individual cannot follow his own selfish desires, but must often sacrifice his own demands in order to serve a cause. However, loyalty can never be wholly impersonal in character. One cannot be devoted to something which is devoid of personal meaning. One cannot be loyal to a mere abstract principle or to a sheer impersonal power. Therefore, he defines loyalty as "the willing and practical and thoroughgoing devotion of a person to a cause." [21] In some sense loyalty must be voluntarily accepted by an individual; a person cannot be forced to be loyal. Loyalty is essentially inner directed or involves the exercise of a person's free will. The autonomous character of loyal action is logically necessary if the individual is to bear any responsibility for his action. However, loyalties do conflict with one another, people can be loyal to morally bad causes. Soldiers in war can be loyal to their respective countries, yet kill one another. People may be deceived into following evil causes. In short, a principle is needed to explain how conflicting loyalties can be overcome and how the service to morally bad causes can be detected and corrected.

Royce argues that when a loyal person follows a bad cause, or when two loyalties conflict with one another, there is, nevertheless, something morally good in the service of loyalty itself. Of course, it would be better if the person who follows a bad cause could instead follow a good one. But even the serving of a bad cause contains the germ of real moral worth, since the individual is loyal. He is morally responsible for his action, and he exercises his free will; this is not only morally good, but absolutely necessary for any moral value. If a person could not devote himself to any cause whatever, if he could not be loyal at all, he would not be a free moral agent. However, when we ask why any particular form of loyal service is bad, or why conflicts between loyalties are not good, the only answer that can rationally be given is that they are incomplete loyalties. Suppose one is loyal to a band of murderers. Why is this not really good? Simply because in being loyal to this cause, other loyalties are destroyed or prevented from existing. Any specific cause can conflict with some other. Loyalty to our country, for example, may require that we destroy the loyalties of our enemies. Consequently, the principle of morality cannot be defined in terms of devotion to a limited or specific cause.

The only acceptable principle of morality is that of loyalty to loyalty itself. This principle implies the devotion to the cause of all loyalties that can be made consistent with one another. According to Royce, the more that men devote themselves to the cause of loyalty itself, the more every individual life will flourish and be allowed freedom. True morality, therefore, not only requires the devotion of individuals to some cause, but it requires a devotion to loyalty as the one supreme cause that binds all individuals together. Loyalty to loyalty involves an infinite community of free individuals united in a single cause. Each individual not only preserves his identity and freedom, but under the principle of loyalty to loyalty each individual contributes to the welfare and life of every other individual.

Royce's absolute moral principle is also a religious principle and a standard of perfection for man's whole social life. Loyalty to loyalty is not a mere formal, abstract concept, but requires reference to the facts of experience to give it meaning. Man's religious, political, legal, economic, and intellectual life—in fact all of human existence—involves a community life. Man apart from any community cannot really be defined or known. Rational insight, therefore, is required to understand how the plurality of many individuals and groups can be harmonized and conceived under one universal form. In his latter years especially, Royce devoted himself to the difficult philosophic problem of defining and explaining the absolute as an infinite community of definite individuals and rational interpretations.

RELIGIOUS INSIGHT AND THE
INFINITE COMMUNITY

Royce insisted that pragmatism, empiricism, realism, and naturalism were all incomplete and essentially defective as philosophies. None of them can give us the proper insight into the whole or absolute truth, so none of them can give us either genuine religious insight or a perfect understanding of humanity. Pragmatism correctly interprets all ideas as plans of action, in terms of their useful workings. But pragmatism does not carry its conception far enough to see that an absolute or infinitely long run of consequences is necessary to determine the complete meaning and truth of ideas. No finite or short run of practical consequences is sufficient to prove the truth of any idea. Empiricism as a philosophy correctly demands that all ideas must be meaningful in terms of experience. But whose experience, we may ask, and what is meant here by experience?

Man's experiences are notoriously limited, and no one directly experiences the past, the future, or other people's experiences. Unless experience here means absolute experience or the infinitely extensive experience of an absolute mind or consciousness, it will be incomplete as a criterion. Empiricism tends to treat the *a priori* as opposed to experience. However, the *a priori* really means rational experience or thinking that consistently carries out the logical implications of ideas. *A priori* truths require an infinite number of finite experiences to establish them. Mathematics uses *a priori* constructions to establish truths that no finite experiences could ever prove. We can know *a priori* that there are an infinite number of odd numbers, that the series 1, 3, 5, 7 . . . has no upper limit. This is a definite fact, but finite empiricism is unable to account for it, as it is unable to account for any absolute or infinite truths.

Realism, on the other hand, correctly demands that true ideas must have an objective reference. True ideas must correspond with the facts. But realism falsely demands that the facts must have existence independent of any mind. Royce admits that the real facts must be independent of what you or I or any finite mind interprets them to be, but holds that they cannot be independent of interpretation by an absolute mind. Real facts that are independent of any mind's grasp of them would be absolutely unknowable. But no facts are truly unknowable, although they may be unknown to any finite experience. We contradict ourselves when we claim that reality is in any way unknowable. To draw any limits to knowledge we must already pass beyond those limits to say that there is something beyond it. If the unknowable is claimed as a real fact, we already know something about it if we claim to know that it exists. How do we know that there is anything unknowable? Merely to raise the question, according to Royce, is to see that we contradict ourselves if we adopt the philosophy of realism and say that reality exists independently of knowledge or mind.

Finally, naturalism is correct in maintaining that the real world must be such that the natural sciences give us more and more reliable knowledge of it. Philosophy cannot ignore nor contradict the careful work and findings of physics, biology, and chemistry. However, naturalism goes astray in claiming that the finite natural world is the sole reality. Naturalism has too narrow a conception of reality since it does not see that the natural sciences themselves require reference to and postulates of an infinite or absolute order of facts. "The acceptance of our natural sciences, as valid interpretations of connections of experience which our form of consciousness forbids us directly to verify, logically presupposes, at every step, that such superhuman forms and unities of consciousness are real." [22] The well-confirmed laws of science require an infinitely long run of verifications that no finite, natural experience can ever show. Science must postulate an absolute truth which it must approximate more and more. Such an absolute or infinite truth is both superhuman and supernatural, according to Royce. However, he also holds that "there is positively no need of magic, or of miracle, or of mysterious promptings from the subconscious, to prove to us the reality of the human and of the supernatural, or to define our reasonable relations with it." [23] Dialectical reason or *a priori* thinking shows us the rational character of the superhuman or supernatural, since it acquaints us with an infinite order of truths that consistently extends beyond our finite experiences and the temporal or natural world.

Religion absolutely requires the superhuman or supernatural according to Royce. If man's finite life or temporal existence could completely satisfy him, then man would have no need of religion. However, man's natural existence is incomplete and unsatisfying. Man has need to realize his potentialities and ideals which are continually frustrated by his natural and limited existence. Every person is a distinct individual, yet no one is able to realize his complete individuality in his natural lifetime. Man longs to be completely free and happy, but his natural existence affords him neither complete freedom nor enduring happiness. Man's need for the absolute, and proper insight into its significance, is most apparent in his need for religion. Man needs salvation not merely in some limited way, but in an absolute way, yet his life is full of obstacles that make his salvation seem remote or even impossible. The questions which Royce continued to probe in his philosophy are, What are the real sources of religious insight? What will give us a genuine understanding of our religious ideals? In dealing with these questions he argues that the proper meaning of what is divine can only be disclosed by rational interpretation. The divine is indeed something ideal to man, but "man needs no miracles to show him the supernatural and the super-human." [24] Idealism as a philosophy can indicate the sources of religious insight only by maintaining a broad and rational viewpoint. Some forms of idealism appeal to irrational sources of religious insight.

It will be remembered that the idealism of Jonathan Edwards found reason insufficient and required recourse to special revelation and miraculous conversion. Emerson's idealism required intuition and mystical insight that passed beyond logical evidence. Royce cannot allow that any genuine insight into religion can follow from mere mystical intuition or miraculous revelation. Religious insight, if it is allowed to exist, must be open to rational methods of testing and interpretation. But he was also opposed to any view of religion which excluded social factors. For example, he argued against James' treatment of religion as an affair primarily concerning the individual. "James is indeed wrong then to neglect the social roads that lead toward the experience of what one takes to be divine." [25] Man in isolation from all society or from any community life would have neither religious insight nor religious need. It is not an accident of history nor an expedient of life that creates churches or organized bodies of religion. Nor is it a mystery why organized religion has had its failures and imperfections. Religion and religious insight are impossible without loyalty. The religious person or group must be devoted to its divine cause. This devotion is both practical and social. It involves the performance of certain actions in accordance with its beliefs, and it involves certain attitudes and forms of behavior toward other individuals. Therefore, Royce argues that "however far you go in loyalty, you will never regard your loyalty as a mere morality. It will also be in essence a religion." [26] Hence, he holds that "loyalty is a source not only of moral but religious insight." [27] Loyalty is a source of moral insight when the principle of loyalty to loyalty is realized as the supreme principle of all moral action.

In a similar way, loyalty becomes a genuine source of religious insight when it is realized that loyalty to loyalty involves what Royce calls the Invisible Church. "I call the community of all who have sought for salvation through loyalty the Invisible Church." [28] Man's moral life and his religious life are not separate or isolated, according to Royce, but are both united under the absolute or infinite community of loyalty. A genuine community is more than a collection of people. It is essentially a historical phenomenon, having both a past and a future which are connected with one another through the lives of its individual members who remember a common past and aspire to a common purpose or future goal. A community requires a time process in order to come into being, but only an eternity of time will suffice to enable any truly religious or moral community to realize itself fully or reach its goal. On the temporal side, men serve their fellow men in order to serve their conception of the divine. But, religion or religious insight also recognizes the existence of suffering and its meaning for salvation. Suffering and service have religious meaning only to the extent that man is related to others, including the divine, who care about and share his suffering. Religion is impossible without ultimate concern for the plights of those seeking salvation. In order to be truly religious this ultimate concern must be both practical and absolute in character. It must be practical in the sense of carrying over into action. Without actual deeds religious concern would be an empty name. But further, this concern must be complete or total; it cannot simply represent a narrow or partial interest. Religious commitment or concern can stop short of nothing save the infinite community in which all lives are harmonized.

In his later works, especially in *The Problem of Christianity*, Royce undertook to reinterpret the traditional ideas and symbols of Christianity in the light of his own system of philosophy. He sought to give a rational interpretation to what he took to be the universal message of the Christian religion. Christianity involves a religion of hope in spite of the deep-seated existence of sin and suffering in the world. Royce has a positive interpretation of sin and suffering: they are necessary because complete salvation can only be won by overcoming them. Like Edwards, he interpreted sin as a metaphysical necessity bound up with man's finite condition. However, unlike Edwards, Royce did not view man as utterly depraved and absolutely unworthy of salvation except through mercy. For Royce, perfect justice requires that men suffer in order to be saved. If men did not suffer or experience alienation, they would have no need of salvation. But if men were not saved, then there would be no rational point to their suffering or alienation. Royce was a rationalist to such an extent that even in matters of religion all conflicts had to be resolved, all disparities harmonized in the absolute.

True religion, then, requires an infinite community of individuals that shall be united and harmonized under the principle of loyalty to loyalty. But this infinite community signifies a unified secular life as well. Royce's concept of the infinite community includes man's whole social life in its political, economic, and educational context. Political problems, economic conflicts, and educational struggles all involve a community of interpretation that must be viewed as infinite and rational.

Throughout his career Royce spoke out on particular American problems, as well as world problems. He saw his philosophy of idealism as applicable to such urgent problems as racial prejudice, industrialization and collectivism, and the outbreak of the First World War. These questions illustrated serious challenges to his absolute idealism. They raised the problem of how thought or reason could deal with violence and the seemingly irrational factors of life. Royce saw that many of these social problems—prejudice, industrialization, war—would increase in proportion to the growth and greater complexity of man's social life. He also saw that any meaningful solution of these problems depended upon a system of rational interpretation. He noted that progress in science resulted from the cooperation of a continuing community of dedicated workers in the field. Science, for Royce, was progressive specifically because it was social in character. By extending interpretation further and further, science progressively turns back the seemingly irrational and makes it more intelligible. It looks at more facts, and it looks at them more carefully. It never stops at raw data and never accepts any limited viewpoint as final. Yet it always assumes that things have an intelligible explanation and that there is a complete truth.

The same method or principle also applies to man's entire social life, according to Royce. Man's social life can be truly progressive if it is interpreted as forming an infinite, rational community. Each existing defect in society should never be viewed as final, but as something to be overcome. Racial prejudice can indeed be surmounted by improved understanding or education. Wars can be overcome by analyzing differences of viewpoint and by devising ways of settling smaller disputes before they accumulate into ones that are too massive. What is final, of course, is the deed that is done. It is an absolute truth that a completed act cannot be undone. But this does not mean that it has to be repeated. Nothing is more apparent in man's social life than the absolute character of social mistakes. However, each mistake implies a lesson that can be learned from thought and proper experience. Mistakes are pointless only if they do not give rise to improved ways of dealing with things.

There is no easy or automatic answer to such problems as racial prejudice, collectivism, or mass society; the only hope of real solution lies in what Royce calls rational interpretation. All interpretation is dialectical (see also pp. 165–173), and interpreting social problems, therefore, requires the three essential terms of *thesis, antithesis,* and *synthesis.* For example, in race problems we must understand the point of view of the victims of prejudice (as one term); the point of view of those holding the prejudice (as a second term); then we must transcend both and find a third term, a higher point of view from which a clearer understanding of the whole problem can take place. Every opposition must have a rational synthesis if we carry our interpretation far enough. Mass society, for example, presents a threat to the individual. But at the same time it compels man to develop his talents in ways to make richer uses of things. "The more the social will expresses itself in vast organizations of collective power, the more are individuals trained to be aware of their own personal wants and choices and ideals, and of the vast opportunities that would be theirs if they could but gain of these social forces." [29] Life involves struggle, and man's social existence is no exception to this rule. Dialectically, the greatest social values show themselves only by their power or ability to overcome injustices, deficiencies, and evils of all kinds. Any opposition between the individual and mass society or individualism and collectivism is triadic or dialectical in character, requiring a third term or a higher synthesis to be found that will reconcile the other two opposing terms. Dialectical reason or rational interpretation applies to all social problems. However, any rational interpretation requires reference to an infinite community of interpretation, as no finite or limited synthesis can ever be final.

Royce also viewed philosophical activity as dialectical, as requiring reference to an infinite community of interpretation. But he deplored the lack of cooperation and mutual enlightenment among philosophers. Philosophy has not been as progressive as science, according to Royce, because it has not produced as good a community of cooperating inquirers.

The philosophers differ sadly among themselves. They do not at present form a literal human community of mutual enlightenment and of growth in knowledge, to any such extent as do the workers in the field of any one of the natural sciences. The philosophers are thus far individuals rather than consciously members one of another. [30]

Royce's great hope for philosophy, as well as for mankind, was that obstacles to cooperation and unity could be rationally overcome by great effort and struggle. There would be no point to philosophical controversy or any human conflict if a higher synthesis could not eventually be achieved. The history of idealism as a philosophy shows in an imperfect manner, as do other movements in philosophy, that progress through cooperation is definitely possible. Royce refused to view any philosophy or any human problem in isolation from any other. He required that all philosophy and all lives be seen as collectively forming their definite part in the infinite community of rational interpretation, since only in this way could an absolutely satisfactory or complete truthfulness be found for all.

THE SIGNIFICANCE AND INFLUENCE OF ROYCE   Josiah Royce is still America's most important and influential idealist philosopher. Through his systematic writings, lectures, and long teaching career at Harvard, Royce succeeded in influencing a good number of other thinkers and students and helped to bring American philosophical thought to a higher degree of sophistication and maturity. Along with James he was one of the first to recognize the importance of Peirce's philosophy. It is important to see the manner in which Royce criticized pragmatism as well as the way in which he incorporated many of its ideas into his philosophy. Royce sided with pragmatism insofar as it treated all ideas or opinions as plans of action, as purposes upon which one is prepared to act. His philosophy, therefore, is concerned with action and practical consequences. We may even say that he transformed idealism by trying to make it as pragmatic, or practical, as possible. However, Royce's achievement is unique because he developed an absolute pragmatism, or a philosophy of action which was subordinate to a fixed and ultimate truth. He criticized pragmatism for its incompleteness and for what he took to be its inconsistencies. In fact, his analyses of pragmatism, along with those of Santayana, represent some of the most trenchant criticisms made by any American philosopher.

Royce's whole approach to philosophy was scholarly as well as voluntaristic. He demanded that philosophy should be thoroughly aware of its own significant past and should carry the responsibility of furnishing a rational guide for all human action. As Royce conceived it, philosophy was for the people as well as for the scholar. Consequently, in his books and lectures he addressed the general public as well as fellow philosophers. He influenced other American idealists such as W. E. Hocking, G. H. Howison and J. Loewenberg. He supervised Santayana's Ph.D. dissertation at Harvard and deeply affected the maturation of Santayana's philosophical thinking. As a close personal friend and colleague of William James, Royce exercised considerable influence on James' thought and caused him to rethink many of his basic ideas. Royce also influenced a number of other important philosophers and logicians, including C. I. Lewis, Henry Sheffer, and Morris Cohen. It was also he who "brought to Harvard the first instruction in symbolic and mathematical logic." [31]

Josiah Royce was elected president of the American Philosophical Association in 1903. In 1915 the Association honored him by a meeting at which papers were delivered by John Dewey, Morris Cohen, C. I. Lewis, W. E. Hocking, and others on various aspects of his philosophy. During 1918–1919 the eminent French philosopher Gabriel Marcel published a series of studies on Royce's metaphysics which has subsequently been recognized as one of the most penetrating analyses of Royce's thought made by any philosopher.

There is no doubt that with Royce's death in September of 1916 American idealism lost its leading light. Since the passing of Royce, philosophical idealism in America has not only been on the decline, but has almost faded out as a viable philosophical movement. Idealism in America, although it began with Edwards and flowered with Emerson and the transcendentalists, was really brought to its height of prestige and articulation by Josiah Royce. As a consequence, his philosophy attracted its greatest following during his lifetime. Idealism was later heavily attacked and eclipsed by realism, pragmatism, and naturalism. However, in recent years there has been evidence to suggest a certain revival of interest in the speculative and dialectical approach to philosophy which Royce promoted. Recently a significant number of studies have begun to appear on various aspects of Royce's philosophy, as well as reprints of his major works.

However, the fact remains that his reputation and significance has not grown with time, as Peirce's has. Peirce was largely neglected during his own time, but now his stature seems to be established as one of the greatest American philosophers. Royce, on the other hand, achieved his greatest eminence during his lifetime.

In large part, Royce's reputation as a philosopher suffers from the fact that idealism has declined as a major philosophic movement. But he also suffers because in effect he defended an older tradition in philosophy rather than starting a new one. He defended a speculative and absolute conception of philosophy which is largely out of tune with more recent times. Twentieth-century life in its political, religious, moral, and philosophic aspects has witnessed more dissatisfactions with and assaults on the "absolute" than any other century. Pragmatism, naturalism, and other anti-absolutistic views have therefore enjoyed a greater prestige and popularity in this century.

However, one cannot assess a philosopher simply in terms of his popularity or current prestige. Royce may be less important today for the general public and trained philosophers than Peirce or Dewey or Santayana or James. But this in itself does not negate his importance for the whole history of American philosophy. Royce's significance must be viewed in two different contexts. On the one hand, he represents an important link in the maturation of serious philosophical thought in America. With Royce, American philosophical scholarship reached a point of definite maturity never previously realized. On the other hand, his significance lies in the context of the dialectical and idealistic philosophy he so well wrote and practiced. Judged as an idealist, he must be rated very highly because he definitely increased the prestige of this kind of philosophy. He gave to idealism a tightly argued position that also claims close relevance to the facts. He therefore throws out a serious challenge to all those who would claim that dialectical reason is fruitless or that idealism cannot prove its case. Royce, we can say, will always appeal to those minds that still believe that philosophy can probe the absolute truth and yet teach us something new and important.

NOTES

1. Josiah Royce, *The World and the Individual, First Series,* p. 311, from Lecture VII, "The Internal and External Meaning of Ideas."

2. Josiah Royce, *The Philosophy of Loyalty,* pp. 16–17, from Lecture I, "The Nature and Need of Loyalty."

3. Josiah Royce, *The Sources of Religious Insight,* p. 203, from "The Religion of Loyalty."

4. *Ibid.,* p. 205.

5. Posthumously published as *Lectures on Modern Idealism.*

6. Josiah Royce, *The Problem of Christianity,* Vol. II, *The Real World and the Christian Ideas,* p. 255, from Lecture XII, "The World of Interpretation."

7. Josiah Royce, *The Spirit of Modern Philosophy,* p. 380, from Lecture XI, "Reality and Idealism."

8. *Ibid.,* p. 377.

9. Josiah Royce, *The World and the Individual, First Series,* pp. 510–511, from Supplementary Essay, "The One, the Many, and the Infinite."

10. *Ibid.,* p. 511.

11. See Josiah Royce, *William James and Other Essays on the Philosophy of Life,* Essay I, "William James and the Philosophy of Life."

12. Royce, *The Problem of Christianity*, Vol. II, *The Real World and the Christian Ideas*, p. 218, from Lecture XII, "The Will to Interpret."

13. Royce, *Lectures on Modern Idealism*, p. 238, from Lecture X, "Later Problems of Idealism and Its Present Position."

14. *Ibid.*, p. 251.

15. Royce, *The Sources of Religious Insight*, p. 89, from "The Office of the Reason."

16. Royce, *Lectures on Modern Idealism*, p. 254, from "Later Problems of Idealism and Its Present Position."

17. Josiah Royce, *The Religious Aspect of Philosophy: A Critique of the Bases of Conduct and of Faith*, p. 409, from Ch. XI, "The Possibility of Error."

18. *Ibid.*, p. 425.

19. Josiah Royce, *Studies of Good and Evil* (Hamden, Conn.: Shoe String, 1898), p. 24, from "The Problem of Job."

20. Royce, *The Philosophy of Loyalty*, p. 20, from Lecture I, "The Nature and Need of Loyalty."

21. *Ibid.*, pp. 16–17.

22. Royce, *The Sources of Religious Insight*, p. 270, from "The Unity of the Spirit and the Invisible Church."

23. *Ibid.*, p. 271.

24. *Ibid.*, p. 272.

25. *Ibid.*, p. 74, from "Individual Experience and Social Experience."

26. *Ibid.*, p. 206, from "The Religion of Loyalty."

27. *Ibid.*, p. 206.

28. *Ibid.*, p. 280, from "The Unity of the Spirit and the Invisible Church."

29. Royce, *The Problem of Christianity*, Vol. I, *The Christian Doctrine of Life*, p. 152, from Lecture III, "The Moral Burden of the Individual."

30. Royce, *The Problem of Christianity*, Vol. II, *The Real World and the Christian Ideas*, p. 254, from Lecture XIII, "The World of Interpretation."

31. Gabriel Marcel, *Royce's Metaphysics*, p. vi, from "Preface" by W. E. Hocking.

QUESTIONS FOR DISCUSSION

1. What does Royce say is wrong with pragmatism? Why does he describe his own philosophy as absolute pragmatism?

2. Why does Royce insist that philosophy must use dialectical reason? Why does he maintain that we need *a priori* truths?

3. Does Royce give adequate justification for his view that loyalty is basic to all moral values? Is his notion of loyalty to loyalty really a practical one?

4. Has Royce given a sound justification for the existence of evil? Is he correct in claiming that evil can serve as a moral good?

5. Does Royce present a good case for the belief that religion requires the "supernatural" and the "absolute"?

6. Why does Royce consider the idea of an infinite community of interpretation so important?

7. To what extent is Royce's rationalism and philosophy of the absolute able to meet objections of the kind James makes against rationalism and any absolute?

8. Does Royce's social and rational interpretation of religion offer a more plausible account than James' psychological and volitional approach?

9. What stature and place does Royce hold in the development of modern American philosophy?

SUGGESTED READINGS

The Spirit of Modern Philosophy. Royce's conception of the nature of philosophy; reality and idealism (General Introduction, Part 1); Royce's views that (1) the world is such stuff as *ideas* are made of, and (2) there is one absolute self or mind, consciously inclusive of all selves and all truth (Lecture XI).

Lectures on Modern Idealism. The concept of the absolute and the dialectical method (Lecture III).

The Religious Aspect of Philosophy. The doctrine of the total relativity of truth and error (Ch. 2, Part 2); the relation of religion and philosophy (Ch. 2); the general nature and religious uses of philosophical idealism (Ch. 10, Part 1).

The Philosophy of Loyalty. Nature and need of loyalty (Lecture I); loyalty to loyalty (Lecture III).

The Sources of Religious Insight. Answer to pragmatism (Part IV, Sec. 5).

The World and the Individual. The struggle with evil (Lecture IX).

William James and Other Essays in the Philosophy of Life. William James and the philosophy of life (Essay I).

Primary Sources

Josiah Royce, *Lectures on Modern Idealism* (New Haven, Conn.: Yale University Press, 1964).

———, *The Philosophy of Loyalty* (New York: Macmillan, 1908).

———, *The Problem of Christianity*, 2 vols. (New York: Macmillan, 1913).

———, *The Religious Aspect of Philosophy: A Critique of the Bases of Conduct and of Faith* (Boston: Houghton Mifflin, 1885).

———, *The Sources of Religious Insight* (New York: Scribner's, 1940).

———, *The Spirit of Modern Philosophy* (Boston: Houghton Mifflin, 1920).

———, *William James and Other Essays in the Philosophy of Life* (New York: Macmillan, 1911).

———, *The World and the Individual*, Gifford Lectures, 2 vols. (New York: Macmillan, 1900–1901).

Secondary Sources

J. E. Creighton, *Papers in Honor of Josiah Royce on His Sixtieth Birthday* (New York, 1916).

Peter Fuss, *The Moral Philosophy of Josiah Royce* (Cambridge, Mass.: Harvard University Press, 1965).

Gabriel Marcel, *Royce's Metaphysics* (Chicago: H. Regnery, 1956).

John E. Smith, *Royce's Social Infinite: The Community of Interpretation* (New York: Liberal Arts Press, 1950).

7 *George Santayana*

Naturalism and Detachment

George Santayana (1863–1952) is the philosopher with by far the broadest cultural background and the most polished literary style that America has yet produced. Born in Spain, Santayana came to the United States at the age of nine and was educated at the Boston Latin School and Harvard University. He pursued his graduate studies in philosophy at Harvard under the guidance of both James and Royce and joined them in 1889 to form what was for about twenty years Harvard's, and perhaps America's, most renowned department of philosophy. His attachment to academic life and professional scholarship, however, was never very strong. In fact, at the age of fifty and at the height of his academic career, Santayana left Harvard to write, travel, and live in Europe for the remainder of his life.

From his earliest published works a definite note of philosophical detachment from nationalities, institutions, and schools of philosophy is apparent in Santayana's basic attitude. This aloofness must not be taken for a mere idiosyncrasy or subjective bias in Santayana since it is critically incorporated into the formation of his entire system of philosophy. Unlike Emerson, whose mystical detachment from life was poetic or romantic and based on intuition rather than analysis, Santayana deliberately, critically, and philosophically cultivated a sophisticated aloofness from life in the manner of Aristotle and the classical Greek tradition. He did this for the sake of understanding life as well as for a rational estimation of values.

191

Like Peirce, Santayana viewed philosophy as essentially involving critical thinking and therefore requiring an objective perspective or distance from matters considered. But unlike Peirce, Santayana did not believe that philosophy was a science. Science is more specialized in its aims and methods than philosophy. Science does not present us with a way of estimating values and does not offer us a conception of the good life. From the time of the ancient Greeks, philosophy was essentially a pursuit of wisdom, an attempt to know and live by that which is really worth knowing and caring for. Santayana accepted this classical definition of philosophy and sought to interpret it in the light of the modern world and careful criticism. To be a pursuit of wisdom, philosophy must cultivate both critical understanding and imaginative appreciation. Philosophy can neither become intoxicated with nor desensitized to the world and its possible values. Philosophy must detach itself from existence in order to bring it into proper focus, but it can never remove itself from the natural order of things. By cultivating his critical thought and imagination the philosopher can try to see what is worth seeing, but at the same time he must avoid being deceived. He must study the significant forms the world presents, but he should always be aware of the difference between form and substance, or symbolic meaning and literal truth. The symbols and myths of man's imaginative or aesthetic awareness should not be confused with the natural or material grounds of all existence. Man has a definite tendency to be carried away by the symbols he uses, the ideas he thinks, and the beauty he experiences. He confuses the way things appear with the way they really are. To mark off this important difference Santayana insists upon what he calls the distinction between *essence* and *existence*.

Essences are pure forms or qualities and as such are detached from the rush and changeability of existence. Essences alone can be directly present to consciousness, and they are the only things which are truly permanent and really recoverable amidst the flux of all temporal things. It is only the form or essence of things, not their material substances, that can actually enter our minds or come into our experiences. Whenever we are conscious of anything, even in our flights of fancy or our dreams, it is only the forms or essences of things that we possess. But whereas existence is remote, changing, and always receding from our grasp, the essences or forms of things are recoverable in memory and thought. Essences may be sensuous (the quality blue), abstract (the number ten), emotional (the quality of melancholy) and may possess any degree of complexity whatever (the idea of infinity). An essence is a universal type or form that is always immutable, whereas any existence is both particular and always subject to change.

The beginning of wisdom therefore is to be able to distinguish the eternal detached forms (essences) of things from their natural temporal ground (existence). To confuse essence with existence is to cut off our sensibility and imagination from undistracted appreciation as well as to distort any possible knowledge of the conditions and material circumstances that make our enjoyments possible. It is Santayana's view that "existence would not be worth preserving if it had to be spent exclusively in anxiety about existence." [1] Unless man can detach himself from existence and become absorbed in the enjoyment of timeless essences or forms, his life would not be worth having. The experience of beauty, for example, would be impossible without detachment since "the beautiful is itself an essence, an indefinable quality felt in many things." [2] Beauty is not itself a material thing or tangible existence, but simply a form or essence that material things may evoke in us. "The most material thing, in so far as it is felt to be beautiful, is instantly immaterialized, raised above external personal relations, concentrated and deepened in its proper being, in a word, sublimated into an essence." [3]

Essences, therefore, or pure enjoyable qualities are not out of place in a naturalistic philosophy. It would be out of place, however, to confuse mere essences or symbols with existing powers or substances. Naturalism would be incomplete as a philosophy if it restricted itself to what merely happens to exist. It would thereby lose all those possible themes which only the imagination and intellect may see. Naturalism therefore is consistent with detachment and prevents philosophy from being either deluded or too narrow. Pragmatism, in its preoccupation with existence, is too narrow, cutting off philosophy from the free play of imagination and aesthetic forms. Pragmatism involves an anxiety about existence and future verification which allows no place for essence and contemplation. Idealism, on the other hand, has the opposite fault of turning essences into existences by falsely giving them a literal, moral, religious, or metaphysical function which they can never have. Essences are symbols, not substances, and as such they are detached from all existence, not bodily involved in any of its workings.

Santayana's earliest philosophical works were concerned with the nature and meaning of poetry, religion, and beauty. He possessed and cultivated a greater sensitivity and knowledge of poetry and other aesthetic forms than perhaps any other American philosopher. His own poetry and prose, in fact, reflect the grace and balanced form which he admired so much in great works of art. Santayana's early fame and reputation rested in large measure on such finely wrought books as *The Sense of Beauty* (1896) and *Interpretations of Poetry and Religion* (1900). Here his charm and skill as a writer matched his philosophical probing and mastery of subject matter. Santayana's polished and graceful style of writing, which he cultivated as earnestly as he did his knowledge of philosophy, has established him as one of the very best of philosophical writers. He possessed a talent for finding the right word or phrase to articulate a complex thought, and insisted on saying things artfully. His longer philosophical works, as a consequence, abound in quotable statements or aphorisms which go to the heart of the themes he discusses. He valued artistry and vision above technical verbalisms or mere argumentation because he always saw philosophy as closer to art and poetry than to science. Some of his best works, therefore, are his short essays which offer critical and reflective interpretations of culture and men. His *Three Philosophical Poets*, published in 1910, has become a small classic, skillfully weaving together the philosophic themes and poetic visions of the poet-philosophers Lucretius, Dante, and Goethe. Santayana's essays on American life and thought, with their detached and critical appraisal of Emerson, James, Royce, and other men, reveal his keen interest in appraising and understanding the significant moments of American intellectual life. His *The Genteel Tradition in American Philosophy* (1911) and *Character and Opinion in the United States* (1920) must be counted as the *first* significant attempt to formulate and assess the development of philosophical thinking in America.

Santayana was sixty years old before he wrote his introduction to his system of philosophy, *Scepticism and Animal Faith*. This work articulated Santayana's theory of knowledge and served as an introduction to his ontology presented in the four-volume work, *Realms of Being*, completed in 1940. These two works contain not only the fruit of over twenty years of careful work, but present his philosophy at its most systematic and skillfully argued. Santayana continued to write and publish up until his death in October of 1952. In 1936 he published his noteworthy novel, *The Last Puritan*, in which the characters symbolize the major themes of naturalism and detachment in his basic philosophy. He never lost his vital concern with the themes of religion, society, or culture. In 1946 he published *The Idea of Christ in the Gospels*, and in 1951, *Dominations and Powers: Reflections on Liberty, Society and Government*.

Santayana's writing and publishing career spans a period of well over fifty years. In fact, his life may be said virtually to reside in his writings and contemplations. His writings were works of art as well as philosophy, but they also embodied a way of life. Basically, he held that the philosopher must detach himself from life in order to appreciate its beauty and understand its nature. A philosopher must seek to live an undistracted life of the mind, but at the same time he should never forget his animal basis or his naturalistic origin.

That Santayana wrote poetry, a novel, and many philosophical reflections concerning art and beauty must not be construed as implying that he advocated an aesthetic detachment from life for poetic or romantic purposes. Aesthetic detachment, as in the feeling of beauty or the appreciation of art, has its own value for Santayana, but this is to be distinguished from philosophy. For Santayana mere contemplation or aesthetic appreciation, no matter how beautiful or satisfying, is nevertheless not equivalent to knowing. Aesthetic detachment is a matter of feeling or imagination and is neither critical nor grounded in facts. Knowledge, on the other hand, is a matter of presumption, not feeling; understanding, not imagining; it must be grounded in the facts. Philosophical detachment must therefore involve a claim to knowledge or truth. In short, it must be grounded in or relevant to matters of fact. Knowledge and philosophic detachment must be indirect and based on criticism; without criticism no distinction between fact and fancy can be sustained. And if criticism is not to be left up in the air, it must assume or base itself upon the facts of the natural world.

The themes of naturalism and detachment are fundamental to Santayana's whole system of thought. They permeate his interpretations of religion, society, man, art, science, and the cosmos. Everything ideal has a natural basis and everything natural has an ideal development. The ideals of man's poetic imagination or rational thought cannot sever their connection with the natural world, but may in fact point out or suggest possible harmonies and fulfillments that might be achieved. Human reason itself can have no higher function than that of discerning, tracing and estimating the forms of all ideas and harmonies that may bring with them some genuine and enduring value to human nature. Santayana's naturalism does not reduce man to mere animal impulses or material facts. Man becomes humanized for Santayana to the degree that his biological needs are rationalized and idealized, and to the degree that the mind and imagination direct and cultivate the satisfaction of desires in orderly and meaningful ways. Society, religion, art, and science are viewed by Santayana as means by which man's basic nature may receive orderly direction and ideal development. Therefore, just as the biological need for warmth and shelter may serve as the natural basis for satisfying this need, the refinements of dress and the arts of building and decoration may become the ideal developments of these biological or natural needs.

Naturalistically, detachment is just as much a part of human life as involvement. Man is rational as well as animal, and therefore lives by his ideas as well as by his actions. Man detaches himself from the present by planning for the future and by surveying the past. However, the bare existence of detachment must be distinguished from its intelligent cultivation. The fine art of architecture may have grown out of the useful art of shelter building, and the science of geometry out of the useful art of earth measurement. However, the point is that these basic needs themselves are transformed by their ideal developments. Although architecture and geometry have a natural basis, it is more detached than those crafts out of which they may have developed. But at the same time, they have become more directly relevant to serving man's rational, aesthetic, and spiritual needs. According to Santayana, we speak of architecture or geometry as liberal arts because they are humanized and idealized and not directly controlled by the immediate needs of life. Man becomes liberated from life, not to the degree that he denies or annihilates his basic naturalistic impulses, but to the degree that he transforms them into ideal, orderly, and harmonious forms. Detachment is necessary for this idealization as it is necessary for what Santayana calls the "good life."

Philosophical detachment itself, therefore, has its natural basis as well as its ideal development. Philosophical thinking, as all thinking, stems from man's basic unreflective impulses. The point of philosophy is not to remove itself from this naturalistic basis but to transform these blind and chaotic impulses by careful, critical investigation. Just as astronomy may attempt to order our shortsighted and confused ideas about the heavens, so philosophy may try to take into consideration all ideas and experiences and attempt to put them into some meaningful conceptual order. Such philosophy will always be naturalistic in basis and humanistic in its ideal end. It can never forget its origin in the natural world and can never go beyond a rational and human interpretation of things that is commensurate with man's powers of observation and reason.

Santayana was extremely critical of the main drifts of American and European philosophy in the nineteenth century. He saw in these developments dependencies which to him indicated too strong an attachment either to the prevalent science or the religion of the day. Santayana identified Emerson and Royce and all forms of idealism with the romantic urge to put philosophy in the service of religion. Idealism was the grand attempt in philosophy to have the spiritual dominate the material. In attacking this idealist movement, Santayana evolved a philosophical realism and naturalism which significantly influenced and contributed to important philosophical developments of the twentieth century. He identified pragmatism, and especially James, with the urge to reform philosophy by buttressing it with the scientific method and by treating ideas as instruments whose truth-measure was found in their useful consequences. Santayana criticized pragmatism for what he called its anti-intellectual tendency to treat all ideas as processes having the simple purpose of adjusting one part of experience to another. This kind of philosophy was too permissive for Santayana as he saw in it the abandonment of rational discipline and dismissal of logical validity concerning ideas.

James, in making the basis of philosophy a matter of temperament and sentiment, had abandoned the critical detachment of philosophy as a life of reason for an "open air" policy that would be receptive to all impulses, however irrational. Santayana sharply distinguished understanding from adjustment, and viewed pragmatism as an attempt to identify the former with the latter. James and his pragmatism had succeeded in solving the traditional philosophical problems of idealism, materialism, rationalism, and empiricism only by dropping them as philosophical problems and by treating them as psychological ones. This psychologizing of philosophy is behind his classification of philosophers into tough-minded and tender-minded. Melioristic pragmatism is offered by James as a psychological solution to the problem of mental health—that it is healthy to balance being tough and factual with a tender-minded affection for moral ideals and religious values. While agreeing with James that Royce and idealism claimed too much for philosophy and represented a dogmatic commitment to sheer reason and mere dialectical argument, Santayana found that James abandoned reason prematurely and *in toto* without observing in what manner reason can be valid and useful in understanding the nature of things.

As teachers and colleagues at Harvard, both James and Royce provided Santayana with fruitful ideas and stimulation from which his own philosophy developed. In fact, it would not be an oversimplification to say that the elaboration of his naturalism and detachment, especially in *The Life of Reason*, represented his attempt to put forth and justify an alternative philosophy to both idealism and pragmatism, the leading philosophies in America in the last half of the nineteenth century. And in developing his conception of naturalism around the turn of the century Santayana succeeded in shaping, along with Dewey, some of the most important concepts of twentieth-century American philosophy.

THE LIFE OF REASON   In 1905 Santayana published the first comprehensive and systematic statement of his basic philosophic position in *The Life of Reason*. It is significant that the subtitle of this work was termed "The Phases of Human Progress," for Santayana attempted here to expound the view that human life receives its only genuine value in becoming harmonious and rational, and that the only terms in which this can take place are those of the natural world. *The Life of Reason* is concerned with those forms of human life which make life worthwhile, and with the means by which these forms can be achieved. Reason is understood throughout this work to be simultaneously an intelligent observer and an imaginative interpreter capable of enlightening and guiding the human animal in the process of living. Reason signifies animal sagacity raised to the power of discerning general patterns and symbolic forms on the one hand, and imagining ideal harmonies on the other. Reason is both intellect and imagination, that is, orderly or rational discernment.

The phases of human progress for Santayana include common sense, society, religion, art, and science. These terms are used in the broad sense to characterize the principal areas wherein life is genuinely satisfying because of the discernment and achievement of intelligible order and harmony. Although distinct, they are not separate or mutually exclusive. In fact, common sense is such a fundamental ordering of life that its presence must be felt in all the others. Within each main phase of human progress there will be alternative and various other orders.

Reason is present whenever a conscious attempt is made to achieve order. Santayana conceives the need for order to be a natural requirement of life at least insofar as experience becomes cumulative so that one strand of experience may be compared with another. Reason presupposes sensation, perception, memory, and imagination. Rational ideas or judgments at the level of common sense concerning persons, places, and things presupposes a common world or relatively permanent frame of reference in the midst of change and variability. Reason is inherently realistic in attempting to refer to or represent external phenomena. It is also inherently practical when it attempts to discern in the flux of existence those patterns of things that are useful and satisfying. Values are discovered when some relatively permanent good is seen as the result of comparison of immediately felt pleasures with distant or more remotely anticipated ones.

However, reason is itself never a literal presentation of a thing or event. Although realistic and based on perception and memory, it also includes imagination. Therefore, the language with which reason interprets and orders experience is often highly poetic and can never escape a metaphorical and emotionally colored rendition of things. In other words, ideas have an aesthetic as well as a cognitive side. We represent the world in terms that are pleasing to us as well as useful. This suggests that poetry, art, and religion are extensions of natural representation and imagination rather than freaks of nature or complete variants from common-sense representations of things.

If reason is present at the level of common sense in our ordinary judgments and understanding of persons, places, and things, it must also be present in what supports the life of common sense, namely society. Every society, for Santayana, has a natural basis and an ideal development. Common sense requires the representation by our ideas of a common world, and every society, however real or ideal, represents an attempt to achieve a common order of interests among individuals. In *Reason in Society* Santayana is intent on tracing the natural as well as the ideal elements necessary to anything that might be called social order. Although reason in some form is present in the organization necessary to any distinctively human society, in the rudimentary forms of social life it is most closely tied to the satisfactions of material wants. Reason and impulse have to be harmonized in order that love, family, or country may achieve a human organization. The most rudimentary order in society relates to satisfactions of man's animal needs, but also tends to serve rational or ideal ends. The family, for example, is a natural order of society as well as a rational one since within it the individual can learn moral ideals and friendship, and become liberalized to participate in a more extensive society outside it. Parental affection, though natural, also becomes idealized so that it may extend, for example, to patriotism. Patriotism, though limited, is nevertheless an ideal affection. And government, whether democracy, aristocracy, or whatever, represents an ideal order.

However, the more rational a social order, the more coherent and universal it tends to become, so that while the individual has roots in some particular, concrete social order, his affinities always extend beyond the limited and accidental bonds of family, locality, and country. The mind tends to find liberal satisfaction in finally detaching itself from all material societies and creates ideal companionships in symbolic societies which are more rational and coherent than any other. In religion, art, and science the rational side of man is liberalized and freed to join societies which transcend both time and space. In religious worship, artistic beauty, and scientific truth man is able to locate symbolic companionships which are more naturally satisfying because they are universal and unlimited. To Santayana, the best justification of any society or government is its tendency to promote the Life of Reason in its richest forms, that is, in religion, art, and science. The pursuit of wealth, security, or power is conceived as subservient to these more ideal ends.

Religion pursues the Life of Reason through the imagination. The Life of Reason is one, while religions are many. To the extent to which any religion is rational, it is a symbolic rendering of the meaning and value of human existence. But Santayana holds that while the symbolic interpretations of religion have great beauty and value when taken poetically, they lead to confusion, contradiction, and conceit when taken for literal transcriptions of reality. The factions and quarrels of religions with one another or with science are as irrational as they are unnecessary, representing as they do a confusion of the purpose of religion within a life of reason. Religion, like poetry, is an ideal rendering of the meaning and value of life, but never a literal report of matters of fact. What life should be and what can lend it eternal value are not matters of fact or history, but imaginative, symbolic interpretations. Thus the ideal goods which are the concern of religion can remain noble and beautiful when taken poetically, but they become debased and false when taken as an imaginative substitute for science.

Santayana, therefore, supports what he would call a rational and naturalistic religion and considers supernatural religion sheer poetry. He offers a purely natural interpretation of prayer and worship and construes immortality in ideal terms. "In rational prayer the soul may be said to accomplish three things important to its welfare: It withdraws within itself and defines its good, it accommodates itself to destiny and it grows like the ideal which it conceives." [4] Rational prayer is a form of contemplation for the purposes of piety and spirituality. Piety is a "man's reverent attachment to the sources of his being and the steadying of his life by that attachment." [5] The proper objects of piety for a naturalistic religion are those on which life and its interests depend: "parents first, then family, ancestors and country, finally humanity at large and the whole natural cosmos." [6] However, piety which looks toward the origins of man's existence is only one side of religion. Religion has a spiritual side that is concerned with an ideal end or what would fulfill man's existence. "Spirituality is nobler than piety, because what would fulfill our being and make it worth having is what alone lends value to that being's sources." [7]

The contemplative side of religion aspires to immortality. It seeks to transcend the accidents of space and time and live in the presence of the eternal. Every genuine ideal is a timeless object called "essence." [8] "He who lives in the ideal and leaves it expressed in society or in art enjoys a double immortality. The eternal has absorbed him while he lived, and when he is dead his influence brings others to the same absorption." [9]

Reason in Art is a vivid illustration of Santayana's basic principle that everything natural has an ideal end and every ideal has a natural basis. The vitality and the beauty of art indicate that rational action may leave traces in nature and enhance the conditions of human existence. Art is a sign of progress in a Life of Reason insofar as it shows to what degree matter can be shaped or given form in ways harmonious to human desires and uses. Accordingly, Santayana refuses to separate the utility of art from its aesthetic value. The fine arts of music, poetry, painting, or sculpture make beauty or the aesthetic element prominent, but they cannot do this rationally at the expense of the practical or the useful. Beauty is defined as objectified pleasure, pleasure regarded as the quality of a thing. Therefore, beauty is a very important type of harmony in life— one that is immediately pleasing or agreeable. Rationally considered, beauty or aesthetic pleasure is also useful to human beings and cannot properly be isolated as a separate good unrelated to other goods.

In a Life of Reason the immediate value of aesthetic goods must harmonize with other less direct values or goods. "If art is that element in the Life of Reason which consists in modifying its environment the better to attain its end, art may be expected to subserve all parts of the human ideal, to increase man's comfort, knowledge and delight." [10] This implies a repudiation of "art for art's sake," since considered rationally and naturalistically, art can have no other purpose than a human one. Though art is useful in securing human happiness, it is also good in itself. The point is that aesthetic values are only intrinsically or genuinely good insofar as they contribute to the perfection of human existence. Rational art then lies between two irrational extremes—spontaneous fancy and utility. Art without discipline is both senseless and useless, mere intoxication, while art that is useful and not graceful or aesthetically pleasing is tedious.

If science is common sense or knowledge extended and refined, it plays an indispensable role in the Life of Reason. Without a true conception of science the rational life will be both incomplete and confused. That is, within the Life of Reason both the capabilities and limitations of science must be understood if science is to be a genuine part of such a life.

Science is distinguished from myth in being capable of verification and correction whereas myth is not. "A chief characteristic of science, then, is that in supplementing given facts it supplements them by adding other facts belonging to the same sphere." [11] By extending and refining our ordinary perception of the world, science seeks verifiable truths that are quantitatively and qualitatively superior to common sense. Both the division of labor and the abstractions of science are understandable and precise. Science can be divided into natural or physical science on the one hand and formal or dialectical science on the other. The natural or physical sciences—physics, chemistry, biology, etc.—although *a posteriori*, nevertheless must make use of formal, abstract ideas to explain events in terms of general laws. "Natural science consists in general ideas which look for verification in events, and which find it." [12] The particular case is studied only to reveal the general rule or principle, but the general principle in natural science must be relevant to and correspond to the particular fact.

Physics or natural science is therefore a kind of applied dialectic or mathematics. Physics makes use of certain ideal mathematical formulas; it gives them a material interpretation. As such, the ideas of pure mathematics or pure dialectic have their validity independent of fact and sense perception. Logical or formal assertions have their validity in their consistency, not in their agreement with observation or fact. Hence, mathematical or formal relations can exist without observable instances. Formal science or dialectic, as Santayana calls it, is concerned only with the intent and consistency of abstract ideas. If all A is B and all B is C, then it logically follows that all A is C. In dialectic we set out to discover the necessary consequences of our assumptions or intentions. The only kind of truth involved in formal reasoning or dialectic is internal coherence or consistency. We try to be true to our intentions. Whether our assumptions or conclusions are true to the facts or in agreement with observation can only be determined by some added material assumption and investigation. This is exactly what the natural sciences are concerned with—not merely the consistency of ideas one with another, but also their agreement with observation.

Santayana views much of traditional philosophy and psychology as confusions of dialectical science with natural science. Natural science rightly uses dialectical relations as a means to an end, but never substitutes a mere formal relation for a material truth. However, what happens if natural facts and science are made means to the end of dialectical science? What happens if philosophy and psychology try to establish matters of fact or existence by mere rational thought or dialectic without observation or empirical evidence? The result is pseudo-science, metaphysics, or literary psychology. To prove dialectically or by reason alone in the manner of Aristotle that the earth is motionless is simply bad physics. To prove in the manner of Royce that the existence of error dialectically establishes the existence of God or Absolute Mind is bad metaphysics. To demonstrate in the manner of Plato that the soul is everlasting because it is by nature a simple substance and as such is incapable of being split into parts is bad psychology. In all these examples we have, according to Santayana, an illicit proof of fact by dialectical means.

Nowhere do we have a more glaring case of illicit science, as far as the Life of Reason is concerned, than in the abortive attempts to make ethics scientific on rational or even grammatical grounds. Therefore, Santayana discusses at great length the possibility of a rational ethics and the place of morality within a Life of Reason. Morality proper, human action insofar as it may be judged right or wrong, good or bad, has a prerational basis. Man practiced morality long before he theorized about it. In fact, the consideration of action in terms of moral standards must begin with the actual desires, impulses, and *de facto* judgments of mankind. That men have moral concerns, or interests in the honesty or justice of deeds, can have no firmer basis than existing fact. That morality, however incoherent, exists, and that it has a naturalistic or pre-rational basis is one thing, but that a truly rational morality has never existed and is not to be expected is another and by far a more important matter from the standpoint of philosophy or a Life of Reason. Santayana assumes that what guides men's actions is always some partial or particular interest and not a purely impartial or rational set of motives. A rational morality would require perfect self-knowledge and a harmony of interests that cannot be attained in practice. "In lieu of a rational morality, however, we have rational ethics; and this mere idea of a rational morality is something valuable." [13]

An ethics in the manner of Socrates, Plato, or Aristotle is only a sketch of a rational morality. Hence, a rational ethics is neither dogmatic nor final, but makes use of critical or dialectical thinking to discover not what is good once and for all but to discover the consequences of whatever estimations of value a man may make. "This method, the Socratic method, consists in accepting any estimation which any man may sincerely make, and in applying dialectic to it, so as to let the man see what he really esteems." [14] The use of reason in ethics or any other estimations of values is not to create values or goods, but to discern possible harmonies between them. Reason is totally incapable of discerning or producing any good by itself apart from man's natural impulses, desires, or interests. We cannot use dialectic or reason as Royce tried to do to establish any absolute moral truth or universal ethical principle since "the ultimate intuitions on which ethics rests are not debatable, for they are not opinions we hazard but preferences we feel; and it can be neither correct nor incorrect to feel them." [15] Since the basis of every moral judgment is vital preference, no moral judgment can literally be true or false, right or wrong; it can only be more or less coherent and sincere.

But reason can direct the existent impulses of man and thereby transform them into enlightened desires and harmonious interests. "When we apply reason to life we immediately demand that life be consistent, complete and satisfactory when reflected upon and viewed as a whole." [16] Rational ethics, therefore, resembles pre-rational morality in being based on natural impulses and desires. It differs from pre-rational morality in being more coherent, complete, and enlightened. Rational ethics, therefore, is not a piece of arbitrary legislation since it does not presume to cancel or subvert our basic preferences, but simply enables them to become more enlightened and sincere. The worst mistake in ethics, according to Santayana, is to fail to see that values are relative to natural, animal interests. This error not only leads to fruitless controversy, but actually encourages the worst forms of intolerance and fanaticism.

However, Santayana observes that men may become disillusioned with the Life of Reason because of its imperfections and yearn for an ascetic or supernatural release from life itself and create what he calls a post-rational morality. Stoic resignation and early Christian asceticism are illustrations of this fundamental despair of having a Life of Reason.

> Pessimism and all the moralities founded on despair, are not pre-rational but post-rational. They are the work of men who more or less explicitly have conceived the Life of Reason, tried it at least imaginatively, and found it wanting. These systems are a refuge from an intolerable situation: they are experiments in redemption. [17]

However, he argues that these post-rational moralities are in effect intercepted or postponed forms of rationalism. Their goal is happiness or well-being, the same as that of the Life of Reason, but their conception of this good is given a set of supernatural conditions. In fact, Santayana argues that the only way that supernatural morality can keep within the limits of sanity is by reinstating "in practice under novel associations and for motives ostensibly different, the very natural virtues and hopes which, when seen to be merely natural, it had thrown over with contempt." [18]

The Life of Reason—reason in common sense, society, religion, art, and science—is nothing more than the union of the rational and the animal in man. To forget or omit either the rational or the animal in human nature is to do violence with the facts or with the very idea of progress in human life. The Life of Reason is the union of impulse and ideations which, if wholly divorced, would reduce man to a brute or maniac. The rational animal is that creature whose ideas have ceased to be spontaneous and undisciplined and whose actions have ceased to be irresponsible and vain. A Life of Reason is the attempt to make man's thoughts responsible to his actions and his actions responsible for his thoughts.

PHILOSOPHICAL POETRY AND REFLECTIONS ON AMERICA   Santayana viewed the main function of philosophy as one of criticism. However, he did not equate criticism with finding or pointing out faults. Criticism implies intelligent judgment concerning the meaning and significance of things and is therefore an indispensable condition of wisdom. Criticism is impossible without both appreciation and analysis. Without sympathetic appreciation, criticism would be entirely negative and empty. Without analysis, criticism would be arbitrary and unenlightening. Philosophical criticism, therefore, must draw upon experience and imagination as well as be able to make careful distinctions between things. But most important of all, philosophical criticism may lay bare its own assumptions or basic principles. No criticism can exist without assumptions although it is easy to lose sight of what they are or how they intervene in one's appraisals. Running throughout all Santayana's criticism of other philosophers, poetry, literature, and social life, consequently, is a clear formulation of his own assumptions and principles. His assessments of literature, poetry, and American intellectual life especially throw clear light on his own philosophical position. They also represent the first searching attempt by an American to subject these matters to careful and extensive philosophical scrutiny.

Very early in his philosophical career Santayana came to three fundamental conclusions from which he never departed. He constantly wove
these conclusions into the themes of many of his later works. First, religion
and poetry are identical in essence however different they may seem in
their accidental or incidental characteristics. Second, "the height of poetry
is to speak the language of the gods"; greatness in poetry is a function of
the scope and richness of its vision, philosophically and religiously. Third,
the task of philosophy is neither to dismiss nor to become converted to
poetry or religion, but rather to appreciate their meaning and beauty
imaginatively and assess their true significance critically. In his *Interpretations of Poetry and Religion* he argued that "Poetry is called religion
when it intervenes in life, and religion, when it merely supervenes upon
life, is seen to be nothing but poetry." [19] Both poetry and religion involve
imaginative and symbolic expressions or interpretations of existence.
Neither offers a literal account of things, but rather an aesthetic and moral
one.

In his *Three Philosophical Poets*, published in 1910, he attempted to
explore the relation between philosophy and poetry by examining three
famous poets who are outstanding for the greatness of their vision as well
as the beauty of their verse. Santayana's choice of Lucretius, Dante, and
Goethe was also guided by his claim that "they sum up all European
philosophy." [20] Lucretius' poem *De Rerum Natura*, Dante's *Divine
Comedy*, and Goethe's *Faust* represent three fundamentally different
world-outlooks. Lucretius sees all things through the eyes of a materialist,
Dante through those of a supernaturalist, and Goethe through those of a
romanticist. Lucretius celebrates the material ground of all things and the
mechanical causes by which they originate, move, and grow. He sees all
things based in the inevitable swirl of material atoms in the void. Even
the soul or mind is explained in terms of its material makeup and origin;
hence it is mortal. Man's true happiness is found in peace of mind and
resignation to the material ground of all existence.

Dante presents a completely different philosophic vision. He sees the
world in terms of its final causes or destination, not in terms of any material ground. He is interested in depicting how the soul will be saved or
damned. Dante's universe is a moral theater where the important actions
are sin and punishment, virtue and reward. He sees human life and the
world in supernatural terms. The soul is immortal, and man's true happiness is to be found not in this world but in paradise. The German poet
Goethe presents still another philosophic vision. He views the world
neither in material origins nor supernatural ends but in the ceaseless **flux**

of the immediacy of experience. Faust depicts the romantic urge to experience life to the full without ever stopping. Goethe is not interested in resignation nor final salvation but in striving always for fresh vistas to uncover, new challenges to overcome. Virtue and vice are both intriguing, but they are only markers along the way of life. Goethe sees human life and the world in romantic terms. The process or flux of life's journey is the central theme, not its origin or its destination.

What are we to say about the philosophic visions of these three poets? Santayana declares, "Each is the best in his way and none is the best in every way. To express a preference is not so much a criticism as a personal confession." [21] "Goethe is the poet of life; Lucretius the poet of nature; Dante the poet of salvation." [22] Lucretius sees the material ground and origin of existence, but there is much he does not see. He does not see the hopes and plights of the soul in its search for deliverance or salvation. But Dante paints the moral and religious tones of life and the world in vivid detail and gives us possibilities beyond those of Lucretius. However, Dante's idea of nature is supernatural and hence illusory. His greatness as a moral poet and artist of the human spirit is won at the expense of viewing nature itself in mythical terms. Goethe, finally, sees much more than the other two poets. Goethe's vision of experience is richer and more immediate than that of Lucretius, and he also sees more of the profusion of life than Dante and does not fix on any single goal. But all is essentially groundless in Goethe; there is no substance behind the appearances, nor any steady, enduring values to be pursued. All is flux.

Santayana contends that although philosophy and poetry have a definite affinity, the philosopher's task cannot be *only* a poetic one. Philosophy requires analysis and drawing of distinctions that the poet may often be impelled to blur or confuse. However, he does claim that the highest philosophy must contain poetic insight and that the highest poetry must supply a philosophic vision. His study of Lucretius, Dante, and Goethe throws much light on his own conception of philosophy. The manner in which he explains and judges their philosophic poems reveals his own penchant for naturalism and detachment. For example, what he admires in Lucretius is the frank materialism and respect for the material ground of all existence. However, he is also critical of Lucretius because of what the Roman poet-philosopher ignores. Santayana claims that just as all ideals have a natural or material basis, so all natural existence has an ideal development. Dante is valued by Santayana because he sees the moral and religious ideals of life in richer and more beautiful forms—despite the fact that he has a false understanding of their basis. Dante is criticized by Santayana because he depicts moral and religious ideals as forces rather than as detached goods. Dante sees more beauty and meaning in the world than Lucretius, but he misconstrues the nature of what he sees. Similarly, Goethe sees more fully the contours and fullness of life than either Lucretius or Dante, but his romanticism gives him no ground or standard for all the richness he sees.

Santayana's own philosophy, therefore, may be viewed as an attempt to reinstate the materialism of Lucretius and the ancient Greeks while at the same time do justice to the richness of things and especially the idealizations possible in existence. Philosophy will never be on sure ground but will only perpetuate deceptions if it confuses the values and beauties that things may display with the causes that produce them. What may make existence worthwhile is one thing, what may bring something into existence or move it is quite another. The enjoyments and beauties of existence are not forces or instruments—they are not means of achieving something else—but definite, valuable ends that make life harmonious and worth having. Music, for example, may be an ideal good, but it nevertheless has a material basis. The beauty of music is not physical; it is detached from existence. Physical sound waves exist behind the music, but it is the pleasure of their form that gives rise to beauty, not the mere sound waves themselves.

Beauty or value is found, therefore, not in existence as such but in an ideal detachment from it. The poet or artist may present us with beautiful verse or pictures, but only if we adopt the proper distance. We can be either too close or too far away to appreciate the beauty. To see the beauty of a storm at sea, for example, we cannot be distracted by fear of drowning. Beauty is objectified pleasure—which means pleasure regarded as the quality of a thing. But unless we are detached observers we can never objectify our pleasures or contemplate them at a distance. However, beauty is only regarded as in the object—it does not really exist there. In fact, beauty or any good is only an ideal appearance without any substance of its own; its substance is something material or natural. Santayana contends that the proper philosophy should make room for the *substance* or material ground of existence as well as for its various *appearances* of beauty and other goods. But it also is the business of philosophy to understand properly and distinguish substance and appearance rather than confuse them. A poetic naturalism can do this very thing. It can make a place for the sublime, the beautiful, and the good in life, while at the same time it will not confuse these ideals with the material substances that give them support or bring them into existence.

Santayana once observed that "After all, it has been acquaintance with America and American philosophers that has chiefly contributed to clear and to settle my own mind." [23] He not only received formal instruction in philosophy from James and Royce, but he made extensive studies and interpretations of American life and thought. In 1911 he delivered an address entitled *The Genteel Tradition in American Philosophy* before the Philosophical Union of the University of California. Later, in 1920, he published further interpretations of American life and thought in his *Character and Opinion in the United States*. These works, along with other essays, show the detached and perceptive manner in which he interpreted many of the salient features of American culture. However, these essays also reveal the mind of Santayana himself, as he frankly admits. His reflections on America, therefore, serve a double purpose of pointing up certain facets of American thought and revealing the premisses and arguments of his own philosophy by which he interprets American ideas.

Santayana views America as a "young country with an old mentality." [24] The genteel tradition in American thinking which he finds in several forms is largely borrowed from older sources. This tradition is a kind of religious idealism that permeates American thinking all the way from Edwards to Emerson and Royce and the transcendental idealists.

> Philosophical opinion in America is of course rooted in the genteel tradition. It is either inspired by religious faith, and designed to defend it or else it is created somewhat artificially in the larger universities, by deliberately proposing problems which, without being very pressing to most Americans, are supposed to be necessary problems of thought.[25]

In Edwards, this idealism took the form of an "agonized conscience" that "oscillates between a profound abasement and a paradoxical elation of the spirit." [26] American Calvinism was, however, also the expression of a pioneering spirit of aggressive enterprise. Young America, therefore, in reality "is a country with two mentalities, one a survival of the beliefs and standards of the fathers, the other an expression of the instincts, practice, and discoveries of the younger generations." [27] American Calvinism, with its deep sense of sin and hope of salvation, encouraged hard work and thus paved the way for enlightenment, growth, and prosperity.

The American Enlightenment, with men like Jefferson and Franklin, emphasized the utilitarian value of virtue and religious beliefs and encouraged optimism regarding man. "Calvinism thus lost its basis in American life." [28] However, according to Santayana, the genteel tradition continued to exist by finding another form. Emerson and New England transcendentalism continued this tradition. It borrowed its inspiration from European romanticism, the mystical tradition, and from intuition. In upholding the doctrine of self-reliance, transcendentalism was truly American. However, Santayana contends that although this American romanticism was sincere and expressed the American spirit, it nevertheless was expressed in "metaphysical fables." [29] Emerson, essentially a poet, did not really turn his transcendentalism into a system. A mystic, he never tried to prove his most cherished insights. He therefore continued the genteel tradition of religious idealism by turning it into pure poetry. Santayana speculates about Emerson, "If he was able so constantly to stimulate us to fresh thoughts, was it not because he demolished the labor of long ages of reflection?" [30] In other words, did Emerson not succeed in buttressing absolute values and religious idealism by default of understanding their nature or ground? Emerson "was not an independent philosopher, in spite of his belief in independence. He inherited the problems and the preoccupations of the theology from which he started. . . ." [31]

Another American thinker, Josiah Royce, did attempt to defend the genteel tradition and religious idealism by making it into a system. Royce, who was trained in German idealism, mastered the dialectical method of argument. He philosophized in such a way as always to come back to the same point—the absolute. Whereas Emerson found the absolute in poetic imagination, Royce required argument and proof. But Santayana sees Royce's proofs and his entire system as false and misguided. Royce wanted to fit the universe into a perfect logical system, while at the same time justifying it on moral and religious grounds. Everything had to be shown to be not only logically necessary, but also morally or religiously good. The existence of evil, for example, became a formidable problem for Royce, as he could neither explain it away nor show it as something good. He therefore never seemed to realize that his whole system of regarding things was based on impossible problems. He never stopped philosophizing, not because he turned up something new, but because he found more and more ways of expressing the same old insoluble problem. Royce's chief problem was to show "that all lives were parts of a single divine life in which all problems were solved and all evils justified." [32] He conceived good as essentially involving a struggle with and mastery over evil, so that if there were no evil there could really be no good. Yet Santayana observes that Royce "could hardly help feeling that all goods are not of that bellicose description, and that not all evils produce a healthy reaction or are swallowed up in victory." [33] Royce's passionate desire to solve the problem of evil was not really based on a search for intellectual clarification, but was rather based upon a lurking Calvinism in his nature.

Santayana contends that "the question why it is right that there should be any evil is itself perverse and raised by false presumptions." [34] It rests upon missing or ignoring the naturalistic ground of all existence and all ideals and substituting for them personified motives and will in a purely mythical sense. It assumes that every catastrophe cannot be explained as a natural event with natural causes, but rather must be given a cosmic reason. This means that an earthquake that may kill thousands of people is not simply a terrible natural disaster, but a cosmic problem that requires some moral justification as to why it was good that this evil should appear. Santayana considers that Royce's solution to this problem must inevitably prove unsatisfactory because it is not a real problem that can be solved, but represents a problem invented for the intellect out of religious or moral emotions.

While Emerson and Royce gave support to the genteel tradition in America in their different ways, Santayana claims that the poet Walt Whitman and the philosopher-psychologist William James clearly broke with it. In Whitman "Bohemia rebelled against the genteel tradition" and "reduced his imagination to a passive sensorium for the registering of impressions." [35] Whitman's poetry is down-to-earth and not based on any secret desire to uphold certain respectable, time-honored absolutes. But one has to turn to William James to find a constructive assault on the absolute and the genteel tradition. Santayana views William James as representing the genuine, long-silent American mind. James understood the psychological basis of the genteel tradition and attacked it as a factually groundless tender-mindedness. He had a healthy respect for empirical fact and the naturalistic basis of the human mind. Santayana considers that the best of William James is to be found in his *Principles of Psychology*.

He saw that experience, as we endure it, is not a mosaic of distinct sensations, not the expression of separate hostile faculties, such as reason and the passions, or sense and the categories; it is rather a flow of mental discourse, like a dream, in which all divisions and units are vague and shifting and the whole is continually merging together and drifting apart.[36]

James thus succeeded in throwing off certain prejudices and pretensions of thinking which for a long time upheld the genteel tradition in America. To Santayana he represents many of the good qualities of the genuine American mind—the spirit of free cooperation, aggressive enterprise, and a vigorous faith in piecemeal future progress. In short, James was genuinely liberal in spirit and progressive in temper.

However, Santayana is not very sympathetic with James' philosophy, particularly his pragmatism and radical empiricism. Pragmatism is good in getting rid of pretended absolutes and thin verbal solutions to problems, he admits, but it fails to provide us with a real ground for our knowledge and fails in its conception of truth. James confuses the changeless or static quality of truth itself with changing events or circumstances in the world. The truth *about* any event or thing can *never* change, even though events and things themselves do change. For example, if it is true *that it rained yesterday*, then this proposition (that it rained yesterday) is still true even though it is no longer raining today. Events change, they come to an end as when the rain stops. Truth, however, according to Santayana does not stop or change. Once something is true, it always remains true. If it is true that it rained yesterday, then it will always be true that it rained *on that date*.

James also confuses our apprehension of the truth with the truth we apprehend. Santayana insists on a sharp distinction between truth and events. Our *apprehension* of some truth, say that George Washington was born in 1732, is a mental event which occurs—it becomes an event in our mental history or biography; also, Washington's birth is a natural event which occurred at a certain time. However, the truth about any event is not itself an event or process that comes into being. All truths are dateless forms in themselves or eternal essences even though the events to which they refer pass in time. If a proposition or judgment is true, it is true forever. This does not mean that it is *a priori* or necessarily true, since all truths of fact are contingent on particular circumstances. But it does mean that any truth is in a different category than what it is the truth *of*—or what it describes. Santayana argues that the truth about any event can never be identical with that event. To be a description of an event, a true proposition must be distinct from what it characterizes; otherwise true propositions would not be true of *anything*.

The proposition that "snow is white" must be distinct from snow's being white as well as distinct from anyone's idea or opinion that it is white. Truth cannot be either a physical event or a psychological one; it is logically distinct from either. James' pragmatism blurs these distinctions which Santayana finds necessary. James wrongly holds that truth is functional or dynamic, that it is a part of experience itself rather than a distinct, impersonal description of things.

Santayana was also critical of James' radical empiricism insofar as this seemed to turn nature and matter themselves into mere parts of our experience of them. James had argued that pure experience needs no substantial support in any way, but is self-sufficient. Santayana considers this tendency to make experience fundamental a psychological or romantic delusion. He claims that no matter how rich and abundant we feel experience to be, it nevertheless requires a ground. Whatever appears must somehow be the appearance of something. Santayana insists that experience must be grounded naturalistically in a material world. The science of physics, for example, does not study only the field of experience, but rather it studies matter in all its detail. Our knowledge of matter may be incomplete and insufficient, but what little there is should not be confused with any mere psychological interpretation of it.

Santayana finds James' humanism acceptable only in part. He is sympathetic with James' attacks on pretended absolutes and excessive rationalism. However, Santayana is unwilling to identify reality with experience or confuse the human with the real. He prefers to conceive human experience as part of a larger natural world. In fact, he considers the recognition of matter and the natural world by common sense to be the beginning of wisdom. Not every desire or wish can be good or wise just because it is demanded or sought. Somewhere distinctions have to be made, and realities have to be taken into consideration. Santayana thus finds that James' pragmatism, however vigorous and liberal it may be, is nevertheless short on wisdom. It is too pluralistic and too permissive. In this sense it is very expressive of the exuberance of the youthful American spirit. It is impatient with the world, and not only looks to the future, but requires that the future be near at hand.

However, Santayana believes John Dewey is the best expression of the American people and their way of life. Dewey is the

> devoted spokesman of the spirit of enterprise, of experiment, of modern industry.[37] The master burden of his philosophy, which lends it its national character, is a profound sympathy with the

enterprise of life in all lay directions, in its technical and moral complexity, and especially in its American form, where individual initiative, although still demanded and prized, is quickly subjected to overwhelming democratic control.[38]

Santayana sees Dewey as both a pragmatist and a naturalist; it is the combination of these factors that makes his philosophy profoundly American, since "the philosophy by which Americans live, in contrast to the philosophies which they profess, is naturalistic." [39] But he observes that Americans, and Dewey also, are naturalists second and pragmatists first. That is, the naturalistic or even materialistic philosophy Americans live by or express in their actions is not founded on theory or interest in analysis, but rather, on utility or practical success. The living philosophy of Americans is the philosophy of aggressive enterprise, a philosophy that must be naturalistic since enterprise involves the monopoly of material activity. But American enterprise is also democratic, upholding the spirit of free cooperation. The philosophy of John Dewey defends all of these traits—it is democratic, naturalistic, and pragmatic.

Santayana finds much that is admirable in Dewey's and America's espousal of democracy and naturalism, but he cannot accept its pragmatic basis or what he takes to be its pragmatic excesses and confusions. "Naturalism in Dewey is accordingly an assumption imposed by the character of the prevalent arts; and as he is aware that he is a naturalist only to that extent and on that ground, his naturalism is half-hearted and short-winded." [40] Santayana is critical of Dewey in the same way he is critical of American life. In both, a naturalistic view of life is imposed by practical circumstances, and is therefore not accepted on the basis of understanding. The pragmatist can offer only a tenuous kind of naturalism since he tends to measure understanding by adjustment and truth by practical success. This kind of pragmatic outlook will have a short-sighted or confused philosophic comprehension, since by treating ideas as instruments and judging them by their success it will inevitably substitute mere cleverness for wisdom or expediency for depth of understanding.

Pragmatism, therefore, tends to distract and confuse the mind which requires leisure and proper reflection to find true wisdom and its proper goods. What these goods may be and how they may be defined and realized are questions that Santayana addressed himself to throughout his life. In his later works, especially, he poses the fundamental questions, How can we know or distinguish what is really worth knowing or caring for? and How can these various goods be put into some meaningful system?

CRITICAL REALISM AND ULTIMATE SKEPTICISM   With the publication of his *Three Proofs of Realism* in 1920 and *Scepticism and Animal Faith* in 1923, Santayana not only laid the epistemological cornerstone of his own system of philosophy, but he became an acknowledged leader in the development of twentieth-century American realism. During the early part of the twentieth century in England and America there developed among philosophers a pronounced interest in problems surrounding the nature of knowledge. A definite reaction set in by a great number of English and American philosophers against the claims of idealism and pragmatism as well. In Britain, Bertrand Russell and G. E. Moore developed strong forms of realism in their critical attacks on idealism and pragmatism. In America in 1912, a group of philosophers wrote a cooperative work called *The New Realism: Cooperative Studies in Philosophy*. It was at this time that Santayana left Harvard and went to England where he remained throughout the duration of the First World War. During this period, he came into contact with English philosophy, but he also kept in touch with a group of American realists; in 1920 he joined with the American philosophers known as the Critical Realists in the publication of the cooperative volume *Essays in Critical Realism*.

Santayana's *Three Proofs of Realism* thus has a double significance. It became the most eloquent and important formulation of the critical realist's point of view, and it represented an important step in the development of Santayana's own systematic philosophy. The gist of his critical realism may be put as follows. Any genuine account of what knowledge is must be *realistic* in the minimal sense of at least assuming that thought and perception can refer to some independently existing object. Knowledge cannot exist unless there is something to know and unless this something or object can be adequately conceived. We may say that realism requires the minimum of two postulates regarding knowledge: (1) independence or transcendence of the object of knowledge, and (2) relevance or adequacy of our ideas in referring to the object known. For example, if memory is to give us true knowledge of a past event, then the minimum of realism asserts that (1) the past event itself as the object of our knowledge is independent of or transcends any present ideas we may have of that event, and (2) our present idea which claims to remember that event correctly must be adequate to conceive that past event. Knowledge can never be *identical* with the object known, but can only be relevant to that object. Knowledge therefore is essentially symbolic. But how can any symbol or idea truly represent a transcendent or absent object?

Santayana admits that all proofs of realism must be circular, that we cannot prove realism or anything else without assuming postulates (1) and (2). However, what can be shown is that every form of genuine cognition takes these postulates for granted. Realism is confirmed biologically, psychologically, and logically. Biologically, animals are equipped with senses that inform them of independently existing objects. Psychologically, illusions or delusions may be the best evidence that our ideas of things are not literal copies of presumed objects. Logically, our ideas of fixed abstract terms such as numbers indicate that, for example, two plus two is equal to four independently of whether someone thinks it is.

Knowledge requires a three-term relationship. If anyone's thoughts or perceptions are to know or give knowledge of an existing object (the number of apples in a certain basket, for example), then the basket of apples itself must be distinguished from the thought or perception of the basket in someone's mind. Here we have two elements—one mental, the other physical. However, since knowledge attempts to leap across the gap between some thought or idea and some independent object, a third term is needed to bridge this gap. If our thoughts are to be adequate to the objects claimed to be known, then our ideas must somehow be connected with or possess something of the object to be known. However, it is a patent fact, according to Santayana and the critical realists, that our thoughts cannot literally possess their objects of knowledge. If I know that a basket contains twenty apples, the basket of twenty apples is not literally contained in my thought of it—my mind does not possess the basket physically. But my mind or my thoughts do possess something—they possess the symbolic form or essence embodied in the basket of apples. Santayana named the third term of the knowledge relation an "essence."

Essences are detached from any kind of existence; they are neither mental nor physical occurrences, but simply ideal forms or universals. The number twenty is an essence—a pure ideal form. It can be distinguished both from physical groups of twenty things and from any mental pictures or thoughts about twenty things. The number twenty is neither mental nor physical, but simply a logical essence that may apply to existences. Universals or essences may be thought by the mind, and they may also characterize physical things. In fact, every physical object must have some form or shape; this would be its essence. Thus, if someone is to know that a certain basket contains twenty apples, then the three terms of this knowledge situation are (1) the thought of the apples as a mental event, (2) the basket of apples itself as a physical existence, and (3) the essence twenty which links the other two terms together.

In other words the mind has before it a certain essence or datum which it posits as embodied in the independently existing physical object. The thought in the knower's mind is thus adequate to the object claimed to be known, since the mind thinks or apprehends a form or essence which actually characterizes the physical object itself. The mind can, of course, be deceived; it can mistakenly attribute an essence to an object which does not in fact have that essence. This is why Santayana called his position critical realism, to distinguish it from other forms of realism, especially from naive realism which assumes that we can directly perceive or know physical objects in a literal manner. Knowledge is not literal but symbolic, according to Santayana; we cannot literally expect to possess in our minds the things we can know. Knowledge is always indirect, based on a three-term relationship. The forms or essences we attribute to things can only be more or less relevant to them —they stand as symbolic representations of things, never as literal duplicates.

In *Scepticism and Animal Faith*, which he published in 1923, Santayana approached the whole problem of knowledge by trying to see how far skepticism could be pushed. He wanted to determine whether a thoroughgoing skepticism would undermine a realistic belief in knowledge or whether it could not be, oddly enough, perfectly compatible with critical realism. He observed that the major forms of philosophical skepticism were superficial and took for granted things they had no right to. The French philosopher Descartes began with a universal doubt but found that he could not doubt his own existence as a doubter who thinks. However, other philosophers had no trouble doubting Descartes' mental substance or *cogito ergo sum*—in fact, the empiricist Hume based his own skepticism on questioning the very existence of such metaphysical entities as a substantial self or soul-substance. Upon introspection, Hume could only find particular impressions and ideas and considered it an immense unverifiable postulate that these impressions and ideas were tied together by some mental substance. Hume therefore carried his skepticism to the point of doubting the existence of internal mental substance as well as external material substance. However, he found that he was left with the existence of impressions and ideas which he did not doubt.

Santayana observes that "scepticism is a suspicion of error about facts." [41] Skepticism in the form of doubt therefore really does not abandon belief altogether, but only certain beliefs. Doubting is accordingly a form of belief, since if there is any point to a doubt, it is because certain facts are believed in. However, can all facts or existences be doubted, can the whole category of fact itself be called into question? Here we must be careful not to believe in any existence or fact. The solipsist, for example, doubts the existence of all things outside his own mind; he banishes all facts or beliefs in any external reality since he finds that he cannot really get beyond or outside his own ideas. The solipsist cannot directly experience a tree, a house, or any other external thing, but only his idea of them. He cannot even know the existence of other solipsists, since he can never experience, think, or perceive them; all he can perceive is his idea of them. However, the solipsist, according to Santayana, still believes in his own existence, and therefore, although he doubts all external facts, his skepticism has not touched the lowest limit. To believe in any kind of existence at all is therefore *not* ultimate skepticism. But to doubt all existence or all facts is still not ultimate skepticism, since even to doubt all existence involves belief in the existence of the doubt itself. Genuine doubt therefore can only be piecemeal, and the doubting skeptic who thinks he has really doubted all facts is only fooling himself.

Does it follow from this that there is no such thing as ultimate skepticism? On the contrary, we have overlooked an important alternative. According to Santayana, skepticism can be carried to the point of solipsism of the present moment, where all existences are banished, even the existence of the skeptic or solipsist. However, this kind of skepticism cannot be based on doubt, but must be based upon suspending judgment altogether. Ultimate skepticism therefore does not believe in anything at all, and it certainly does not believe in doubting all facts or existences. It suspends both belief and doubt and makes no claims or judgments about anything. Santayana calls this suspension of judgment the intuition of essence. Intuition is a passive awareness of anything that comes before the mind, but is totally unconcerned with existence or anything ulterior. Intuition makes no distinction between what is illusory and what is real, between what is a dream and what is not. Intuition is mere contemplation or aesthetic appreciation. Sounds and colors, for example, are listened to or contemplated in detachment from where they may come from or what they may lead to. Intuition is merely the timeless appreciation of pure qualities. If one becomes self-conscious and pays attention to the fact that one is having an aesthetic experience or intuition, then one has already passed beyond it and made a claim for some fact. If one interprets a quality or essence as signifying something else, then again one has passed beyond intuition into belief of some kind.

Ultimate skepticism therefore is a suspension of judgment from any existence or fact. It is, nevertheless, an absorbing awareness, so absorbed that it involves no distractions of any kind. Intuition, consequently, is all enjoyment with no worries about anything at all. Santayana claims that intuition is involved, however weakly, in all conscious attention. It can be heightened by various means, even by a child who loses himself in the enjoyment of playing or by a man who becomes absorbed in his work. Since all conscious awareness involves the passive attention to qualities or forms or essences in some measure, it follows that ultimate skepticism is not incompatible with a realistic belief in knowledge. Ultimate skepticism, which hits rock bottom by allowing the mind simply to gaze on some essence, does not undermine or conflict with knowledge of facts or existences since it involves no belief contrary to any belief in knowledge. Ultimate skepticism bypasses knowledge for something else; it does not presume to challenge any knowledge or conflict with any belief in facts or existences. Philosophically, Santayana's whole purpose in pushing skepticism to its ultimate point in pure intuition is not to show that knowledge is impossible, but rather to show in a clearer light exactly what it is or what it involves. Intuition is not knowledge because it makes no claim, involves no intent to fathom or figure anything out. Belief or cognitive intent is thereby shown as necessary to knowledge. Knowledge always involves a presumption regarding something beyond a mere intuition. Intuitions of essences are neither true nor false—they are what they are and nothing else.

Santayana's ultimate skepticism and critical realism meet one another from opposite directions in the notion of "essence." Ultimate skepticism is reached by suspension of all belief and by entering into the detached, passive intuition of some essence. Critical realism is discovered by venturing a belief or knowledge-claim that some essence or symbol entertained by the mind actually applies to some fact and state of affairs. Essences or pure universals, therefore, are just as necessary for knowledge as they are for contemplation. Mere contemplation or intuition are not knowledge since they only involve an aesthetic awareness of some form or quality such as listening to music or enjoying colors. The music is not true or false, nor the colors correct or incorrect—but only more or less beautiful or aesthetically pleasing. Cognitive intent or knowledge-claims and beliefs, however, are either true or false, correct or incorrect. Knowledge always involves a presumption that something is correctly described or truly characterized. However, nothing could be described or characterized at all without the use of universals (essences). To describe something as large or small, hard or soft, brown or green is to make use of general descriptive terms that can be used again and again. Every term of general description is simply an essence or universal.

Santayana defines knowledge as true belief grounded in experience. Knowledge is a kind of "faith mediated by symbols" where the symbols are essences taken as applying to or describing some fact. He therefore described knowledge as a kind of "animal faith" or presumption that is precipitated by the natural need to seek and find information about existence. The animal (and man is partly animal in nature) simply cannot live or survive by mere intuition or contemplation alone. The passive awareness of mere essences must be converted to the active pursuit of real substances if knowledge is to be obtained.

> All knowledge, being faith in an object posited and partially described, is belief in substance, in the etymological sense of that word; it is belief in a thing or event subsisting in its own plane, and waiting for the light of knowledge to explore it eventually, and perhaps name or define it.[42]

Substance means matter for Santayana. The hungry animal, for example, in pursuit of food must be concerned with finding material substances and not mere appearances or essences. The material or naturalistic ground of all knowledge is at the same time a requirement of life and a measure of sanity in any philosophy. Philosophical theories, if they are to explain anything at all, must see that all ideals (including any ideals of knowledge) have a naturalistic basis. But philosophy should also be expected to see that all natural things have ideal fulfillments or idealizations. Animal sagacity, therefore, although it may be the basis of all human knowledge, is certainly not its highest form. Knowledge grows by sophistication and by abstraction from the concrete practical needs of living and survival. Pure mathematics and science, as refinements of cruder and common-sense ways of apprehending things, may extend and improve our knowledge in many ways. Philosophy may do the same thing by detaching itself from particular existences and surveying things in a more general manner. The philosopher is not really interested in knowing all the facts or existences he possibly can, since many of these may be trivial. Although the philosopher cannot desire to be deceived and must "wish to know the whole unvarnished truth about relevant matters," [43] he is not any mere fact-worshiper.

The philosopher also has ideals to contemplate and pursue. Essences or ideal forms in their own right are objects worthy of philosophical attention. And the fact that these essences are detached from existence simply means that they are more congenial to the mind and imagination than many things that only happen to exist and vanish, appear and disappear. The philosopher must be concerned with what is possible as well as with what is actual. The awareness of essences or ideal forms expands our perspective on things, which would be narrow or impoverished without contemplation. Santayana observes that it is not naturalism that would reduce man to an animal or brute existence, but that mere fact-worship or total preoccupation with and anxiety about existence would tend in this direction.

Ultimate skepticism thus has its value in showing that knowledge of facts and existences is not the only avenue open to the mind, and that even when we do presume to have knowledge it can never be absolute and literal. Knowledge is impossible without faith in some existence and without symbolic use of some essence to depict or render that existence. Skepticism shows that knowledge involves a presumption which is always liable to error, but skepticism also shows that man can enjoy a release or suspension from the presumption to know or believe in existences altogether. This detachment from existence, although never a source of knowledge, is nevertheless necessary in order to see better by contrast exactly what knowledge involves. Contemplation, or the intuition of essence, far from interfering with knowledge or existence, gives man a heightened sense of what knowledge and existence really are; it shows that they are not everything, that the mind can enjoy its own life by often being free of the cares of existence and knowing.

REALMS OF BEING: ESSENCE, MATTER, TRUTH, AND SPIRIT

"Josiah Royce, who had kept a kindly but troubled watch over my youth, once said to me that the gist of my philosophy was the separation of essence from existence. This was one of those rare criticisms that open one's eyes to one's own nature." [44] This quotation from Santayana's last reply to his critics not only shows the fundamental character of the distinction between essence and existence in his philosophy, but it shows as well his basic concern to construct an ontological system—a philosophy that would carefully distinguish various modes of being. Peirce began an ontological system, but never brought it to completion. James inveighed against system-making as such and never composed a philosophic system. Royce, on the other hand, had a system composed of an amazing wealth of detail, and he struggled to tie the various parts together. But judged by Santayana's standards, Royce's system was essentially metaphysical and religious and consequently impure.

Santayana required an ontological system that would be just what Royce's was not, both detached and naturalistic. For Santayana a system of honest ontology would have to be consistent with the Life of Reason. Any attempt to distinguish and analyze the different orders of being could never succeed if it contradicted its own natural basis or if it missed the significant ideals and forms of things by being partial only to certain ones. Detachment from all existence is thereby seen to be a prerequisite for any philosophy that would hope to be comprehensive and fair. Naturalism is equally necessary for any philosophy that would claim relevance to the world in which we actually live.

Beginning with *Scepticism and Animal Faith: Introduction to a System of Philosophy*, Santayana completed his system of ontology with the successive publication of *The Realm of Essence* (1927), *The Realm of Matter* (1930), *The Realm of Truth* (1938), and finally *The Realm of Spirit* (1940). These works are not only masterpieces of the polished and graceful philosophical prose for which Santayana has become famous, but they also present the most systematic and elaborately argued version of his philosophy as a whole. The four volumes of *Realms of Being* run to well over eight hundred pages and thus any brief summary of their contents cannot do justice to the great wealth of philosophical material they contain. It is possible, however, to indicate exactly how Santayana thought these four realms of being should be distinguished and also why he thought they were worth distinguishing.

The cornerstone of Santayana's ontology or realms of being is his sharp distinction between essence and existence. Existence refers to whether something occurs or has duration; thus it is always temporal and changeable. Mental events as in thoughts, desires, or actual feelings are existences as are physical events such as earthquakes, rainstorms, or the digestion of foods. Essence, on the other hand, refers to mere quality or *what* something is—never to whether it exists. Hence, essences are not temporal at all, but are eternal objects, free of time. Since essences do not occur in time they do not exist at all or change in any way. An essence is a purely ideal object and is always a universal, whereas any existent is not ideal but real and is always particular. The number ten, for example, is an essence and does not exist in any particular place or time; otherwise it could not be used at all to characterize different groups of ten things such as tables, chairs, horses, and apples, which do exist at different times and places. The essence green, for example, should not be confused with green pigment or green light, since they are physical and hence existents. The essence green is an ideal quality that always remains the same even when green pigment is dissolved or when green light is dispersed. Even changing, particular thoughts or ideas must be distinguished from essences. Someone may begin to think about the number ten, or may stop thinking about that number. The thought process or sequence of ideas, since it occurs in time, has at least a psychological existence to it. But essences do not even possess psychological existence or changeability. Existence is either mental or physical according to Santayana, but essence is neither since no essence exists.

If essences do not exist, then how do we know there are any? What evidence is there for these non-existent things called essences? Although essences do not have existence they nevertheless have *being*. The being which Santayana attributes to essences is pure being—being only in the sense of self-identity. Every essence is perfectly identical with itself and never loses that identity. By contrast, existents over periods of time lose or change their identity and never preserve any perfect identity. The identity of any existent is contingent upon circumstances. A tree, for example, may not only change its appearance in the color of its leaves, but it may cease existing altogether. Essences never run the risk of losing their identity since their identity is only tautological—each essence is only what it is and not anything else. This logical identity or pure being is internal and by definition inviolable. The essence blue can never cease being blue, nor can the essence round cease being round. We can know then that there are essences if we can know anything else, since universals or essences are involved in or necessary to anything's existence. If we can know that an apple is red, we must be able to know the tautology or identity that red is red. If red were not red, then nothing else could be red in any meaningful sense.

In his *Realms of Being*, Santayana distinguished four different orders of being, two of which pertain to existence in time and two which are not existential.

> The simple dissolution of superstition yields three of my realms of being: matter, as the region and method of power; essence, as the proper nature of appearances and relations, and spirit, as the witness or moral sensibility, that is subject to the double assault of material events and dramatic illusions. There remains the realm of truth, which is the total history and destiny of matter and spirit, or the enormously complex essence which they exemplify in existing.[45]

The realms of matter and spirit are existential in the sense that material events as well as conscious or mental events both occur in time. The realms of essence and truth, on the other hand, are not existential, as such, since essences do not exist and since the realm of truth is merely one segment of the realm of essence. Truth, for Santayana, is neither a material thing nor a mental existence, but simply that system or set of essences which happen to depict or characterize existence. Truth is not itself a process or a thing that may change. Any truth is just as static or eternal as any essence. "That which without existing is contemporary with all times is *eternal*. Truth is dateless and eternal, but not timeless, because, being descriptive of existence, it is a picture of change. It is frozen history." [46] For example, if it is true that George Washington was born in 1732, then this proposition is true forever. That is, once a proposition is true, it always will be true. Every existing thing or event which occurs in time must exemplify some form of essence. If George Washington existed, if he was actually born, then he must have had certain characteristics or have exemplified certain essences. Any truth about him therefore would then be a certain set of essences or characteristics that in fact depict or represent what he was or did.

Events should not be confused with any truths about them. Future events themselves, when they occur, fall into the realm of existence either as material events or mental ones. The truth about them (and truth is always secondary to existence or events) is not itself another event, but a complex essence which depicts their form, order, and relationships. Every truth, moreover, is contingent rather than necessary because as a depiction of existence truth can only characterize whatever facts occur. Truths of fact cannot simply be deduced from logic because then there would be no guarantee that they point to or describe actual events. There is an infinity of essences, and the problem of knowing which of these truly describe the world of actual events depends upon observation. It cannot be simply decided by reason alone.

The realms of matter and spirit refer to what is distinct from the realm of essence. The complex essence, round-square, for example, can never be exemplified in existence since it represents an impossible combination. However, things in the realm of matter or the realm of spirit, if they exist at all, have to exemplify some form. As existents, material things are much more than their mere form. Form has no power to do anything. Green apples may make someone sick, not because they exemplify the essence green, but because their material composition is difficult for the body to digest. Matter acts on matter in the very way that no essence ever acts on any other essence. The realm of matter is the whole field of action in nature where things move, grow, and react. It exhibits blind mechanisms or repetitions, as in the revolutions of the planets, as well as unconcious teleology or purpose, as in the web-building of spiders. Matter is anything but static, and anything but mere appearance.

Santayana does not pretend to know what the innermost nature or ultimate constituents of matter really are. He claims that it is the business of physical science to probe the depths of matter. Common sense grants that matter is very real and operative but common sense only has a rough and short-sighted view of what matter is. Santayana also holds that it is idle for philosophers to object against the very existence of matter on the grounds that human ideas are inadequate to grasp its nature. No human idea or any idea can grasp the essence of matter, because matter is always something more than any essence can show. Matter is opposed to the very being of any mere essence, since it is dynamic, ulterior, and recondite. Essences are all surface with no substance, but matter, just because it operates, moves, and grows, shows itself to have substance at least this far.

The firmness of Santayana's materialism is not only based on the fact that he requires matter as one kind of existence, but also on the fact that he holds that all existence, even mental, is dependent upon, or a function of, matter. Matter is asserted to be the ground of all existence. This means that all things which exist have matter behind them. However, Santayana does not claim that matter is the only thing which exists; his materialism does not deny or discard mental existence. He distinguishes between the being proper to spirit or consciousness from that which is proper to matter alone. For example, a thought or feeling about a painting is not that painting. All of conscious awareness has an existence which, although dependent on matter, is not identical in nature with it.

The existence of matter is spatial as well as temporal. Material things exist in a material context or space of some kind. However, the realm of spirit refers to existences which, while they do exist in time, do not exist in physical space. Santayana holds that while the brain and physical nervous system underlie thought and make its existence possible, they do not define or locate its center of existence.

Consistent with this view is his distinction between what he calls the psyche and spirit or consciousness. The human psyche refers to the vital mechanisms in man which maintain his life. All of man's life functions —breathing, eating, sleeping, walking—define the material agency of the psyche. These functions or activities of the psyche are all in principle observable and would be studied by the behavioral sciences, biology and psychology. However, it is also a salient fact about man's existence that he experiences certain feelings, ideas, and images along with his biological functions. These experiences are not observable in the way that his behavior or biological makeup is. Man's experience or spirit does not exist in any publicly observable space; rather, this experience is subjective. A distinction between physical time and what Santayana calls specious time will help make this point clear. The actual physical time as measured by the clock that indicates how long a person has been taking a walk may in fact be quite different from the specious time he feels may have elapsed. The feeling of time is personal and pertains to the realm of spirit; the actual physical time is objective and pertains to the realm of matter. The realm of spirit, therefore, is distinguishable from that of matter and has its own quality of existence.

Spirit, as Santayana defines it, is the realm of conscious experience and is free to roam, as the imagination or fancy may indicate, in ways in which matter or the body cannot. Spirit is essentially reflective and poetic whereas matter, although dynamic, is essentially dumb or blind. Matter as matter does not have awareness or spirit, but nevertheless supports it and makes it possible. Spirit or awareness, in turn, does not support or sustain itself—it needs some material machinery for that—but in existing it adds a new dimension to existence by virtue of the many perspectives it sees or the ideas which it thinks. Spirit is therefore powerless to do anything, just as all essences are powerless. Spirit lives and flourishes, however, by being aware of things. It is that which is aware of both essence and existence. Intuition, for example, is a mental or spiritual event. Memory, as a form of knowing something about the past, is a mental or spiritual event. Prayer and contemplation, while truly spiritual in quality, are certainly not the only kinds of spiritual experiences; all thinking and all conscious experience is spiritual in quality however lofty or ordinary their intentions may be.

Santayana insists that his materialism is not metaphysical. However, he asserts that "I do not disclaim being metaphysical because I at all dislike dialectic or disdain immaterial things: indeed, it is of immaterial things, essence, truth and spirit that I speak chiefly." [47] It is a distinct feature of his materialism that it makes room for spirit as an immaterial existence, and allows essence and truth to possess a being or status that is non-temporal and immaterial. Essence, truth, and spirit are important modes of being, but they have no power to force things to happen. Immaterial things like poetry or symbols or thought do not intervene in material events, but merely supervene upon them as ideals to be enjoyed and reflected on. Materialism or naturalism "will break down, however, so soon as words, ideas, or spirits are taken to be substantial on their own account, and powers at work prior to the existence of their organs, or independent of them. Now it is precisely such disembodied powers and immaterial functions prior to matter that are called metaphysical." [48]

The question remains, Why does Santayana think that these four realms of being—essence, matter, truth and spirit—are worth distinguishing? To answer this question it should first be remembered that Santayana has a definite respect for common sense. He does not believe that philosophy can or should construct a system with no basis in the time-honored accumulated wisdom of man's experiences with the world of affairs. Philosophy can never justify itself as a purely specialized pursuit that withdraws from actual life. Philosophy ought to bring wisdom, but it will have little or nothing to teach us if it ignores the sane counsels of common sense. However, philosophy must also recognize that our common-sense apprehensions of things are very rough, in need of definite pruning and refinement. The whole point, then, of carefully distinguishing between different kinds of being is to achieve a more stable and coherent type of wisdom on the basis of what common sense can assure us. Philosophy is neither honest nor a source of wisdom unless it pertains to how we should live our lives and how we may obtain some definite good by living. Knowledge merely for its own sake is idle for a philosopher who should not properly busy his mind in mere facts. The philosopher must seek such distinctions that are grounded in the way things are and that have some point to them.

Santayana thinks the realm of essence worth distinguishing basically because essence is the principle of distinguishability itself. Since every essence is a distinct form, we could not distinguish anything else without attending to essential differences. Also, essences as enjoyable qualities open to awareness are a source of good in life, since without them every-thing would be chaotic. Existence itself would not be worth having. The realm of matter is worth distinguishing because it supports our existence. Since men must recognize that they have bodies which can be helped or harmed by other material bodies, it would be insane or whimsical not to respect the realm of matter as the source of power, growth, and all change. The uses to which matter can be put are best seen by looking to art, since art is one of the most important phases of human progress and indicates in tangible ways how matter can be shaped for human uses and enjoyments. The realm of matter is fallaciously denied by all those idealists who either expect matter to be what it can never be—some pure essence—or who condemn matter because it stubbornly resists our efforts to understand and control it. These complaints can only be seen as futile when we have carefully distinguished matter from other orders of being and when we give it credit for being in full measure just what it is, the substance or ground of all existence.

The realm of truth is worth distinguishing as a mode of being distinct from material events and from any of our mere opinions about things. Only through misunderstanding could truth itself be materialized and confused with that of which it is the truth. Events are neither true nor false; rather, propositions are either true or false of them. Truth would have no subject matter if it were not secondary to the passage of events. But propositions could not even misrepresent or falsify events unless a total, correct system of representations was assumed. Truth (the whole) must be an ideal description of events and can neither exist in experience nor in any mind; by merely existing, any experience or thought implies the truth about itself, which it could not do if truth were not distinct from that which thinks or experiences it. For example, if someone thinks that it is true that Abraham Lincoln was born in 1809, this proposition about Lincoln is not true because someone thinks it is. The thought or opinion itself is an existence that gives rise to a further truth, namely the true proposition that someone in fact at a certain time had that thought or opinion.

Santayana contends that the realm of truth is worth distinguishing as one segment of the realm of essence, in order to avoid what he takes to be the mistakes of pragmatism and idealism. Pragmatism, in making truth a functional part of experience, confuses truth with experience or the realm of spirit. Experience or spirit is ever changing and thus the pragmatists assert that truth itself is dynamic and changing. This is contradictory, according to Santayana, since it is events which change and not the truth about them. If the truth about events changed, then some truths would be false, which is absurd. Similarly, idealism, which makes truth a mental reality (existing in some mind which knows it), confuses truth with thought or the realm of spirit. The idealists claim that the existence of truth logically requires a mind that comprehends it, since an incomprehensible truth is no truth at all. The mistake here is to treat truth as something which exists or occurs in the first place, and second to confuse ideal comprehension with an actually existing thought or mind. Truth has being, of course, since it is a complex essence or set of relations, but it does not have existence. It only depicts existence.

But the whole truth, as that complex essence which depicts all existence, cannot be comprehended by an existing thought, since any existing thought implies a further truth about itself as an actual thought. Santayana allows that truth is comprehensible, but only ideally; That is, while in principle every truth is knowable, not every truth is actually known. Actual knowledge is a function of animal faith or naturalistic conditions which set limitations on our knowledge. These limitations do not affect the being of truth itself, but merely its being known. Further, Santayana considers that Royce and the idealists are mistaken in their view that truth can be logically deduced or that there are necessary truths. Deduction or logic only informs us about the implications of our discourse or symbols; it only judges the consistency, not the truth value, of our ideas. Since false ideas can be logically consistent with one another, the only measure of truth in ideas is reference to existence or actual facts. However, no fact is logically necessary, since necessity, too, is a function of discourse or the way symbols are defined. No proposition is rendered true simply by definition, since we are free to define terms as we choose, whereas truth has to refer to what occurs in time.

Finally, Santayana considers the realm of spirit worthy of careful distinction since spirit is the most distinctive feature of human existence. Of all four realms of being, only spirit is characteristically human. The pure being and infinity of essences mark them as detached from all existence. Matter, although existent and the ground of all existence, is physical in character rather than human and underlies the existence of inanimate things as well as animate. The realm of truth is impersonal and as a whole well beyond man's limited power or even interest to know or see it all. Spirit, however, is only present when conscious experience is aroused. Spirit, although it may roam poetically and imaginatively far afield, nevertheless has a moral focus and human bias that marks it alone as the center of man's life. Spirit does not have the power to make things change or to compel the body to act. Rather, it is the function of spirit to feel and conceive things dramatically and with human meaning. Spirit can even complain that it is attached to a certain body or any body at all, since in contemplation it can easily imagine itself as free of all matter and all cares of the world. But spirit can only imagine itself as cut off from the body; it cannot effect any such severance, according to Santayana. Spirit lives on borrowed time, but imagines itself living forever. Spirit is essentially poetic and is ever finding symbols for itself which are congenial to its purposes.

The great value of spirit is that it can remain free even when it is disciplined, although it is only when spirit is disciplined by knowledge and common sense that it can become coherent and avoid confusion and unnecessary frustration. The spiritual life must certainly be consistent with a life of reason. The true life of the spirit for Santayana involves the careful cultivation of self-knowledge to achieve detached and disillusioned enjoyment while at the same time maintaining a proper respect for the world or the sources of its own existence. Spirit cannot be free or enjoy well-being if it is fooled or deceived. But the worst enemy of spirit is itself, since self-deception disperses the mind's grasp of other things. False hopes, despondency, tragic desires, and vain estimations all stem from over-estimation or under-estimation of self. Distraction and anxiety beset spirit, but they must also be recognized as inevitable in animal life.

Intuition or undistracted enjoyment requires detachment from existence and time. The good life for man is impossible without harmony or order in life. Enjoyment therefore requires a set of conditions that are in conflict with one another. Existence would not be worthwhile if it did not bring any immediate enjoyment with it. But immediate and undistracted enjoyment requires not only the leisure to pause and enjoy things, it requires a detachment from the passage of time and from the existences that are merely instrumental to its happiness. One cannot watch the clock or be anxious about his existence and at the same time enjoy what he is doing. Enjoyment or the good life, according to Santayana, must be timeless in quality, but it takes time and concern with more than mere quality to possess and sustain any good life. Philosophy, therefore, must enlighten us about both essence and existence—all the realms of being—

if it is to be truly helpful and not short-sighted or confused. Only then will philosophy be in the truly classical sense a love or pursuit of wisdom.

THE SIGNIFICANCE AND INFLUENCE OF SANTAYANA Santayana is today one of the major figures not only of twentieth-century American philosophy but of the twentieth century as a whole. This fact was acknowledged during his lifetime with the publication in 1940 of *The Philosophy of Santayana* in *The Library of Living Philosophers,* a work specifically devoted to the recognition of the most outstanding world-figures in philosophy. This volume on Santayana contains the efforts of numerous philosophic scholars who offer their interpretations of the meaning and significance of his thought. The great number of other books which either discuss Santayana's philosophy or include portions of his writings testify to the fact of Santayana's contemporary prominence.

Many of his works continue to be published in new editions. *The Sense of Beauty,* for example, originally brought out in 1896, continues to be published today in paperback form which means that it circulates to a wider reading audience. *The Life of Reason,* originally published in five volumes in 1905–06, was revised by Santayana for a compact one-volume edition which appeared in 1953. *Scepticism and Animal Faith,* first published in 1923, has subsequently been issued in paperback form as have been other of Santayana's works.

The continued publication of Santayana's writings not only indicates the endurance of his ideas, but indicates something of his appeal to the reading public as well. His writings have become accepted as examples of philosophical writing at its very best. He is as enjoyable as he is profitable to read. His works demonstrate that philosophy does not have to be academic or difficult in a technical sense, but that it can state its case for all intelligent readers to understand. Santayana's greatness may therefore be taken to reside in this fact: he refused to make philosophy esoteric while, at the same time, he maintained the highest standards of excellence for philosophic composition and thinking. Santayana's high regard for Aristotle and the classical Greeks is a case in point. What he admired in Aristotle and the ancient Greeks was their love of wisdom and beauty, their respect for a life of reason. Socrates, Plato, and Aristotle conceived philosophy as based on reflective thinking and refused to entertain or construct a philosophy they could not live by. Santayana respected the classical quality of these ancient Greek philosophers precisely because they raised man to be a lover of the rational, that is, the orderly and enduring forms or essences of things.

Santayana's writing and publishing career extended for a period of more than fifty years, longer than any other American philosopher except John Dewey. The great number of gracefully written works from *The Sense of Beauty* (1896) to *Dominations and Powers* (1951) have established Santayana as one of the very best and most readable of philosophers. Along with Dewey's, Santayana's critical naturalism stands as one of the most important and comprehensive philosophies of the present century. Also as a critical realist Santayana is one of the key figures in the development of twentieth-century realist epistemologies.

Santayana's place in the development of American philosophic thought is unusual. As first a student and later a colleague of both James and Royce, Santayana represents an important link in the maturing of philosophical thinking in America. Santayana is unique in that he is the only major American philosopher to have grown to his intellectual maturity under the guidance of two of the greatest American philosophical thinkers. However, he became a disciple of neither James' pragmatism nor Royce's idealism, but developed his own brand of critical naturalism in opposition to both of their positions. Yet what is most unusual about Santayana as an American philosopher is the manner in which he remained detached or aloof from American culture as a whole. There is no sense of struggle, enterprise, or involvement in human affairs in his philosophy such as one finds in the works of James, Royce, and Dewey. Santayana is without doubt the only modern American philosopher whom we can describe as perfectly serene. However, his serenity and urbanity did not narrow his philosophical perspective; rather they gave it wider scope and clearer vision. Santayana utilized his detachment to view America and all things with greater freedom and impartiality.

The Life of Reason in many ways may be regarded as Santayana's finest achievement. This work has become a classic of twentieth-century philosophical naturalism; it has deeply influenced other leading naturalists and received high praise from such prominent American philosophers as John Dewey, Morris Cohen, John Herman Randall, Jr., Ernest Nagel, and others. Morris Cohen, writing of the whole American philosophical tradition, asserts that Santayana's *"Life of Reason* is the only comprehensive, carefully articulated, philosophy of life and civilization which has been produced on these shores." [49] John Dewey also paid high tribute to Santayana when he wrote, "No modern thinker has pointed out so persuasively as Santayana that 'every phase of the ideal world emanates from the natural,' that 'sense, art, religion, society, express nature exuberantly.' " [50] Santayana's influence on Dewey and other naturalistic philosophers is an important factor in the prominence of naturalism as a viable philosophical movement in the twentieth century. Many naturalists including Dewey are fond of quoting many of Santayana's well turned statements to articulate their own positions. They admire Santayana's talent for expressing a complex thought in clear graphic terms. Although Dewey diverged from Santayana's philosophy on certain points, he thought their agreement was far more important. One significant agreement between these two philosophers concerns the natural basis of all ideals. Dewey stated, "One of the not least of the many merits of Santayana's *Life of Reason* is the consistency and vision with which is upheld the doctrine that significant idealism means idealization." [51]

Santayana's influence has remained strong in aesthetics and in those circles where philosophy is cultivated as an art as well as an intellectual discipline. His essays in literary criticism have not only continued in print, but they have been made a special object of study and have been collected in a single volume by Irving Singer, *Essays in Literary Criticism by George Santayana*. Special issues of the *Journal of Philosophy* in 1954 and 1964 have been devoted to assessments of Santayana's philosophy. However, it is his wider appeal to individuals interested in man, life, and art that indicates his best side. The publication of *Atoms of Thought* in 1950 and *The Wisdom of George Santayana* in 1964, both of which contain his beautifully succinct statements of complex ideas, indicates the manner in which he has become admirably quotable. His aphorism concerning fanaticism is a good illustration: "Fanaticism consists in redoubling your effort when you have forgotten your aim." [52] Santayana's humor and sharpness of expression is an essential part of his wisdom. The philosopher must try to see things for what they are, but this does not mean that he cannot enjoy what he sees. His statement about superstition exemplifies the peculiar brand of his wisdom that does not fail to bring in a note of laughter. "Men became superstitious not because they had too much imagination, but because they were not aware that they had any." [53]

In conclusion, we may say that Santayana is one of the very few twentieth-century philosophers who has completed an entirely consistent and comprehensive system of thought that is not esoteric and highly technical. Santayana's enduring impact resides in his poetic naturalism which compels respect both from common sense and from man's ideal or imaginative aspirations. Although he was detached from existence and neither intoxicated nor really in love with it, he was neither a pessimist nor a cynic. He celebrated the true and the beautiful while at the same time placing them upon a naturalistic basis—for the sake of understanding as well as for pure enjoyment.

NOTES

1. George Santayana, *Realms of Being,* One Vol. Ed., p. xii.
2. *Ibid.,* p. 8.
3. *Ibid.*
4. Santayana, *The Life of Reason, or the Phases of Human Progress,* One Vol. Ed., p. 198.
5. *Ibid.,* p. 198.
6. *Ibid.,* p. 258.
7. *Ibid.*
8. *Ibid.,* p. 264.
9. *Ibid.,* p. 296.
10. *Ibid.,* pp. 303–304.
11. *Ibid.,* p. 384.
12. *Ibid.,* p. 409.
13. *Ibid.,* p. 456.
14. *Ibid.,* pp. 456–457.
15. Santayana, *Winds of Doctrine and Platonism and the Spiritual Life,* p. 144.
16. Santayana, *The Life of Reason,* p. 462.
17. *Ibid.,* pp. 466–467.
18. *Ibid.,* p. 480.
19. Santayana, *Interpretations of Poetry and Religion,* p. v.
20. Santayana, *Three Philosophical Poets,* p. 12.
21. *Ibid.,* p. 203.
22. *Ibid.,* p. 204.
23. Santayana, *Character and Opinion in the United States,* p. vi.
24. Santayana, *Winds of Doctrine and Platonism and the Spiritual Life,* p. 187.
25. Santayana, *Character and Opinion in the United States,* p. 88.
26. Santayana, *Winds of Doctrine and Platonism and the Spiritual Life,* p. 189.
27. *Ibid.,* pp. 187–188.
28. *Ibid.,* p. 191.
29. *Ibid.,* p. 196.
30. Santayana, *Interpretations of Poetry and Religion,* p. 225.
31. *Ibid.,* p. 230.
32. Santayana, *Character and Opinion in the United States,* p. 100.
33. *Ibid.,* p. 106.
34. *Ibid.*
35. Santayana, *Winds of Doctrine and Platonism and the Spiritual Life,* p. 203.
36. Santayana, *Character and Opinion in the United States,* p. 68.

37. Santayana, "Dewey's Naturalistic Metaphysics," in Paul Arthur Schilpp, ed., *The Philosophy of John Dewey,* p. 247.

38. *Ibid.,* pp. 247–248.

39. *Ibid.,* p. 248.

40. *Ibid.,* pp. 252–253.

41. Santayana, *Scepticism and Animal Faith: Introduction to a System of Philosophy,* p. 8.

42. *Ibid.,* p. 182.

43. *Ibid.,* p. xii.

44. Santayana, "Apologia Pro Mente Sua," in Paul Arthur Schilpp, ed., *The Philosophy of George Santayana,* p. 497.

45. Santayana, *Realms of Being,* p. 834.

46. Santayana, *Scepticism and Animal Faith: Introduction to a System of Philosophy,* p. 271.

47. *Ibid.,* p. vii.

48. Santayana, "Dewey's Naturalistic Metaphysics," in Schilpp, ed., *The Philosophy of John Dewey,* p. 246.

49. Morris Cohen, *American Thought: A Critical Sketch* (New York: Collier, 1962), p. 390.

50. John Dewey, *Experience and Nature* (New York: Dover, 1958), p. 58.

51. John Dewey, *The Influence of Darwin on Philosophy and Other Essays in Contemporary Thought* (Bloomington: Indiana University Press, 1965), p. 224.

52. Santayana, *The Life of Reason, or the Phases of Human Progress,* p. 13.

53. Santayana, *Interpretations of Poetry and Religion,* p. 108.

QUESTIONS FOR DISCUSSION

1. Why could Santayana not accept either James' pragmatism or Royce's idealism?

2. How does Santayana's "Life of Reason" show his basic naturalism and detachment?

3. How cogent is Santayana's interpretation of religion as poetry?

4. How valid are Santayana's interpretations of American intellectual life? Are his criticisms of other American philosophers such as Emerson, James, and Royce valid?

5. Is Santayana inconsistent when he defends knowledge as animal faith, after having arrived at ultimate skepticism by suspending judgment or belief altogether?

6. Why does Santayana consider the distinction between essence and existence so important? Is his distinction sound?

7. Why can Santayana not accept James' theory of truth, or Royce's? Is his conception of truth superior to theirs?

8. What is Santayana's stature and place in the development of American philosophy? To what extent is he an American philosopher at all?

SUGGESTED READINGS

A General Confession. The best brief statement of Santayana's basic position. [In Schilpp, ed., *The Philosophy of George Santayana,* pp. 1–30.]

The Life of Reason or the Phases of Human Progress. Reason in common sense. The birth of reason (Ch. 1). Reason in society; ideal society (Ch. 8). Reason in religion; how religion may be an embodiment of reason (Ch. 1). Reason in art; art and happiness (Ch. 11). Reason in science; the validity of science (Ch. 10).

Character and Opinion in the United States. The moral background (Ch. 1); William James (Ch. 2); Josiah Royce (Ch. 3).

Winds of Doctrine. The critique of pragmatism (Ch. 4, Part 3); the genteel tradition in American philosophy (Ch. 6).

Interpretations of Poetry and Religion. Emerson (Ch. 8).

Dewey's Naturalistic Metaphysics. [In Schilpp, ed., *The Philosophy of John Dewey,* pp. 243–261.]

Scepticism and Animal Faith. There are no first principles of criticism (Ch. 1); ultimate scepticism (Ch. 6); the discovery of essence (Ch. 9); knowledge is faith mediated by symbols (Ch. 18); belief in nature (Ch. 22); the implied being of truth (Ch. 25); discernment of spirit (Ch. 26).

Platonism and the Spiritual Life. Detachment, disillusionment, and the eternal aspect of things (Ch. 23).

PRIMARY SOURCES

George Santayana, *Apologia Pro Mente Sua,* in Schilpp, ed., *The Philosophy of George Santayana,* pp. 495–605.

————, *Character and Opinion in the United States* (New York: Anchor Books, 1956).

————, *Dominations and Powers* (New York: Scribner's, 1951).

————, *A General Confession,* in Schilpp, ed., *The Philosophy of George Santayana,* pp. 1–30.

————, *Interpretations of Poetry and Religion* (New York: Harper Torchbooks, 1957).

————, *The Life of Reason, or the Phases of Human Progress* (New York: Scribner's, 1955).

————, *Realms of Being* (New York: Scribner's, 1942).

————, *Scepticism and Animal Faith: Introduction to a System of Philosophy* (New York: Dover).

————, *The Sense of Beauty* (New York: Scribner's, 1896).

————, *Three Philosophical Poets* (New York: Anchor Books, 1953).

————, *Winds of Doctrine and Platonism and the Spiritual Life* (New York: Harper Torchbooks, 1957).

Paul Arthur Schilpp, ed., *The Philosophy of George Santayana* (New York: Tudor, 1940).

————, *The Philosophy of John Dewey* (New York: Tudor, 1939).

SECONDARY SOURCES

Willard E. Arnett, *Santayana and the Sense of Beauty* (Bloomington: Indiana University Press, 1955).

Milton K. Munitz, *The Moral Philosophy of Santayana* (New York: Columbia University Press, 1958).

Paul Arthur Schilpp, ed., *The Philosophy of George Santayana* (New York: Tudor, 1940).

Irving Singer, *Santayana's Aesthetics: A Critical Introduction* (Cambridge, Mass.: Harvard University Press, 1957).

8 John Dewey

Naturalism and Instrumentalism

John Dewey (1859–1952) is the most productive and influential philosopher that America has produced. His active career as author and teacher extended for more than seventy years, and his ideas and influence have become firmly imbedded in American life. The application of Dewey's philosophy to the problems of men and the world in which he lived are entirely consistent with the naturalistic and instrumental conception of philosophy that he so staunchly advocated. No one claimed more application for philosophy in the world than Dewey, and no one has insisted as profoundly that philosophy can have relevance *only* in relation to the natural world. Dewey's entire effort as a philosopher, therefore, must be viewed as an attempt to show that all of man's experiences and actions take on increased meaning when understood naturalistically and when viewed as functions or instrumentalities for solving his problems and enriching his life. The themes of naturalism and instrumentalism, which are complementary to one another, are central to all Dewey's thought. Whatever exists or has meaning and values must have a naturalistic context; nothing can have meaning, truth, or genuine value unless it operates or serves instrumentally to dispel confusion in life and produce clarity and order.

John Dewey was born in Burlington, Vermont in 1859, the year that Darwin published his *Origin of Species*. After his graduation from the University of Vermont in 1879, Dewey taught high school for several years before he embarked upon his graduate work in philosophy. In

1882 he began his distinguished publishing career with the article "Metaphysical Assumptions of Naturalism," published in *The Journal of Speculative Philosophy*. This same journal devoted to original philosophic thought was the same one in which Peirce published his earliest philosophical essays. Encouraged in his study of philosophy by W. T. Harris, the editor of the journal, Dewey entered Johns Hopkins University where he received his Ph.D. in 1884. While at Johns Hopkins he took two courses in logic under Charles Peirce, but it was G. Stanley Hall, the psychologist, and George S. Morris, the idealist philosopher, who had a greater influence upon Dewey's early development. Under the influence of Hall, Dewey developed an interest in scientific or experimental psychology, and in 1887 he published his first book, *Psychology*. Under Morris' influence, Dewey went to the University of Michigan where he eventually became Chairman of the Department of Philosophy. During this period he became more and more concerned with problems of education and applied psychology. In 1889 he published a work entitled *Applied Psychology: An Introduction to the Principles and Practice of Education*.

He had an early and continued interest in the interrelationship between theory and practice. During these formative years it gradually became more and more evident to Dewey that theory and practice were not two separate things, but that a vital interaction must exist between the theoretical and the practical, between how we think about things and how we work with them. His growing concern with educational problems made him see the need of integrating theory and practice and provided him with an excellent series of test cases for his own theories. Of extreme importance to Dewey, at this time and later, was the idea that every body of learning should have an application for some other. Real learning must involve a thorough-going inquiry, drawing on results from other inquiries and furnishing results for further inquiries.

Consistent with his concern for the integration of knowledge is the important fact that in 1894 Dewey was appointed Chairman of the Department of Philosophy and Psychology at the University of Chicago. Also included in his appointment was the responsibility to develop educational theory and practice. At Chicago Dewey originated the University Elementary School, the first experimental school of education known as the Laboratory School. During his stay at Chicago he developed and published a long series of works on philosophy, psychology, and education. The titles of these works indicate both the broadness of Dewey's interests and his basic concern to interrelate different bodies of knowledge: *Psychological Method in Ethics; The School as Social Center; The Psychology of Number and Its Applications to Methods of Teaching Arithmetic; Ethical Principles Underlying Education; Psychology and Philosophic Method; Evolution and Ethics,* etc. Two important works which Dewey published while at Chicago and which reflect his impact on the world of education and in philosophy are *The School and Society* (1899), which has been translated into more than twelve languages, and *Studies in Logical Theory* (1903) which became one of the most influential and important works in the development of American pragmatism in general and Dewey's own instrumentalism in particular.

In 1905 Dewey moved to Columbia University where he continued to write and teach, and where he became America's most prominent philosopher. Along with James he was an acknowledged leader in the development of American pragmatism with the publication of such essays as *The Realism of Pragmatism* (1905), *Experimental Theory of Knowledge* (1906), *What Does Pragmatism Mean by Practical?* (1908), *The Bearings of Pragmatism upon Education* (1908), *The Pragmatic Movement of Contemporary Thought* (1909), etc.

Dewey's output of articles and books during this period and after is staggering. In 1908, in collaboration with James H. Tufts, he published his famous *Ethics,* and in 1910 he published *How We Think,* later translated into French, Russian, Spanish, Chinese, Polish, and other languages. In 1916 he published his influential *Democracy and Education* and his *Essays in Experimental Logic* which established him as a leader in education as well as in philosophy. Dewey's published works and interests kept him in intimate contact with intellectual developments and practical affairs of the time. Like Jefferson, Dewey was in tune with and exercised leadership in educational, political, philosophic, and all important human affairs. He actively supported Theodore Roosevelt for the presidency in 1912, and in 1915 served as the first president of the American Association of University Professors. He traveled and lectured in Japan, China, Turkey, and Russia, where he influenced the course of world education both in theory and practice.

In 1920 he published *Reconstruction in Philosophy* which together with *Human Nature and Conduct* (1922) and *Experience and Nature* (1925) gave mature and extended formulation to his fundamental naturalism in philosophy. In 1927 he published *The Public and Its Problems,* in which he formulated his important and influential idea of the "great community" or the "great society," and in 1929, the year in which he retired from teaching and became a Professor Emeritus at Columbia University, he published his famous book, *The Quest for Certainty*. After his retirement from teaching, Dewey continued to write and publish influential books and articles until his death in 1952 at the age of ninety-two. His *Philosophy and Civilization* appeared in 1931, and in 1934 he published his famous *Art as Experience* and *A Common Faith*. These two books have subsequently come to be recognized as among the most important works in this century in aesthetics and the philosophy of religion respectively. Dewey continued to publish outstanding works in social philosophy with his *Liberalism and Social Action* in 1935 and *Freedom and Culture* in 1939. He continued his efforts in the field of education with his *Experience and Education* in 1938. He also published in 1938 *Logic, the Theory of Inquiry*, presenting his instrumentalism in its most complete form. In 1939 he published *Theory of Valuation*, which has become a work of importance in contemporary philosophy.

Dewey's long philosophical development is too complex to be indicated by any simple outline. However, what may be shown are some of the important influences on his thought as well as something of the way he not only received these influences but reconstructed them into a unified and comprehensive philosophy. Early in his career, Dewey came under the influence of dialectical idealism. Like Royce, he was impressed by its attempt to see things whole and integrated. Dewey also was impressed by the attempt of idealism to include the social, religious, scientific, artistic, and, in fact, all important realms within the scope of philosophic inquiry. However, his own studies of psychology, along with his growing interest in experimentation and the study of empirical results, more and more convinced him that the methods and conclusions of absolute idealism were faulty and in need of revision. It gradually became apparent to Dewey that the methods and conclusions of absolute idealism were inconsistent with the methods of genuine inquiry or problem-solving and in reality defeated the purposes of inquiry.

> The claim to formulate *a priori* the legislative constitution of the universe is by its nature a claim that may lead to elaborate dialectical developments. But it is also one that removes these very conclusions from subjection to experimental test, for, by definition, these results make no difference in the detailed course of events.[1]

In rejecting the claims and methods of idealism, Dewey did not reject the hope that intelligent methods could be found to integrate and unify our understandings of things. He retained the idealists' confidence in intelligence and intellectual methods as well as their goal of seeing things unified. However, he was left with a serious problem which he continued to study for the rest of his life, that of devising a method of intelligence that would do justice to the complexity of experience and nature and at the same time put things in order and unity. A method was needed that would apply to all subject-matters and that was, in addition, self-corrective and objectively testable. He came to see that both the scientific and pragmatic methods fulfilled these requirements, but that a theoretical and practical demonstration was needed to show that this was the case. Dewey interpreted the works of Darwin as showing that living things, including man, were definitely susceptible to understanding through naturalistic and scientific methods. The concept of evolution not only signified that life and man were truly natural, but that a dynamic continuity exists between man and nature, or experience and the external environment. Human experience is neither an exception to natural processes or events, nor an isolated, self-enclosed, ghostlike phenomenon; rather, it takes place in nature and involves transactions or interactions with the natural world.

> Experience is *of* as well as *in* nature. It is not experience which is experienced, but nature—stones, plants, animals, diseases, health, temperature, electricity and so on. Things interacting in certain ways *are* experience; they are what is experienced. Linked in certain other ways with another natural object—the human organism —they are *how* things are experienced as well.[2]

All of our experiences involve a situational context that is not only spatial and temporal, but continually changing and potentially rich in meaning, knowledge, and value. The important feature of our experiences is that they have continuity and future consequences. Experience signifies a building up of habits and thoughts in response to the needs of living and growth. As such it is always changing, indicating a dynamic interaction between the organism and its environment. Hence, there is not just one kind of experience; rather, experience is multi-sided involving social, aesthetic, intellectual, moral, or religious meanings. However, Dewey does claim that there is only one kind of useful or progressive experience—the experience of intelligent problem-solving, that is, the scientific method. Scientific or intelligent experience accepts change and problems as part of the conditions of all existence. The advantage of the scientific method or approach, however, is not just that it accepts or admits change, but that it actually induces changes experimentally in order to predict and control results. This means that the scientific method is operational or pragmatic in character since it sets up certain operations to be performed and then looks to experienced or observable results as tests of its hypotheses.

Dewey gives credit to Peirce for originating the pragmatic or operational method as the only objective way of determining the meaning of concepts. He further gives credit to James for broadening the pragmatic method to include a theory of truth and making it applicable to all of man's basic life concerns. Dewey claims that "it lies in the nature of pragmatism that it should be applied as widely as possible." [3] He agrees with Peirce that "everybody uses the scientific method about a great many things, and only ceases to use it when he does not know how to apply it." [4] The scientific method is pragmatic inasmuch as it gives meaning to its ideas in terms of their anticipated consequences. And the pragmatic method, because it is experimental, is scientific; it calls for exclusively operational tests of meaning.

For Dewey the pragmatic and scientific methods are not two separate methods with restricted applications; rather, they both signify the method of intelligent inquiry which selects the appropriate means for achieving worthwhile purposes. This is Dewey's instrumentalism, that all meaningful, true, or valuable ideas are experimental instruments for the intelligent solution of problems. According to him, thinking itself only arises in the face of problematic situations. As a consequence, the only proper goal of thought is to dispel confusion and doubt and to work to a clear and certified conclusion. However, instrumentalism also signifies that the development of intelligent ways to solve problems is no easy matter and that the solution of one problem gives rise to further problematic situations. Problems and their solutions are interrelated, and they always involve an existential context which is cultural or social as well as biological. Problems neither arise nor can they be solved in a vacuum. Here is where Dewey's naturalism meets his instrumentalism.

Ideas as mental instruments are not mere subjective existences in some mind, but rather they are objectively discoverable modes of interaction occurring in the natural world. The ideas and thoughts of men not only do not occur without the brain and other biological functions, but these biological functions in man are themselves interactions with an external world that is both natural and social. Man's thinking is socially or culturally conditioned just as much as his conduct is. Human life as we know it would not be possible without the acquisition of habits both in terms of how we think as well as how we act. Without habits every effort of thought or action would be discontinuous with every other, and man would be reduced to a creature of pure impulse or erratic behavior. However, according to Dewey, not only are habits necessary to human nature and conduct, they are also excellent examples of interactions between the organism and its surroundings. Habits are naturalistic as well as instrumental—natural because they are interactions between an organism and its actual environment, and instrumental insofar as they are useful in the organism's dealings with environment.

However, the bare existence of habits, whether of action or of thought, should not be confused with their intelligent cultivation. Dewey's basic philosophic effort may in fact be viewed as an attempt to face and meet the "repeated struggle between the active force of scientific knowledge and technical power and the deflecting force of the lag and inertia of institutionalized habits and beliefs." [5] One of his most often repeated themes is the need to eliminate outmoded ways of thinking and doing things and to devise newer and better modes of thought and courses of action. Philosophy has a most important role to play as general or comprehensive criticism. Without intelligent criticism, human life can only repeat itself; it cannot really improve.

The advance of science in solving problems means that any responsible philosophy will have to be scientific in character. However, since knowledge must be integrated and applied as widely and intelligently as possible, the advance of science requires the advance of philosophic effort as well. Scientific specialization must be balanced by a general or philosophic understanding. Also, the advance of science and technology requires the advancement or improvement of learning. Accordingly, Dewey asserts that "philosophy may even be defined as the general theory of education." [6] Philosophy must be instrumental both in theory and in practice. In the field of education he believes that this is readily apparent. Philosophy must provide intelligent guidance in the broadest sense in order to avoid the narrow extremes of (1) theory without application, (2) repetition without understanding, and (3) education without meaningful values.

This means that philosophy can never succeed if it attempts to become isolated from life. Dewey's naturalism assumes that all meaningful inquiry begins and ends with the natural world. His instrumentalism assumes that inquiry itself must be conceived in the broadest sense as working to provide useful methods of problem solving. However, what Dewey terms the deepest problem of modern life, the problem of coordinating facts and values, is fundamentally philosophic in character.

> The problem of restoring integration and cooperation between man's beliefs about the world in which he lives and his beliefs about the values and purposes that should direct his conduct is the deepest problem of modern life. It is the problem of any philosophy that is not isolated from that life.[7]

Traditionally, philosophy has separated facts and values, and insofar as it has done so, it has not been of real service to man. So-called philosophical resignation or detachment from the affairs of the world is not only useless, but is philosophically baseless as well. It represents a failure to understand the natural and instrumental character of all genuine thinking. Similarly, we must expect more from philosophy than mere consolation and misleading platitudes. Philosophy, if it is true to life, cannot be merely high sounding or less energetic than life. In short, philosophy must be existentially concerned with the world and experimentally oriented to deal with it intelligently.

Dewey's own philosophical development represents, therefore, a remarkable combination of reconstruction as well as creation. His naturalism and instrumentalism developed from Peirce and James. Clearly his philosophy is pragmatic. However, it is not a mere reworking of Peirce and James, but goes far beyond them. Neither Peirce nor James worked out a comprehensive or integrated theory of values or social philosophy. Peirce showed that concepts required logical and operational tests of their meaning; James showed that truth as well as all life concerns required humanistic and functional tests of their meaning. Dewey attempted to show how a comprehensive experimental philosophy could integrate all these factors (meaning, truth, and value) and at the same time give them application to man's social life. His philosophy, therefore, is more comprehensive since it is social or cultural in emphasis and includes the logical and psychological within its naturalism. If Peirce's pragmatism calls for logical and experimental consequences, and if James' pragmatism demands concrete and humanistic results, then Dewey's pragmatism may be said to require social applications as well.

THE INTEGRATION OF EXPERIENCE, THOUGHT, AND SCIENTIFIC METHOD — Dewey's early studies in psychology set the stage for his instrumental and integrated view of all knowledge. It became apparent to him that psychology could not properly study the mind and experience by treating them as purely isolated and subjective phenomena. Introspection or the mere passive contemplation of mental states is not only faulty because it cannot be objectively verified, but it is mistaken in believing that we can study the mind in a vacuum or outside a natural context. For Dewey, our study of the mind is limited to seeing how it functions in its contexts. This means that experience and thinking can only be known instrumentally in terms of what they accomplish and how they involve an interaction between the organism and its environment.

Psychology is the study of behavior and not the study of the mind in separation from nature. Behavior, whether it be emotional or sensory, rational or habitual, always implies a context and something which in principle is objectively observable. However, behavior must be studied experimentally, according to Dewey, since mere passive observation is superficial and does not engage in problem-solving. Experimentation, whether simple or complex, involves the assumption of a problem to be solved as well as the carrying out of operations to work to the solution of that problem. Unlike passive observation, experimentation is directed to some practical purpose and therefore involves active problem-solving. Dewey assumes that without problem solving the quest for knowledge of any kind would not occur. However, experimental problem-solving is inherently operational and always entails an interaction between experience and some environment. Thought and action therefore are not opposed, but are both operationally defined in terms of their purposes. In fact, experimentation is a prime example of the cooperation of thoughts and actions. A thoughtless experiment would be a contradiction in terms. But an experiment which did nothing at all, which implied no action in any way, would be just as contradictory.

It follows that there is no gulf between theory and practice or between theoretical knowledge and applied knowledge. Any separation that is made between the theoretical and the practical is based on misconceiving the instrumental and integrated character of all genuine knowledge. Consider psychology as an example. According to Dewey, psychology can only study experience in terms of behavior. It therefore must study what the organism does under experimentally controlled situations. But this means that psychology has to consider the biological and social environment without which no experiences would occur. The psychological, biological, and social factors of experience must be integrated if our knowledge of what experience really is, is to be in any way complete and factual. Psychology is therefore a social science just as much as it is biological. The need for integration in our knowledge of experience is based on the observable facts of a dynamic continuity or integration of factors in existence. This point may be pushed even further by observing that psychology is also a physical science in the sense that biological knowledge is intimately dependent on and connected with chemistry and physics.

The unity of the sciences also implies a unification of theoretical and applied knowledge. No idea can be true in theory and false in practice, although true theories may be falsely applied. Psychology, for example, may give us true ideas about learning under certain conditions which may be falsely applied to learning situations under different conditions. However, Dewey contends that theoretical and applied knowledge are intimately connected with one another, for they are both instrumental and operational. True theories are simply intellectual instruments which work to unify facts. Every true theory, in order to be true, must operate to lead the mind to find certain clarifications and orderings within experience. A true theory about learning, for example, must be instrumental in tying the relevant, observable facts together. But such a theory also has potential to throw light on the problems of applied psychology. In fact, without theories or ideas that are instrumentally true there can be no applied knowledge and hence no applied psychology. Applied psychology refers to the use of theoretically and experimentally ascertained knowledge of behavior for the proper guidance of conduct in such areas as education, industry, and the treatment of mental illness. Applied psychology involves operational or instrumental knowledge that depends, as do other sciences, upon the experimental resolutions of problems.

Dewey admits that the experimental method has not been as thoroughly or successfully used in the solution of problems in the whole area of human affairs as it has been in the study of physical nature. However, this does not mean that there is an inherent separation between human affairs and nature or between theory and practice. It only means that our operational knowledge is incomplete. Operational knowledge, since it views all thinking in terms of problem-solving, deliberately looks for and finds more and more connections between theory and practice or between one area of problems and another. The only problems which it allows to be called unsolvable are those that cannot be operationally and experimentally defined. If knowledge is truly operational, then improvements in psychology, for example, should furnish ground for improvements in education. Historically, the search for one kind of knowledge has led to the discovery of other kinds. In fact, Dewey argues that excessive preoccupation with theory to the neglect of practice or vice versa has led to detrimental results. In the science of physics, for example, preoccupation with pure theory among the ancient Greeks not only meant that technology was left relatively undeveloped, but that physical theory itself was left without experimental enrichment; hence, the physical theories of the Greeks were faulty in many ways. Similarly, excessive preoccupation with practical results to the exclusion of theory has led to disastrous results in political and economic affairs. The assumption that some things, such as politics or business, are purely practical affairs having no connection with theory is as erroneous and disastrous as the view that some things are purely theoretical.

The pragmatic character of Dewey's philosophy may be clearly seen in his insistent objection to all forms of dualism that would fragment and scatter our understanding of things. He insisted that a truly pragmatic philosophy would have to be applied as widely as possible. He concurs with Peirce that all intellectual concepts, all concepts that we can reason logically with, must have their meaning located in experimental consequences. He agrees with James that all truths and life values must be found in definite consequences within experience. However, Dewey demanded more of pragmatism than did either Peirce or James. He required that logical thinking and experience be more satisfactorily integrated than is provided for by either Peirce or James. Peirce, for one, severed logical thinking from experience insofar as he held that certain vitally important topics such as morals or religion were matters for feeling or instinct that could not be justified by any intellectual or logical methods. In other words, Peirce did not conceive logical thinking as relevant to all experience or all problems. On this point, James agreed with Peirce but he went even further than Peirce in claiming a break between logic and life or intellect and experience. James not only agreed that experience has more volume than thoughts, but he gloried in this fact since it gave him an opportunity for a "piecemeal supernaturalism." In other words, James cut off science and thought from the whole of experience in order to save religion.

Dewey, however, refuses to accept any break between logic and life, intellect and experience, or science and religion. He cannot accept any conception of experience which is not integrated with logical thinking, because he holds that logical thinking is thoroughly naturalistic in its context, instrumental in its workings, and experiential in its felt quality of existence. He contends that if logical thinking or intellectual thought is properly conceived (i.e., as experimental problem-solving), then there is no reason to view it as opposed to life or inadequate to the solution of all meaningful problems. For example, it is false to say, as James did, that moral problems cannot wait for sensible proof, since this would mean that impulse has more value than accumulated knowledge in human affairs, which is patently false. It is also false to say, as Peirce did, that the practical man cannot understand what science is all about, since this would mean that chemical engineers could accomplish their results without the intelligent use of chemistry, which is not true. If logical thinking is not relevant to life or human problems, then, according to Dewey, the reason for this cannot be found by erecting an unbridgeable gap between the two, but rather the reason is located in our failure to forge an adequate logic. Of course, Dewey admits that no logic will solve all problems infallibly and automatically. But logical thinking will not even be tried or consulted if we decide *a priori* that it is not equal to the task.

During the decade between 1920 and 1930, Dewey published three major works which expound his views on the need for integration between experience, thought, and scientific method. *Experience and Nature, The Quest for Certainty,* and *Reconstruction in Philosophy* all develop his basic instrumental theory of knowledge as well as his principal objections to dualism. Dewey's opposition to dualism is central to his broad philosophic outlook and consistent with his call for integration of knowledge and reconstruction in thinking. It is his view that many traditional philosophic problems that have caused endless controversy are predicated on the basis of false dualisms. The quest for certainty and the search for an absolute in philosophy are both based upon disparaging ordinary experience. A gulf is then set up by the philosopher between the absolute, perfect truth and inferior copies of it.

One form of this dualism upholds reason against sense experience. Pure reason is fixed, universal, and unified, while the senses are changing, partial, and full of disparity. However, Dewey argues that nothing positive is gained by disparaging sense experience. What is really needed is a method of integrating the senses with intelligent thinking so that our experiences can become more continuous and relevant to one another. Experience does not exclude thought and no thoughts can be so pure that they outrun experience. Our most poetic and imaginary thoughts are wedded to what we have experienced, and here Dewey is in full accord with Santayana in maintaining a natural ground or context for all experience no matter how idealized or imaginative it may be. Poetry has been falsely idealized by the romantics as passing beyond experience and as even revealing insights that can never be found in mere experience. Dewey does not deny that poetry may involve a more heightened or a more unified and beautiful kind of experience than may ordinarily be found, but he refuses to accept any bifurcation between poetry and life which makes them entirely separate. Any separation of the so-called ideal from real experience is not only incapable of being verified, but is also a source of confusion in practical affairs as well as in theory.

The history of logic may be used to illustrate what is wrong with separating the ideal from the real. Historically it has been assumed that the science of logic teaches us how we ought to think rather than how we actually do think. According to Dewey, the preoccupation of logic with pure and perfect forms of thinking to the exclusion of any content or application to fact only leads to the unfortunate result of turning logic into petrified science. The study of purely formal logic, empty of any contact with fact or experience, cannot lead to new discoveries either in theory or in practice. Ideal reasoning that is not relevant to experience or tested by real facts is limited to repeating itself or arguing in a circle. We can only study the forms of how we ought to think by referring to and testing the forms by which we actually think. There is no need to separate the ideals of thinking from our real thoughts. The two must instead be brought closer together so that our actual thinking will approximate more and more what it ought to be, and so that our chosen ideals of thought will have some possible application. Logic when it is conceived as truly experimental will not be purely formal or abstract but will have both form and content which means general as well as concrete application. One of the real values of logical thought is, indeed, its formal or generalizing power. If, for example, we know that A is larger than B, and B is larger than C, then formally it follows that A is larger than C. The value of this general result is of course that it works for anything named by A, B, or C. But this means that it also works for particular cases of fact and is, therefore, not a mere ideal but rather an ideal form with real application.

According to Dewey, philosophy can play an important role in the improvement or reconstruction of logic. Philosophy can be expected to see the value of perfecting both the theory and practice of logic. Philosophy should be able to indicate how improvements in devising logical methods themselves can lead to improvements in things to which these methods can be applied. The study of techniques as worthwhile ends in themselves should not be seen as conflicting with the possible use or application of these methods to other things. For example, the concern with the techniques of logical reasoning or inference cannot be profitably divorced from the whole problem of education or the question of how these techniques can be learned and taught. Unless the methods of logic are formulated in ways that can be efficiently and intelligibly communicated, then not only will applications be blocked, but logical theory itself will not advance or even be tested by any community of investigators. In fact, although Peirce never devised what can be called a systematic social philosophy, Dewey points out that Peirce is to be given credit for seeing the social character of logic. As a method of inquiry logic should be conceived as both normative and factual and as theoretical and practical. On its normative side logic will be in search of efficient and intelligent standards of thinking. But as normative in devising intelligent methods concerning how we ought to think, logic will also have to be factual and study the actual means by which we do think. Normative and factual logic as integrated with one another will then imply a social factor, since any experimental logic will have to be open to testing by a continuing community of inquirers. A fully integrated logic, one that is sound in theory as well as in practice, will have to be social as well as experiential. Its methods will have to be made more and more rigorous or precise, and its applications will have to be made as comprehensive as possible.

Dewey's view that all thinking is a form of behavior that arises only in the face of problems implies that thinking is essentially an indirect mode of response. Thinking arises when an uncertainty, confusion, or problematic situation is first objectively recognized and looked into, and, second, when some method is devised for dealing with the problem at hand. Thinking takes time, and intelligent thinking takes careful study and consideration of the relevant factors that may lead to a resolution of the problem. Real thinking is, therefore, contrasted with impulsive behavior which merely reacts to confusion or trouble without locating the objective source of the problem.

> Here is where ordinary thinking and thinking that is scrupulous diverge from one another. The natural man is impatient with doubt and suspense: he impatiently hurries to be shut of it. A disciplined mind takes delight in the problematic and cherishes it until a way out is found that approves itself upon examination.[8]

Immediate reactions or experiences are not sources of knowledge since they do not really involve problem solving. Dewey defines knowledge as "warranted assertability," since, in order to know what is the case, consequences have to be anticipated and tested. He insists that knowledge must be objectively and operationally defined. Immediate feeling or passive experience is unreliable and subjective. If we could know things immediately or directly, then there would be no need of thinking or experimentation. But we often confuse a "feeling of certitude" with a "certified situation." Feelings of satisfaction, or merely feeling that something is true, do not give any objective warrant for truth or the experimental resolution of a problem. Here there is only one suitable method by which we can arrive at warranted assertibility or a certified situation. Knowledge in all forms must be obtained by the use of the scientific method.

The scientific method, however, must not be narrowly conceived as only dealing with certain subject matters, such as chemistry, physics, or biology. The scientific method is simply a name for the intelligent processes of problem solving no matter what the subject matter may be. The virtues of the scientific method are its objectivity and correctability, not its absolute certainty in dealing with problems. The scientific method conceived in the broad sense is the only method for solving theoretical as well as practical problems. It is essentially an active method since it pursues all questions of meaning, truth, and values in terms of their consequences. Here is where Dewey combines Peirce's theory of meaning with James' theory of truth to make a comprehensive instrumentalism. For Dewey all meanings, truths, and values must be operationally defined and experimentally tested.

No exceptions are made by Dewey in his demand that the scientific method be used to solve all problems. It might be thought, for example, that the scientific method is too technical and exacting to apply to ordinary problems, that science deals with things like atoms, electrons, and neutrons, not with tables, chairs, and windows. Science seems to eliminate the familiar objects and qualities of experience and substitutes highly abstract and quantitative terms. We see colors or hear sounds, but physics talks about light waves and sound waves which we do not see or hear. Dewey believes that this is a false position regarding the relation of science to ordinary experience. To set up a gulf between the two is only another example of false dualism which would also separate theory from practice. If science says that a table is composed of atoms, electrons, etc., moving at velocities we do not see in ordinary experience, this does not mean that science posits a second table separate from the one we can see or touch. There is only one table, but it may be viewed in various ways relative to our interests and purposes regarding it. Dewey admits that science *per se* represents a more sophisticated and symbolic way of looking at things, but this does not mean that it breaks with ordinary experience. The carpenter who measures his wood for cutting and the cook who determines how much sugar to put in the cake are using the scientific method in a basic way. The established sciences such as astronomy or chemistry require measurements and techniques of experimentation that are more refined and precise than ordinary life. But this only proves that there are many levels and uses of scientific method; it does not prove that science and ordinary experience are split in two.

ETHICS AND VALUATION   Of all the pragmatist philosophers, Dewey has given the most extensive and careful attention to the problems of ethics and valuation. Not only did he subject the problems of moral theory and value theory to methodical analysis in their own right, but throughout all his major works he strove to see the moral implications of his basic concepts and attempted consistently to integrate facts with values and morality with science. His *Theory of the Moral Life* and *Theory of Valuation* offer detailed, systematic accounts of his general theory of values. His main purpose in his whole philosophy of value was not only to integrate theory with practice, but also to integrate genuine values with one another, always within experience.

The deepest problem of modern life as well as philosophy is to bring values and facts into proper relation with one another. Our factual knowledge in physics, astronomy, chemistry etc. has grown by the use of intelligent experimentation, but our knowledge of political, economic, moral, and other values has lagged far behind. This is partly due to the fear of change and the acceptance of traditional answers to value questions. In science, what Dewey calls the "changed attitude toward change" means that change is no longer feared or merely accepted, but actively sought and studied by making changes in order to study predictable consequences. However, man's moral life, his entire political and social existence, is still lived in fear of change; as a result, the method of intelligence or scientific method has not been really tried in the solution of value problems.

The importance of a comprehensive theory of values can be seen by observing what Dewey means by the word "value" itself. He understands by value "whatever is taken to have rightful authority in the direction of conduct." [9] Values do not designate any narrow class of things or some specialized subject matter. Rather, values apply to the whole field of actual and possible experience where some human interest can pertain. This means, of course, that there can be no real values apart from interests or preferences, but at the same time interests and preferences alone do not constitute values. A value is not simply any object of any interest, since interests obviously may be misguided, impulsive, or bad. If things became values merely because they were felt to be good, then critical thinking about values would be superfluous. On the other hand, if values were located or constituted by mere thinking or *a priori*, then there would be no guarantee that they apply to experience. If values pertain to what in fact should regulate conduct, then they must be found in experience and be open to critical thought. Real problems about values, therefore, can never be only theoretical or only practical problems; rather, they must be both. Neither can so-called moral values be separated from economic or political values, nor can so-called aesthetic values be separated from instrumental values. Just as false dualisms prevent the integration of knowledge, so they also invade the realm of values and make unbridgeable gaps between the higher and lower, the intrinsic and extrinsic, or between ends and means. The notion that only certain things are good as ends and that other things are only valuable as means is a source not only of intellectual confusion but also of confusion and trouble in practical affairs.

Means and ends are not separated from one another; they can only be meaningfully conceived as a continuum. Obviously, nothing is a means by itself but only in relation to something else. Nothing can be only a means; it must be a means for some purpose. But equally, nothing is in itself or absolutely an end but is only an end in relation to the possible means by which it could be realized or brought into existence. Means and ends are relative to each other. Learning may be cited as an example. Learning how to read a foreign language may be an end-in-view, something which is sought for enjoyment or self-fulfillment. Obviously, as an end it would have to be related to certain means by which it could be achieved. But this end-in-view could become a means to another end or further ends without losing its value as a worthwhile end or goal. Learning a foreign language may be valued as a means to earning a living or getting more out of traveling. In other words, all values must be instrumentally conceived. Social, educational, aesthetic, or moral values must be conceived in terms of a means-ends continuum and not in terms of a means-ends separation. For example, the social value of justice as a means of achieving order and equity in life must be integrated with the moral value of justice as intrinsic and pertaining to the integrity and dignity of the individual. The utility of social values as means to certain ends cannot contravene the moral rights of individuals, but rather, should work in harmony with these rights. At the same time, the rights of individuals should not be conceived as self-enclosed or as not operating in a natural and social environment.

The same principle of coordination or cooperation of values applies to the problem of intentions versus consequences. Philosophers have long debated the problem as to whether the moral value of an action is to be located in its motive or in its consequences. One school of thought argues that good motives are the sole measure of the moral worth of actions. Another school argues that consequences alone are to be considered. Dewey rejects any separation between motives and consequences or character and action since morally speaking both are involved. Consequences would not be moral in character if they were not derived from motives, and motives themselves would not be morally definable apart from consequences or anticipated consequences. Moral actions should be viewed pragmatically as interactions between thought and action or choice and conduct. Good conduct must be measured both in terms of the motives behind it and the consequences which follow from it. This means that moral values and conduct cannot be determined by any simple method. The solution of moral problems in theory as well as in practice must be sought by applying the method of intelligence or the scientific method to find the relevant facts and principles. Moral principles, like those in science, must be testable in experience. But moral facts or experiences themselves must be related to intelligent principles to take on meaning and value. The interplay between facts and theories, actions and principles, is as necessary in morals as it is in science. This means that inquiry and criticism in moral matters should be viewed as a positive good rather than as a necessary evil. The use of scientific methods as objective and self-corrective is the only intelligent means by which moral problems can be understood and solved.

The problem of determining what is the source of value or what can have rightful authority in the direction of conduct is not solved by stating that only the scientific method can have such rightful authority. What has to be shown, according to Dewey, is why this is the case and why other alternative methods must prove unsatisfactory. Philosophers have long debated the problem of the nature and sources of values. The rationalists upheld the importance of intellect or intelligence in locating their source. Traditionally, however, the rationalists required transcendent and *a priori* principles that could not be tested in experience. It was believed that, rationally, values had to be absolute and eternal and therefore located in reason independent of experience. On the other side, the empiricists upheld the importance of fact or experience in determining the source of values. Empirical theories, however, tended to identify values with desires or enjoyments which resulted in subjective and completely relative standards of value.

Dewey accepts neither the overly rationalistic nor the empirical theory. Both fail to locate the real source and nature of values. The rationalist's account of values is unacceptable because it makes values unverifiable in experience. The empiricist's account is rejected because it holds values down to past experience and fails to make them relevant to and testable in terms of future experience. Here Dewey makes an important distinction between the desired and the desirable or between the enjoyed and the enjoyable. To say that something is desired or enjoyed is only to make a judgment of fact. Such judgments are not, properly speaking, value judgments at all. If one person asserts that he enjoyed the play and another that he did not, there is no value disagreement here but merely two statements about two facts. If, however, someone asserts that a thing is desirable or enjoyable he is making a value judgment. If an engineer, for example, asserts that a certain building material is desirable in making a certain kind of bridge, he is not merely asserting that he desires it or that he likes this building material. Rather, he is making a prediction that it will satisfy certain conditions that are testable in terms of future experience. Value judgments, therefore, can be verified if they are interpreted as predictions. In fact, to conceive value judgments as predictive is to interpret them as practical or instrumental in terms of concrete fact.

However, value judgments are predictions of a specific kind. If someone asserts that it will rain tomorrow, he is not making a value judgment; he is simply making a prediction about the weather. Value judgments make predictions about possible future enjoyments, or what will be found and judged to satisfy certain desires or demands. This holds for all kinds of value judgments in all human affairs. To judge that a certain action is morally good, to assert that a certain fiscal policy is sound, to judge that a specific kind of foreign policy is good for the country, etc., all would be examples of value judgments that involve predictions about future possible enjoyments. To interpret value judgments as kinds of predictions is to bring them into relation with the scientific method. According to Dewey, this not only makes them objectively verifiable or testable but leaves room for correction and improvement. This removes subjective bias and arbitrary opinion from the problem of settling value disputes. However, it also means that valuations cannot be justified or proven merely because they are traditional or customary. If the conditions of life or society change, then valuations must pertain to these changes rather than simply ignore them.

Valuations cannot, however, simply follow or accept changes without intelligent anticipations of future experience. This means that value judgments cannot hope to be sound apart from attempts to integrate necessary forms of knowledge. Sound or judicious valuations depend upon taking as many relevant factors into consideration as possible. However, valuation would be paralyzed if it feared the possibility that it might have to be corrected or improved upon in some way. The practical character of value judgments signifies that something has to be done, that something as it now stands is in some way unsatisfactory. For example, in the field of education something can always be done to improve the conditions and methods of learning. New methods would not be needed if older ones were entirely satisfactory. But the devising of newer or better methods is itself never entirely free of the opening up of new problems. Intelligence or the scientific method can only hope to make some improvements and anticipate new problems, but it cannot (nor can anything else) completely solve all problems.

Valuations in ethics and in all human affairs are therefore non-terminating in several important senses. Valuations imply an on-going continuum of means-end relationships that is open at the end for more development. Ends-in-view and means toward those ends should never be statically fixed or conceived as stationary, according to Dewey. Some ends take precedence over others, but this itself can only be intelligently determined by referring to a non-terminating series of possible growth in the widest possible sense. This means that the validity of any single value (e.g., the value of justice or music, etc.) cannot be tested or proven apart from its relation to other values and apart from its tendency to promote the general growth of values. Specific things therefore take on a disvalue or become bad to the degree to which they prevent the existence and growth of values in general.

For example, one may indeed grow to be a better and better pickpocket, but the question is whether this kind of growth is consistent with the widest possible growth of other things, including society. Obviously, when society is considered, it becomes apparent that the pickpocket must not only function in a social context, but is himself a product of a social context with which he comes into conflict or works against. Criminal behavior therefore is not bad or a disvalue because it is wrong in itself, or in isolation from other things. It is bad or wrong specifically because it conflicts with the existence and growth of other values including the preservation of society, without which such conduct could not even exist. Consequently, nothing is really good or bad in itself, according to Dewey. Music, for example, is not good in itself but only good in experience where experience itself always involves an on-going series of interactions between persons and their environments. Finally, valuations are also non-terminating in the sense that an indefinite series of predictions must figure in their having operational meaning. For example, if a physician makes a judgment to the effect that a certain medicine is good for the treatment of a certain disease, then he is making a prediction not just that it will work in one or two cases, but that it will be helpful in an indefinite series of cases.

Dewey's ethics, like that of William James, is essentially liberal and humanistic. He agrees with James that a moral philosophy cannot be dogmatically worked out in advance of experience, but rather must keep in close touch with the relevant facts. However, he diverges from James and goes well beyond him in systematically addressing himself to the problem of how to determine the relevant facts in moral matters and in value questions. James and Peirce conceived the application of the scientific method in rather narrow terms. Essentially, they both considered that value judgments were outside the realm of scientific methods. For James, science tells us what is, but morality is concerned with what ought to be. James even gave a personal interpretation to what ought to be, because he placed a definite emphasis on the individual. Dewey, however, tries to see the individual in context and never as an isolated person. He contends that without proper social influences individuality would not appear or develop. The individual should not be set above society, but rather the two should be understood in interaction and relation with one another. Any unbridgeable opposition between society and the individual is similar to the false dichotomy between "what is" and "what ought to be."

For example, it is false to say that science is only concerned with facts and has no need or ability to make value judgments. Science must decide what constitutes a good measurement, a good experiment, or a good explanation. If such judgments could not be made by science, it could not carry on its work. But the point can be pushed further. If scientific methods must make and verify value judgments in carrying on their own work, what is to prevent these methods from being applied to other problems, human problems? Granted they cannot be transferred or automatically applied without intelligent design and invention. But Dewey would ask why should scientific methods only be applied to certain value questions and not to others? The growth of knowledge and the success of experimentation in physical inquiries suggest to Dewey the need and encouragement to apply science also to human affairs. But no less does Dewey require the application of philosophy to human problems. One important danger in the attempted application of science to human affairs is the temptation to oversimplify human situations and falsely conceive them as neatly falling under certain mechanical or artificial explanations. The search for predictable outcomes or simple formulas may easily lead to the false or even disastrous use of science in guiding human affairs. This can only be avoided by the integration of knowledge and by the use of general philosophic criticism. As science tends to become more and more specialized, the need for general and philosophic thinking becomes all the more necessary.

It would be erroneous therefore to assert that Dewey advocates a scientific ethics or value theory without the assistance of philosophic theory and criticism. He does not advocate turning moral problems over to biologists or chemists. Moral problems generally are man's problems and not the possessions of a privileged group. For this reason Dewey refuses to isolate morality and values from general education, since the only hope for moral improvement lies in better education. It is therefore instructive to see the manner in which he attempts to integrate value concerns with education and art. Moral conduct and decision-making should be conceived as a matter of art as well as science. To cut asunder scientific methods from artistic production would be an unwarranted dualism. Moral problems and value concerns in human life are so complex that no real headway can be made toward adequate solutions until science, art, and education in theory and in practice cooperate with one another. But no cooperation is possible unless these endeavors are viewed philosophically as making use of intelligent and testable methods.

ART AND EDUCATION   Dewey's own philosophical development illustrates his basic principle of the interplay between theory and practice. This is especially the case in his view on art and education. His thoughts and theories on these subjects were developed and clarified through close contact with education and the arts. Among philosophers he is outstanding for his involvements in and influence on the field of education. But his comprehensive and practical interest in the meaning and significance of art makes him one of the leading interpreters of art in the present century. The titles of two of Dewey's major writings in these fields point out how he sought to relate these phenomena to life.

His *Art as Experience* and *Experience and Education* indicate the experiential orientation which he deems essential to a proper understanding of art and education.

Any philosophy or understanding of art is doomed to failure if it erects false dualisms between art and nature, art and science, fine art and useful art, etc. In fact, the tendency to view art as something precious and unique, something to be held on a pedestal, can only be seen to be false by locating the actual existence of art within the experience of society or culture. Man's understanding of art must stem from his contacts with it. If his contacts are superficial and disconnected, if social conditions persist in encouraging or only allowing art to be experienced on special occasions or at rare moments, then it is understandable that art should be conceived as something ethereal, something removed from life. Philosophical interpretations of art have not been immune from cultural influences, nor have they avoided setting up false dualisms as keys to understanding the nature and significance of art. To expose these false dualisms is to go a long way toward the proper understanding of art.

Dewey claims it is unfortunate that we have no word to cover both the artistic and the aesthetic. This itself reflects a tendency to view the two in isolation from one another and even in opposition to one another. Aesthetic experience thereby comes to be viewed as a passive enjoyment or contemplation of beauty detached from working or making anything practical. Aesthetic experience may even be likened to a dream or state of suspended animation where all realities are banished and where all thoughts and cares are thrown aside. In this way the aesthetic experiences of beauty may even be opposed to intellectual efforts to gain knowledge or understanding, with the result that aesthetic experiences are labeled as mere indulgences. For Dewey, "the enemies of the esthetic are neither the practical nor the intellectual. They are the humdrum; slackness of loose ends; submission to convention in practice and intellectual procedure." [10] He cannot accept Santayana's view that aesthetic experience or beauty involves the intuition of timeless essences which are detached from existence or which do not exist at all. "An experience has pattern and structure, because it is not just doing and undergoing in alteration, but consists of them in relationship." [11] An aesthetic experience is not a special kind of experience; all experiences whether intellectual, practical, or emotional are aesthetic insofar as they have an immediately felt quality of unity and run their course to fulfillment.

Thinking, far from being opposed to any aesthetic experience, must have an aesthetic character if it is to have any felt unity and if it is to come to a meaningful conclusion. The same principle applies to experiences and actions that are predominantly practical. Cutting wood or fixing a fence may have aesthetic quality if they are experienced as continuous or unified and if they run their course to fulfillment. As long as man's experiences are disjointed or fragmented without any feeling of unity, they will not be aesthetic in character. Also, as long as man's experiences are only mechanically connected or merely repetitious they will not possess any aesthetic quality. Dull routine or disconnected, inchoate experiences are the two opposites from the aesthetic sense. The aesthetic is not in any way detached from life, but rather the aesthetic implies the fullness of living or actual enrichment in existence. Aesthetic values therefore are not opposed or irrelevant to moral, economic, or social values, but are present whenever any genuine value is found. Man's moral and social life can only be enhanced by making them more aesthetic, since this would mean that they had become more continuous, enjoyable, and fulfilling.

If logical thinking, in order to be continuous and to arrive at a conclusion, must possess an aesthetic character, then it is false to place art and science in opposition. Art as skill in overt doing or making is doubly aesthetic, for we may enjoy both the process by which something is made and the completed object in its own right. Aesthetic experiences enter art from the side of creation as well as appreciation. However, art as a form of creation is just as much involved in scientific thinking and activity as it is in the creation of so-called "fine art." The mention of "works of art" suggests special objects placed in museums or heard in concert halls.

However, this tendency to separate works of art from other works or from the rest of life is only another example of those false dualisms which break up experience and scatter any proper understanding of things. Intelligent art must be related to life as well as to practical affairs. If art is judged as impractical, this can only mean that humanity is not in any way benefited from it. All good art serves some human purpose and all great art serves as a source of enduring enrichment. However, if art is falsely separated from science and education, and if it is divorced from culture or any social function, then it will only deteriorate into a precious indulgence of the few rather than serve as a source of enjoyment and fulfillment for the many. Art loses by being divorced from science if science is thought of as intelligent inquiry and technology. At the same time, science loses by being divorced from art if art is thought of as skillful construction that is both aesthetic and useful. Good art may indeed be opposed to bad science, or good science may be opposed to bad art. However, this signifies that good art and good science are integrated or have something very important in common. What they have in common is the devising and using of intelligent means to produce worthwhile human ends.

The disastrous results of falsely separating science and art can be clearly seen in educational theory and practice, according to Dewey. What educational theory and practice need most of all are the widest possible use of intelligent methods. A progressive type of education cannot be scientific at the expense of the artistic and aesthetic, or artistic at the expense of the scientific or experimental. Insofar as art and science are useful at all, they will be indispensable in education. But their real use will only extend to the point where they are successfully coordinated or used without conflicting with one another. Conflicts and misunderstandings are all too frequent between the humanities (arts) and the sciences in education. In fact, it is even supposed by some that a talent for the one precludes a talent for the other. This kind of separation can educate no one well, but only serves to produce bad artists, bad scientists, and poorly educated individuals.

Dewey observes that not only does the state of education reflect the lack of working cooperation between theory and practice or between the various branches of knowledge, but that education is itself the very place where progress can be started to unify and integrate knowledge. It was not by accident that the famous Greek philosopher Plato hit upon the idea of an educational program as necessary to the pursuit of knowledge and the good of society as well. However, Plato's idea of education involving the establishment of an intellectual elite or leadership class, as well as including a separation between the practical and the theoretical, was based on mislocating the true social value of education as guided by scientific methods. Plato disparaged sense experience, physical doing or making, as well as democracy. In their place he upheld purified rational thought, perfect immaterial forms, and an intellectual aristocracy. For Dewey, Platonic education and philosophy was based on a whole series of untenable dualisms.

Dewey firmly maintains that education must be based on and applied to experience. If life implies growth, and if education is necessary to the full and continued growth of human beings, then education cannot be simply a prelude to adult life or the attainment of some narrow vocation.

Education in the good sense as well as the bad continues for an entire lifetime. Therefore, the problem for any theory of education is not how it will be brought to a conclusion, but how it may better serve and continue to serve all the processes of living that contribute to their widest possible growth. Consequently, Dewey points out that education is just as much in need of general philosophic guidance as it is in need of practical techniques to solve particular problems. One of the worst gulfs in the field of education is that which separates needful theories from equally needful techniques. Preoccupation with mere practices to the exclusion of theories has led to the stultification of students and teachers alike and in turn, to sterile applications as well as the illusion that education is synonymous with mere talking well and writing well.

If thinking and doing are given operational meaning, then no philosophy of education should seek to compartmentalize them by subject-matters or by classes of students, but rather education should seek meaningful ways in which thought and practice can be united with one another. No student can learn to think if his thinking is untested by and unsupported by performance. Writing, reading and speaking should be thought of as kinds of performances wherein thinking can be expressed or tested. In this way, thinking will not be considered as merely subjective or private, where anyone is entitled to any opinion he wants. It is Dewey's view that thoughts only take on a self-enclosed or subjective character to the degree to which they do not or cannot function in the performance of problem solving. It is well known that it is easier to teach the solution of a problem than to instruct the student in the methods by which he could arrive at the solution himself. This means that any truly progressive education will attempt not only to teach the student how to use previously worked-out methods of solving problems, but will also try to teach the student to understand methods themselves. Dewey conceives progressive education as a dynamic process of interaction between thinking and experiencing, planning and performing, etc., all of which must be geared to the future and to social meaning. A first principle of progressive education is that it never reaches an end. Dewey defines the educated person not as someone who possesses a certain quantity of knowledge, but rather "an educated person is the person who has the power to go on and get more education." [12]

Educational methods, therefore, not only have to be criticized and revised, but they must be related to one another and to the future. Methods, just as values, require integration and continuity. This requires a philosophy of education that is continually tested by experience. For this reason, Dewey believes that one of the best ways of defining philosophy itself is to assert that it is a general theory of education. This implies that philosophy is given the practical function of guiding the learning of integrated forms of knowledge and values. In this way there will be no need to construe the moral, social, economic, aesthetic, intellectual, or even the religious components of education in isolation or in opposition to one another. Dewey argues that an experimental notion of inquiry as well as an operational conception of all knowledge can only lead more and more to the same result of unending development. This means that democracy and education are completely complementary to one another. Like Jefferson, Dewey viewed a democratic society as impossible without the fullest possible education of all the people. But Dewey also maintains that educational growth cannot be fully realized apart from social conditions which promote free inquiry and the liberal dissemination of knowledge. Inherent in the notion of democracy is the idea of free opportunity for human beings. This does not mean that the idea of democracy is the simple solution to all educational problems. It means rather that the idea of a free people is the only idea in terms of which educational problems will get a genuine chance of being worked on to the full and solved in progressive ways.

Two of Dewey's most influential books on education, *The School and Society* and *Democracy and Education,* signify the strong sense in which he viewed the problems of education in a social context and within his own comprehensive social philosophy. The intimate relation between school and society or education and culture is confirmed in his basic principle of interaction. Just as the individual responds to his environment by changing it some way in return, so the school or education is both affected by and in turn affects the society or culture wherein it exists. Dewey came more and more to see the dynamic character of this interaction as only explainable and controllable in terms of operational or instrumental thinking. This means that social and educational problems have two very important elements in common. They both require an integration of knowledge so that the relevant facts can be used to determine what to do, and they both require the intelligent control of the applications of knowledge in concrete cases. Knowing *what* to do or what values should be maintained is useless without knowing *how* to attain them. It is Dewey's strongest claim that integrated, operational thinking will serve both purposes since it sees them as the same in principle.

DEMOCRACY AND RELIGIOUS EXPERIENCE   Santayana caught the distinctively American and democratic character of Dewey's philosophy when he wrote, "The master burden of his philosophy, which lends it its national character, is a profound sympathy with the enterprise of life in all lay directions, in its technical and moral complexity, and especially in its American form, where individual initiative, although still demanded and prized, is quickly subjected to overwhelming democratic control." [13] However, Santayana criticized Dewey's naturalism for its practical moral and social focus. He alleged that because Dewey's naturalism was dominated by a pragmatic or instrumental interpretation of the nature and purpose of all experience and all ideas, it was, therefore, only "half-hearted" or "short-winded." Dewey's basic concern with the practical functioning of all ideas, including the moral and social, was interpreted by Santayana as giving a false dominance to the foreground in naturalism. Santayana could not admit that human experience of any kind could be anything more than a symbolic transcript (foreground) and never a literal agency of power or action (background). Matter, and matter alone, for Santayana was the only real agency of power, and the realm of matter, as he viewed it, was not essentially human at all but a dark, unfathomable agency beyond man's power to grasp. It is important to note how Dewey sought to meet these and similar criticisms of his philosophy. He not only replied to Santayana,[14] but he continuously sought to dispel the misinterpretation that his philosophy was a partisan defence of Americanism or a glorification of technology and practical affairs.

No one more than Dewey spoke out against the falseness of a merely nationalistic philosophy. In fact, he has called attention to the need of locating problems in their comprehensive or human context rather than in the context of some one nation's or people's interests. No sound philosophy can be merely national in character, although no philosophy can escape the influence of society or culture. Because philosophy cannot operate in a vacuum but must be relevant to all existence, Dewey maintains the necessity for a comprehensive framework for the philosopher's task. For example, in reply to Santayana, he refuses to accept any separation between experience and nature or human experience and the realm of matter that would present matter as an unfathomable power or recondite substance. Dewey claims that Santayana's description of knowledge as "animal faith" involves an exaggerated and unnecessary concession to irrationality at exactly the point where intelligent methods are needed and where they can prove their usefulness. He detects in

Santayana's separation of essence and existence a falling back on those false dualisms that impede inquiry as well as practical affairs. The notion of eternal essences standing outside of time and existence is not only irrelevant to natural events and the affairs of the world, but existence itself becomes an unwarranted mystery in Santayana's theory by being referred to as picking up and dropping timeless and non-existent essences. Dewey attacks the unwarranted relativism and irrationalism in Santayana's theory of values for the same reason.[15] If value is not found in existence (and Santayana claims that it is not), but rather in timeless and nonexistent forms then all value judgments will be equally groundless since existence will not be thought of as intelligible or intelligent in any way. But Dewey claims that it is a mistake to separate intelligence from existence. Real knowledge and real values are denoted by intelligence and existential application.

Knowledge and values therefore cannot be based on irrational impulses or eternal essences, but are rational to the degree to which they control all the affairs of life. But this means that knowledge must be conceived instrumentally as warranted judgment or certified belief and that value judgments must be interpreted as intelligent predictions. For the guidance of understanding or the control of action, eternal essences or irrational impulses prove to be useless and even disastrous in experience. Dewey insists that knowledge and values must be interpreted as social in order that they may be objective, intelligent, and practical. It is precisely the non-social and non-practical character of essences or animal impulses that makes them unfit as genuine philosophical categories.

The importance of Dewey's social philosophy for a proper understanding of his philosophy as a whole can be seen in his insistence that social science should not be separated from natural science. Not only are societies definite aspects of the natural world, but all existence is *associated* in character, and existents are never found in total isolation from one another. Associated existences or groupings of things are found throughout all nature and not merely in human societies. Electrons and animals, insects and plant life do not exist in isolation from one another. The tendency of philosophers to look for ultimate data is not only false to the way things exist, but it also leads to unverifiable controversies and thwarts the integration of our knowledge in theory as well as practical application.

Dewey therefore claims to use "the social as a ranking philosophic category on the ground that it is indicative of the widest and richest range of association empirically accessible." [16] Or again he asserts, "I do not say that the social as we know it is the whole, but I do emphatically suggest that it is the widest and richest manifestation of the whole accessible to our observation." [17] In the light of this it is understandable why social philosophy occupies not only a central point in his own works, but why he also conceived it as central to philosophy as such.

Social thought, like logic, has suffered from a tendency to isolate it from other fields of inquiry. Just as the science of logic, as the study of how we ought to think, has been falsely separated from inquiries into how we carry on our thinking, so social inquiries into what should be done have been falsely separated from inquiries into what actually is done. One disastrous consequence of this bifurcation is that intelligent methods of social planning and social action either have not been tried at all or have lagged far behind improvements in technology and science. Outmoded models of explanation and obsolete plans of action are characteristic of the tendency to separate the social from other fields of knowledge. Conservatism is not the only force that impedes social progress or social understanding; the narrowness of certain forms of liberalism is just as noteworthy. Conservatism in social affairs, if it means holding to rules and customs irrespective of intelligent criticism and changing conditions of life, is indeed bad and indefensible. However, liberalism in calling for social action will be no better if it fails either to anticipate new problems or to devise means of organizing knowledge and controls of action in methods consistent with the way things unfold.

Social science is often depreciated because it lacks predictive power to anticipate accurately what will happen. It is usually compared unfavorably with physical science as lacking intelligent measurements. Astronomy, for example, can predict exactly when the next eclipse of the moon will occur and where it can be observed. Social science, on the other hand, cannot tell us the date of the next war or depression. Human affairs are consequently considered too complex and variable to be explained by scientific methods. Dewey claims that this is a false view of social science. He points out that natural science itself only succeeded in making great advances when it adopted a "changed attitude about change" and began to make changes by active experimentation. Astronomy has been able to obtain more and more exact knowledge by devising instruments and ways of obtaining information. Modern astronomy is not a passive study of the heavens, but an active science improved by the use of operational concepts and instruments.

However, the insecurity of social life with its corresponding fear of change and experimentation implies that social problems have not been operationally studied or solved by the use of scientific method. Dewey argues that dynamic methods of investigation can be and should be intelligently devised and applied to all social problems. For example, he claims that man's inability to anticipate social conditions or consequences can be helped by devising experimental ways to manage and control social affairs. He argues that recent history presents us with examples which are only too clear of being able to anticipate social consequences. Totalitarian states which exercise tight and overriding control over the important aspects of human life clearly show, by morally bad examples, that social consequences can be predicted and controlled. Propaganda techniques, control of news media, secret police, economic pressure, and mass murder are all examples of how social life can be controlled.

Dewey argues that only under free and intelligent democratic control can social life make any real progress and at the same time be morally healthy. Democracy signifies the moral right of each individual to share in society's benefits as well as the moral responsibility of each individual to cooperate freely in society's total growth. Dewey's idea of democracy is neither a utopian dream separated from the actual conditions of social life nor a partisan glorification of American society. His idea of democracy, like Jefferson's, is a working experiment of real life. In fact, Dewey cites Jefferson as the first to conceive of democracy in completely moral and experimental terms. He interprets Jefferson's demand for the natural rights of man as a call for specifically moral rights. Democracy, therefore, is not conceived by Dewey as applying to any one group of people but to all humanity. The first premiss of democracy is equal rights for all men—each man's right to life, liberty, and the pursuit of happiness. However, this also implies the responsibility to respect the rights of others. Democracy in America is only an imperfect realization of equal rights and free cooperation. Dewey views American life as engaged in democratic pursuits, though needing much improvement. He gives much credit to Jefferson for seeing the democratic experiment as a comprehensive plan of action. Jefferson realized that a free society depended upon the growth of science and education. Dewey contends that only in a free democracy can the moral and comprehensive growth of human life really occur. Equal rights and free cooperation can only flourish if science and education are also advanced in theory and practice. Enlightened freedom for Dewey, as for Jefferson, implies the responsibility to use knowledge and experiment in the deepest as well as in the widest possible sense for unending growth of human welfare.

However, Dewey goes well beyond Jefferson in his analysis of democracy and freedom. Unlike Jefferson Dewey cannot tie the democratic ideal to an agrarian society nor to any fixed conception of human nature. Democracy, like freedom, is something which comes into being. Democracy and freedom depend upon growth and the interaction of many factors. Dewey, in fact, considers fallacious the belief in *innate,* natural rights, powers, and needs. He asserts that

> since actual, that is, effective, rights and demands are products of interactions, and are not found in the original and isolated constitution of human nature, whether moral or psychological, mere elimination of obstructions is not enough. The latter merely liberates force and ability as that happens to be distributed by past accidents of history.[18]

Dewey claims that there can be no effective freedom without organization and intelligent social planning. However, because social problems are complex and changing, intelligent planning must be an on-going or continuous affair. Freedom is inseparable from culture; it essentially involves a whole series of ongoing transactions between persons and groups, politically, morally, commercially, etc. Free culture, or democracy, therefore, cannot be conceived or realized by merely isolating some one factor, e.g., the political or economic, from all the rest. The test of the value of democracy consequently cannot be whether it simply promotes economic opportunity or political liberty but rather its measure must be sought in terms of intelligent growth. Does democracy promote the intelligent expansion of human life morally, politically, economically, etc.? Can democracy meet the ongoing challenges of industrialization, population increases, education, and world tensions? Not in isolation but in continuous interaction must the nature and value of freedom and democracy be sought. For this very reason, freedom cannot be prized as merely an affair of the individual, or as some philosophers have interpreted it, a question of only the "will."

According to Dewey, preoccupation in the history of philosophy with the so-called free-will problem is based on isolating one factor of freedom and failing to see the rest of the context. Freedom, of course, requires individual choice, but unless choice is made intelligent and translated into public or social action, it will not be worth very much. What is gained if we have free will or free choice but no freedom of action? Further, what is gained if we possess individual or personal freedom but no social freedom in any public sense? But most important of all, what would be the value of freedom of choice and even action if we lacked the intelligence and education to make good choices or perform worthwhile deeds? Merely to mention these points enables us to see that freedom is a function of a number of interrelated factors, rather than something simple and isolated. Freedom depends on choice, action, and intelligence. Without intelligence, choices and actions cannot be in any significant way free. But, further, freedom in any real sense depends upon a social factor; it depends upon the cooperation of human beings. Cooperation does not mean the thwarting or lessening of individual freedom; when joint efforts or cooperative actions are guided by intelligence, they work to the mutual benefit of persons and groups.

Dewey frankly admits that his idea of democracy and faith in its enduring value is essentially religious in character. But this point can only be understood by grasping the sense in which he defines the term "religious." "Any activity pursued in behalf of an ideal end against obstacles and in spite of threats of personal loss because of conviction of its general and enduring value is religious in quality." [19] Dewey refuses to isolate the religious quality of experience from the rest of experience, and he refuses to define it in supernatural terms. It will be remembered that he argued that aesthetic experience does not involve the enjoyment of special objects on special occasions, but that any experience is aesthetic if it has a felt quality of continuity and if it runs to fulfillment. In a similar way, Dewey argues that the religious quality of experience does not involve any special objects which are worshipped on special occasions, but that any experience is religious if it involves the pursuit of an enduring and comprehensive ideal for humanity. An enduring ideal for Dewey means a non-terminating end-in-view, one that is capable of perpetual growth, such as democracy. A general or comprehensive ideal signifies an end-in-view which includes all human values. In fact, Dewey defines the irreligious as "that which attributes human achievement and purpose to man in isolation from the world of physical nature and his fellows." [20] Here he agrees with Santayana that all meaningful ideals must have a natural basis and no ideal is a literal description of fact, but rather involves an imaginative interpretation. However, religious ideals for Dewey cannot simply be imaginative; they must also intervene in life and "lend deep and enduring support to the processes of living." [21]

He requires that a distinction be drawn between the noun "religion" and the adjective "religious." He claims that there is no such thing as religion in the singular. There are, instead, various religions, which are so disparate and even contradictory to one another that no single meaning can be found to define the noun "religion." Belief in a supernatural power, for example, Dewey contends cannot be used as a defining characteristic of religion, not only because this conflicts with science, but also because this belief has been interpreted in too many different ways, some of which are even amoral or clearly immoral in character. A supernatural power could be conceived as a source of evil, rather than one which is benevolent. However, Dewey argues that even a so-called benevolent supernatural power is inadequate since as supernatural it could be only miraculously or irrationally connected with the natural world. Any supernatural being and any absolute would be in conflict with the method of intelligent human inquiry. The supernatural versus the natural is a glaring example of the kind of dualism that blocks the road to intelligent inquiry and prevents the integration and application of knowledge from taking place. However, Dewey argues that this is not the case with the meaning he attaches to the adjective "religious."

The religious aspect of life is humanistic but also unending. But insofar as the religious dimension of experience admits of unending growth, it must be naturalistic and instrumentally defined. Faith in human intelligence and free cooperation are truly religious in quality. What makes them truly religious is simply their enduring and general value. However, this enduring quality must include their potential to grow, and their general value must include their relevance to all humanity. The perfection of human intelligence and the cultivation of free cooperation are essentially growing ideals and hence naturalistic and instrumental as well as democratic. Consequently, Dewey feels no need to apologize for having excluded the supernatural from his conception of religious experience. On the contrary he claims that intelligence demands an honestly naturalistic interpretation of religion. Religion cannot include the occult and supernatural any more than democracy and education can. It is one of Dewey's strongest claims that superstition and outmoded customs are not only useless and impractical, but they are morally and socially defective as well. In the modern world democracy and education are in definite need of intelligent ways of handling their complex problems. Fear of change as well as fear of failure often prevent the best use being made of intelligence and free cooperation. However, proper respect for human intelligence and free cooperation would add to their effectiveness and value. To place human intelligence and free cooperation at the level of religious ideals would not lower man's way of life. It would contribute to its widest possible growth.

"John Dewey is unquestionably the pre-eminent figure in American philosophy; no one has done more to keep alive the fundamental ideals of liberal civilization; and if there could be made an office as that of national philosopher, no one else could be properly mentioned for it." [22] This tribute by Morris Cohen, one of America's leading philosophers in this century, points up the magnitude of Dewey's significance and influence. His impact on other philosophers and on the general public as well is greater than any other American philosopher. As an original thinker Dewey is unique in the number of contributions he has made to virtually every aspect of philosophic study. But further, Dewey is also unique in that he became a *leading figure* in virtually all the main areas of philosophical concern in recent times.

For over half a century Dewey was an acknowledged leader in the development of American pragmatism. In agreement with Peirce he viewed pragmatism as providing a logic of inquiry. Ideas must be brought to a test in terms of their experimental consequences. Consequently, one of Dewey's most important contributions to philosophy has been his careful and extensive work in experimental logic and theory of knowledge. Dewey's instrumentalism adds new and important dimensions to pragmatism by calling for a comprehensive social philosophy and systematic theory of value as well as by insisting on the supremacy of the scientific method for the solution of all genuine problems. Dewey goes well beyond both Peirce and James in his attempt to *apply* pragmatism as widely and as thoroughly as possible.

This point is best observed in his philosophy of education. He is outstanding for the thoroughness with which he maintained the view that philosophy itself must be defined as a general theory of education. The primary function of philosophy must be practical in the educational sense. It must add to the widest possible growth of human life by enlightening men about all the significant conditions of their existence. However, there is only one way in which the educational function of philosophy can be successfully carried on. This is in terms of intelligent or scientific criticism. Philosophy cannot succeed in its educational function if it imposes false limits on the use of the scientific method. Education can be progressive only if it adopts a workable problem-solving approach to all vital human concerns and continually subjects all of its theories and practices to careful criticism.

The scientific method, according to Dewey, is the only method suited to the solution of all meaningful problems precisely because it is correctable in theory as well as practice, and because it is objective in always consulting *experience* for the relevant facts. Experience must be the testing ground for education, democracy, science, and philosophy itself. But here experience must be viewed as neither self-enclosed nor merely subjective in character, but rather as a form of interaction that is both pragmatic and social in its meaning. Dewey's philosophy is distinctive in calling for a newer and broader approach to the questions of the nature of experience and the bearing it has on the solutions of human problems. Experience for Dewey is neither simple nor static; it is not one thing but *many*, depending upon its contexts and relations. Experience may be religious, aesthetic, intellectual, or social in character depending upon the kind of interaction it involves or interpretation that is given to it. However, the important thing about experience is that it may be *meaningful*, cognitive, and valuable. In fact, only when an experience has meaning, affords knowledge, or offers value, is it truly practical in Dewey's sense of the word. Consequently, Dewey's major writings emphasize the central position of experience for philosophy. Three of his major works, *Experience and Nature*, *Art as Experience*, and *Experience and Education*, emphasize this point by their very titles.

John Dewey was much esteemed during his lifetime. In 1939 he was honored with the publication of *The Philosophy of John Dewey* in *The Library of Living Philosophers*. This volume notes a great number of Dewey's contributions to all the major fields of philosophy. As a writer Dewey's works have circulated among an amazingly wide audience. His major books continue in print today, many in paperback form. However, Dewey never possessed a graceful and polished literary style like that of Santayana, nor did he write with the personal persuasiveness and energetic clarity of William James. Dewey's great influence consequently cannot be attributed to his skill with words, but rather to the power of his ideas. As a writer he resembles Peirce in that he requires the reader to follow many long and involved analyses of problems. Like Royce there is a constant note of seriousness in Dewey's writings that calls for an equal seriousness on the part of the reader. However, despite the great demands that he makes on the reader he has had a greater following than any other modern American philosopher. In large measure his prominence in this century is based on the fact that he pioneered work in not just one but two major strands of twentieth-century thought —pragmatism and naturalism. Both the social and scientific developments of the present century called for a philosophy that could integrate the rise of natural science with the complex changes occurring in man's social life.

Dewey's naturalism and instrumentalism were intended to deal with this very problem. In fact, it was Dewey's purpose to make philosophy as relevant as possible to the changing conditions of man's existence. His prominence in the twentieth century as the philosopher of democracy and progressive education stems from his skill and painstaking care in making philosophy fit the needs of the times.

Any consideration of Dewey's achievements would have to note that his impact on education is of prime importance. In fact, his efforts in education indicate in large measure the theoretical as well as practical significance of his whole philosophy. Dewey's theories have not only notably influenced the course of twentieth-century education, but he stands also as the most important philosopher of education that America has yet produced. As an empirical philosopher he is outstanding for his concern with the social role of science and for his concern with larger issues. His capacity for dealing with difficult problems of theory while at the same time elucidating the complexities of practice shows something of his enduring importance. His ability to make careful distinctions between things and yet avoid the pitfalls of isolating things that require to be integrated has, however, not always been properly appreciated. In fact, in the field of education itself Dewey's influence has not always been good, often because of superficial understandings of his ideas. His idea of progressive education has been wrongly interpreted in certain ways to mean permissive learning and premature use of scientific methods in learning and instruction. Certain of his key concepts—growth, interaction, enrichment, learning by doing—have been used as mere jargon or without his intended meaning to present a misleadingly easy and yet seemingly scientific solution to educational problems. To the extent to which Dewey's concepts on education have become jargon or platitudes, they fail to represent his true intentions and only indicate the need of a thorough-going problem-solving approach to educational matters.

Dewey's impact on other philosophers is too great to be indicated in detail. Some of the best creative work and scholarship in twentieth-century American philosophy has been affected by Dewey. Included in the impressive line of contemporary philosophers he influenced are Morris Cohen, an outstanding American naturalistic philosopher; C. I. Lewis, one of the leading figures in contemporary epistemology and value theory; George H. Mead, a leading American pragmatist; J. H. Randall, Jr., one of the leading American scholars in the history of philosophy; and Sidney Hook, one of the most prominent contemporary American political and naturalistic philosophers.

However, Dewey's significance for philosophy tends to be clouded by his immense influence. Any philosopher as dominant as Dewey is bound to be misinterpreted, and his real worth is likely to be scattered and hidden in many ways. However, this means that his thought calls for continued reinterpretation. The worst mistake in gauging Dewey, therefore, is to mislocate the precision of his thought. His basic concepts are in a certain sense elusive because he tried to tie so many different things together. The fact that he attempted to do more with concepts like experience, democracy, education, etc., than any other empiricist or naturalist obviously leaves him open to possible criticism on this very point.[23] However, it must be remembered that Dewey, unlike the idealists or rationalists, never tried to explain things *a priori* or absolutely in such a way as to block further inquiry. His significance for philosophy must be located in his empirical approach to unifying our ways of looking at the world and its problems. Admittedly, any empirical philosophy is open to correction by better methods of consulting experience. Dewey's account of experience is no doubt incomplete and in need of some correction. However, he was always receptive to criticism based on intelligent ways of consulting experience. In fact, Dewey was not opposed to the idea of cooperative efforts in philosophy as is proved by his actual collaboration with other philosophers. This only indicates his own social conception of inquiry itself—as always in need of intelligent testing by a larger and larger community of inquirers.

NOTES

1. John Dewey, *The Influence of Darwin on Philosophy and Other Essays in Contemporary Thought* (Bloomington: Indiana University Press, 1965), pp. 17–18.
2. Dewey, *Experience and Nature*, p. 4a.
3. Dewey, *Essays in Experimental Logic*, p. 307.
4. Charles Sanders Peirce, *The Collected Papers of Charles Sanders Peirce*, Vol. 5 (Cambridge, Mass.: Harvard University Press, 1931–1958), p. 243.
5. Paul Arthur Schilpp, ed., *The Philosophy of John Dewey*, p. 522.
6. Dewey, *Democracy and Education*, p. 328.
7. Dewey, *The Quest for Certainty*, p. 255.
8. *Ibid.*, p. 228.
9. *Ibid.*, p. 256.
10. Dewey, *Art as Experience*, p. 40.
11. *Ibid.*, p. 44.
12. Dewey, in R. D. Archambault, ed., *John Dewey on Education: Selected Writings* (New York: Modern Library, 1964), p. 4.
13. George Santayana, "Dewey's Naturalistic Metaphysics," in Paul Arthur Schilpp, ed., *The Philosophy of George Santayana* (New York: Tudor, 1940), pp. 247–248.

14. See John Dewey, "Half-Hearted Naturalism," in *The Journal of Philosophy*, Vol. XXIV, No. 3 (February 3, 1927).

15. See John Dewey, *Theory of Valuation*, pp. 39–40.

16. Dewey, *Philosophy and Civilization*, p. 83.

17. *Ibid.*, p. 92.

18. *Ibid.*, p. 281.

19. Dewey, *A Common Faith*, p. 27.

20. *Ibid.*, p. 25.

21. *Ibid.*, p. 15.

22. Morris R. Cohen, *American Thought: A Critical Sketch* (New York: Collier, 1962), p. 364.

23. For recent critical studies of Dewey, see Charles W. Hendel, ed., *John Dewey and the Experimental Spirit in Philosophy*.

QUESTIONS FOR DISCUSSION

1. What new dimensions and directions did Dewey add to pragmatism and American philosophy as a whole?

2. Is Dewey's naturalism compatible with Santayana's?

3. Why does Dewey so strongly insist that philosophy must be experientially and scientfically oriented?

4. Does Dewey make out a good case for the objectivity of values and the verification of value judgments?

5. Is Dewey's interpretation of aesthetic experience sound? Is his analysis of aesthetic value as penetrating as Santayana's?

6. Why does Dewey insist that philosophy should be defined as the general theory of education?

7. Why does Dewey believe that philosophy must have a social emphasis?

8. Does Dewey present a reasonable justification for democracy?

9. Is Dewey's naturalistic and humanistic interpretation of religion sound?

10. What accounts for the immense influence of Dewey's philosophy in the twentieth century?

SUGGESTED READINGS

Essays in Experimental Logic. What pragmatism means by practical (Ch. 12).

Philosophy and Civilization. The development of American pragmatism (Ch. 2).

Experience and Nature. Experience and philosophic method (Ch. 1).

Reconstruction in Philosophy. The scientific factor in reconstruction of philosophy (Ch. 3); the significance of logical reconstruction (Ch. 6); reconstruction in moral conceptions (Ch. 7); reconstruction as affecting social philosophy (Ch. 8).

Theory of Valuation. Propositions of appraisal (Ch. 4); the continuum of ends-means (Ch. 6).

Democracy and Education. The democratic conception of education (Ch. 7); intellectual and practical studies (Ch. 20).

Art as Experience. Experience as esthetic quality (pp. 35–43).

A Common Faith. Religion versus the religious (Ch. 1).

The Quest for Certainty. The supremacy of method (Ch. 9); the construction of good (Ch. 10).

Half-Hearted Naturalism. Dewey's reply to Santayana. [In *The Journal of Philosophy* Vol. XXIV, No. 3 (February 3, 1927).]

PRIMARY SOURCES

John Dewey, *Art as Experience* (New York: Capricorn Books, 1958).
————, *A Common Faith* (New Haven, Conn.: Yale University Press, 1960).
————, *Democracy and Education* (New York: Macmillan, 1961).
————, *Essays in Experimental Logic* (New York: Dover, 1958).
————, *Experience and Nature* (New York: Dover, 1958).
————, *Freedom and Culture* (New York: Putnam, 1939).
————, *Human Nature and Conduct* (New York: Modern Library, 1930).
————, *Individualism Old and New* (New York: Capricorn Books, 1962).
————, *Liberalism and Social Action* (New York: Capricorn Books, 1963).
————, *Philosophy and Civilization* (New York: Capricorn Books, 1963).
————, *The Public and Its Problems* (Denver, Col.: Alan Swallow, 1954).
————, *The Quest for Certainty* (New York: Capricorn Books, 1960).
————, *Reconstruction in Philosophy* (Boston: Beacon Press, 1960).
————, *Theory of the Moral Life* (New York: Holt, Rinehart & Winston, 1960).
————, *Theory of Valuation* (Chicago: University of Chicago Press, 1939).

SECONDARY SOURCES

George R. Geiger, *John Dewey in Perspective* (New York: Oxford University Press, 1958).
Charles W. Hendel, ed., *John Dewey and the Experimental Spirit in Philosophy* (New York: Liberal Arts Press, 1959).
Sidney Hook, *John Dewey: An Intellectual Portrait* (New York: John Day, 1939).
Jerome Nathanson, *John Dewey: The Reconstruction of the Democratic Life* (New York: Scribner's, 1951).
Paul Arthur Schilpp, ed., *The Philosophy of John Dewey* (New York: Tudor, 1939).

Guide to Further Reading

With the deaths of George Santayana and John Dewey in 1952, an important phase of American philosophical thought came to an end. Within their comprehensive and carefully formulated viewpoints they helped to bring American philosophy to its real maturity. Both Santayana and Dewey have become *world-figures* in philosophy. They have made a greater impact on the general public and on other philosophers than was ever before the case in American philosophy. The quality and quantity of their published works are of such a nature that it will be difficult indeed for others to equal or surpass them. As American philosophers, Dewey and Santayana are unique in the great number of contributions they have made to virtually every area of philosophical concern. But equally important is the fact that they have managed to reach an extremely wide audience and have consequently exercised a marked influence on twentieth-century thought. However, the greatness of their work does not mean that no significant contributions have been made by other contemporary American philosophers. Quite the reverse is the case.

American philosophy has come to maturity through the quality and quantity of meticulous philosophical work produced by *many* philosophers during the twentieth century; this work by far surpasses that which preceded it. Recent studies take in the whole range of philosophy—logic, ethics, metaphysics, aesthetics, epistemology, etc.—but some of the finest examples are found only in such journals as *The Philosophical Review, The Journal of Philosophy*, and *Review of Metaphysics*. The diversity and complexity of viewpoints imply that no simple summation can do justice to what has thus far transpired in twentieth-century American philosophy. However, some guide to further readings in this area can be given. The purpose of this guide is to show in some measure where the great wealth of careful philosophic work by recent American philosophers can be located.

The main characteristic of recent philosophic efforts in the United States has been analytical precision, especially care and study of the language, methods, and concepts needed to propound any philosophical problem about ethics, religion, science, or anything else. The critical analysis of fundamental concepts is now the dominant conception of the purpose or function of philosophy. However, there is considerable difference of opinion concerning how this critical analysis should go on and what results it may lead to. Some philosophers favor a more speculative approach while others restrict metaphysical speculation and claim that philosophy should instead center its attention on linguistic analysis and clarity.

An excellent source of readings by recent American philosophers is *American Philosophers at Work*, edited by Sidney Hook. This book is divided into three main parts and contains efforts of over twenty-five individuals with diverse viewpoints writing on (1) logic and scientific method, (2) metaphysics and theory of knowledge, and (3) ethics and social philosophy. For example, this volume contains selections from Rudolf Carnap ("Meaning and Synonymy in Natural Languages") and Willard Quine ("Logical Truth"), two of the leading figures in recent logical theory. Selections from some speculative philosophers such as Brand Blanshard ("The Nature of Mind") and Paul Weiss ("The New Outlook") are also included in this volume, as well as an essay by F. S. C. Northrop ("Ethical Relativism in the Light of Recent Legal Science"), one of the leading social or cultural philosophers in recent times.

Another source of readings is *The American Pragmatists*, edited by Milton Konvitz and Gail Kennedy. This work not only presents selections from earlier pragmatists such as Peirce, James, and Dewey, but offers readings from other and more recent pragmatists. For example, it contains George Herbert Mead's "The Genesis of the Self and Self-Control." Mead is not well known but nevertheless was a very creative and careful thinker of whom Dewey thought very highly. Also included in this volume is an essay by Clarence Irving Lewis ("A Pragmatic Conception of the *A Priori*") whose careful work in logic and epistemology has had considerable influence in recent philosophy.

Naturalism and the Human Spirit, edited by Yervant H. Krikorian, contains essays showing some of the most important explanations and defences of naturalism by recent American philosophers. This book is dedicated to Morris Cohen whose *Reason and Nature* and other works have established him as one of the best examples of analytical precision in recent times. Contributors to this volume include, among others, Sidney Hook ("Naturalism and Democracy") and Ernest Nagel ("Logic Without Ontology"). Sidney Hook is outstanding for his efforts in analyzing and criticizing social and political concepts, while Ernest Nagel is one of the leading contemporary philosophers of science.

Sources of Contemporary Realism in America, by Herbert Schneider, is an excellent guide to the best work done by American realists in this century. The efforts of the "new realists" and "critical realists" are discussed; short excerpts of their work and helpful bibliographies are also included. For further readings from various American realists and other recent philosophers, *Contemporary American Philosophy: Personal Statements*, Volume II, edited by George P. Adams and William P. Montague, is an excellent source. For example, this volume contains essays by Arthur Lovejoy ("A Temporalistic Realism") and Ralph Barton Perry ("Realism in Retrospect"), two of the leading figures in critical realism and the new realism respectively.

Although idealism has declined as a viable movement in this century, *Contemporary Idealism in America*, edited by Clifford Barrett, is a valuable source for further study of the issues and implications of idealism and its approaches to various philosophical problems. This volume is dedicated to Josiah Royce and contains among others an illuminating essay by W. E. Hocking ("The Ontological Argument in Royce and Others"). Hocking, who has written eloquently in defence of idealism, points up in this short essay one of the central issues that cuts across Royce's philosophy as well as that of Santayana—the relation between essence and existence.

Another excellent source of recent American philosophy with discussions of ethical theory, philosophy of science, metaphysics, and linguistic philosophy is *Philosophy* in the series *Humanistic Scholarship in America: The Princeton Studies*, containing essays by Herbert Feigl, William Frankena, Manley Thompson, and others. For example, this volume contains a chapter on "Naturalistic Metaphysics" in which some of the important differences between Santayana's and Dewey's naturalism are discussed. Other sources of the recent tendency in linguistic philosophy are *Language and Philosophy* by Max Black and *Knowledge and Certainty* by Norman Malcolm; these men are two of America's leading figures in linguistic philosophy.

Charles Stevenson's *Ethics and Language* is a good illustration of some of the best and most careful analysis recently done in the field of moral philosophy, while Morton White's *Foundations of Historical Knowledge* and Susanne K. Langer's *Feeling and Form* are among the best examples of careful analysis as applied to philosophical problems of history and art. Excellent sources of recent interpretations of American values and intellectual life are *American Thought: A Critical Sketch* by Morris Cohen and *American Ethics and Public Policy* by Abraham Kaplan.

No outline of readings in twentieth-century American philosophy would be complete without reference to Alfred North Whitehead. Along with Santayana and Dewey, Whitehead has become recognized as a world-leader in twentieth-century philosophy. In 1941 he was honored with the publication of *The Philosophy of Alfred North Whitehead* in *The Library of Living Philosophers* which contains essays by many outstanding American philosophers who discuss virtually every aspect of his philosophy. Although he was born and educated in England and did not come to the United States until he was sixty-three years old, Whitehead has made a considerable impact on recent American philosophy. In 1924 he accepted an invitation to join the Philosophy Faculty at Harvard University. Thereafter he continued to live in America, and produced some of his most important philosophical works here up until the time of his death in 1947: *Science and the Modern World* (1925); *Religion in the Making* (1926); *The Aims of Education* (1929); *Process and Reality* (1929); *Adventures of Ideas* (1933); *Modes of Thought* (1938); *Essays in Science and Philosophy* (1947). The fact that Whitehead remained in the United States is further evidence of the real maturity of American philosophical activity in this century. His tributes to the high quality of work done by American philosophers with whom he became acquainted are in marked contrast with the low opinions held previously by many European thinkers. Whitehead's influence on other American philosophers has been considerable. This is in large measure due to the fact that he combined an expert knowledge of mathematics and science with a profound concern with system-making and speculative philosophy. His *Process and Reality* is perhaps the greatest work done in this country in speculative cosmology and metaphysics.

Philosophical activity in America in this century has already come to genuine maturity, but it still continues to grow. It definitely exhibits a continuity with work that has preceded it. However, no single type of philosophy can be identified as making up this continuity. Pragmatism, naturalism, realism, idealism, and empiricism possess more continuity than other developments, but there is great diversity within each of these major movements. But further, recent philosophy in the United States has witnessed great dissatisfactions with previous methods and systems of philosophy. Greater attention than ever before has been paid to the analysis of words and language which philosophy uses to carry on its work. This linguistic turn in American philosophy has been greatly influenced by recent developments in British philosophy. A rich exchange of ideas and visiting scholars has made England and America together the center of linguistic and analytic philosophy. Whatever the results of this approach to philosophy may be—and the evaluation will take considerable time—there are indications that it already has changed the face of Western philosophy and that it will continue to grow. More and more it is possible to discern among many philosophers a heightened concern as to the purposes and possibilities of philosophical inquiry based on the careful study of the forms and functions of language.

This critical concern with the meaning and purpose of philosophy itself does not mean that recent philosophy is pointless; rather it means that today philosophy has become hypersensitive and has arrived at a deepened sense of its own shortcomings and responsibilities. American philosophers today still attempt to throw light on man, religion, morality, free will, etc., the same themes dealt with by Jonathan Edwards and other early American philosophers. However, today philosophers tend to approach these themes much more indirectly. Instead of directly asking, for example, whether the will is free or how freedom can be proved or disproved, they prefer to ask what we are *asserting* when we say the will is free or not free, or what we are *saying* when we claim that freedom can be proved or disproved. We are advised to make our assertions as explicit as possible and distinguish between characteristically different kinds of assertions, since as one contemporary linguistic philosopher says, "Philosophy is a much more purely verbal activity than is a science that collects facts about chemical reactions, social structures, or rock formations. Verbal discussion is the philosopher's laboratory, in which he puts his ideas to the test. It is not surprising that the philosopher should be especially sensitive to flaws in his major instrument." (William P. Alston, *Philosophy of Language*, Englewood Cliffs, N.J.: Prentice-Hall, 1964.) Today philosophy tackles its themes much more critically, analytically, and cautiously than ever before. Recent philosophy in America therefore may be less bold and more filled with the statement of qualifications. But this only means that it is attempting to be more careful and thoughtful—carefulness and thoughtfulness, in fact, define the principal virtues of its best recent work.

SUGGESTED READINGS

Sidney Hook, ed., *American Philosophers at Work: The Philosophic Scene in the United States* (New York: Criterion, 1956).

Milton R. Konvitz and Gail Kennedy, eds., *The American Pragmatists: Selected Writings* (New York: Meridian, 1960).

Arthur Lovejoy, *The Thirteen Pragmatisms and Other Essays* (Baltimore: Johns Hopkins University Press, 1963).

Andrew J. Reck, ed., *George Herbert Mead: Selected Writings* (New York: Bobbs-Merrill, 1964).

Clarence Irving Lewis, *An Analysis of Knowledge and Valuation* (LaSalle, Ill.: Open Court, 1946).

Yervant H. Krikorian, ed., *Naturalism and the Human Spirit* (New York: Columbia University Press, 1944).

Morris Cohen, *Reason and Nature* (New York: Harcourt, Brace, 1931).

Morris Cohen, *American Thought: A Critical Sketch* (New York: Free Press of Glencoe, 1954).

Sidney Hook, *The Quest for Being and Other Studies in Naturalism and the Human Spirit* (New York: St. Martins, 1961).

Ernest Nagel, *Logic Without Metaphysics, and Other Essays in the Philosophy of Science* (New York: Free Press of Glencoe, 1954).

Clifford Barrett, ed., *Contemporary Idealism in America* (New York: Russell, 1964).

William Hocking, *The Meaning of God in Human Experience: A Philosophic Study of Religion* (New Haven, Conn.: Yale University Press, 1912).

Brand Blanshard, *The Nature of Thought*, 2 vols. (New York: Macmillan, 1939).

Herbert Schneider, *Sources of Contemporary Philosophical Realism in America* (New York: Bobbs-Merrill, 1964).

Ralph Barton Perry, and others, *The New Realism: Cooperative Studies in Philosophy* (New York: Macmillan, 1912).

Arthur O. Lovejoy, George Santayana and Others, *Essays in Critical Realism: A Cooperative Study of the Problem of Knowledge* (New York: Macmillan, 1920).

Ralph Barton Perry, *General Theory of Value, Its Meaning and Basic Principles Construed on Terms of Interest* (New York: Longmans, Green, 1926).

Arthur O. Lovejoy, *The Revolt Against Dualism* (New York: Norton, 1930).

George P. Adams and William P. Montague, eds., *Contemporary American Philosophy: Personal Statements*, Vol. 2 (New York: Russell, 1930).

Alfred North Whitehead, *Science and the Modern World* (New York: Macmillan, 1925).

Alfred North Whitehead, *The Aims of Education and Other Essays* (New York: Macmillan, 1929).

Alfred North Whitehead, *Process and Reality: An Essay in Cosmology* (New York: Macmillan, 1929).

Alfred North Whitehead, *Religion in the Making* (New York: Macmillan, 1926).

Paul Arthur Schilpp, ed., *The Philosophy of Alfred North Whitehead* (New York, Evanston, and Chicago: Northwestern University Press, 1941).

Andrew Reck, *Recent American Philosophy: Studies of Ten Representative Thinkers* (New York: Pantheon, 1964).

Roderick Chisholm, and others, *Philosophy: Humanistic Scholarship in America,* The Princeton Studies (Englewood Cliffs, N.J.: Prentice-Hall, 1964).

Paul Arthur Schilpp, ed., *The Philosophy of Rudolf Carnap* (LaSalle, Ill.: Open Court, 1963).

Rudolf Carnap, *Foundations of Logic and Mathematics,* in *Encyclopedia of Unified Science,* Vol. 3 (Chicago: University of Chicago Press, 1939).

Willard Van Orman Quine, *From a Logical Point of View: 9 Logic-Philosophical Essays* (Cambridge, Mass.: Harvard University Press, 1953).

Paul Weiss, *Modes of Being,* 2 vols. (Carbondale: Southern Illinois University Press, 1958).

Max Black, *Language and Philosophy Studies in Method* (Ithaca, N.Y.: Cornell University Press, 1949).

Max Black, ed., *Philosophy in America: Essays* (Ithaca, N.Y.: Cornell University Press, 1965).

Norman Malcolm, *Knowledge and Certainty: Essays and Lectures* (Englewood Cliffs, N.J.: Prentice-Hall, 1963).

William P. Alston, *Philosophy of Language* (Englewood Cliffs, N.J.: Prentice-Hall, 1964).

F. S. C. Northrop, *The Logic of the Sciences and Humanities* (New York: Meridian, 1949).

Charles Stevenson, *Ethics and Language* (New Haven, Conn.: Yale University Press, 1944).

Morton White, *Foundations of Historical Knowledge* (New York: Harper, 1965).

Susanne Langer, *Feeling and Form: A Theory of Art* (New York: Scribner's, 1956).

Abraham Kaplan, *American Ethics and Public Policy* (New York: Oxford University Press, 1963).

INDEX OF NAMES

INDEX OF TERMS

287